chp. 5-7

5.00

FROM CHARITY
TO SOCIAL WORK
IN ENGLAND AND THE
UNITED STATES

STUDIES IN SOCIAL HISTORY

edited by

HAROLD PERKIN

Lecturer in Social History, University of Manchester

FROM CHARITY TO SOCIAL WORK

IN ENGLAND AND THE UNITED STATES

by

Kathleen Woodroofe

Senior Lecturer in History
University of Adelaide

Routledge and Kegan Paul

LONDON

First published 1962
by Routledge and Kegan Paul Limited
Broadway House, 68–74 Carter Lane
*London, E.C.*4

Printed in Great Britain by
Percy Lund, Humphries & Co. Ltd., London & Bradford

Contents

Acknowledgements

T<small>HIS</small> book is the outcome of visits to Chicago and London during a year's study leave from the University of Adelaide. I would like, therefore, to thank the University for freeing me from routine duties and for giving me this opportunity to study abroad. My thanks go also to the University of Chicago and the London School of Economics for allowing me to use the magnificent resources of their libraries, and to the Family Welfare Association in London, which placed at my disposal its private library at Denison House. My colleagues, too, at the University of Adelaide have often helped me in different ways. Four, in particular, have acted as a gentle scourge. I would therefore like to thank—but not implicate—Hugh Stretton, W. G. K. Duncan, Kenneth Inglis and Peter Phillips.

Adelaide,   KATHLEEN WOODROOFE
South Australia.
15 September 1961.

PART ONE

The English Origins

We may our ends by our beginnings know.'

SIR JOHN DENHAM: *Of Prudence*

(17th century)

I

In the Midst of
Victorian Plenty

ALTHOUGH the matters with which it is concerned are old,
social work as a profession is very young. Its beginnings are to
be found within the Charity Organization movement which
developed in England during the 1860's as one answer to the
question of how to tackle poverty in the midst of Victorian
plenty.

This was a problem which engaged only intermittently the
attention of the choice and master spirits of the age. To them,
England's wealth was indisputable, and poverty, when noticed
at all, was accepted as a temporary lapse from prosperity, an
unfortunate necessity, or as proof of individual aberration. Certainly in the years between the Great Exhibition of 1851 and
the onset of depression in 1873, there might have been some
justification for thinking along these lines. For England it was
a period free from national cares. Her population increased from
18 million in 1851 to more than 22 million in 1871. Her exports,
£71 million in 1850, had grown, twenty years later, to nearly
£200 million. Invisible exports mounted no less rapidly, and,
as a result, England acquired substantial credit balances overseas. As she did most of her own carrying and much of that of
the rest of the world, the shipping which entered and cleared
from English ports increased from 14 million tons in 1847 to

3

36½ million in 1870. Certainly there might have been one or two flies in the commercial ointment. A North Staffordshire ironmaster, for instance, lamented in 1867 that the Belgians have 'superseded us everywhere', sending iron to America and even securing an order from St. Thomas' Hospital 'for what are called girders',[1] but his words, inspired, it would seem, by a grudge against trade unions, were contradicted by overall statistics, which told the cheery tale of an increase in the value of iron and steel exports from £5 million in 1850 to £23 million in 1872. Likewise the value of cotton and woollen exports increased from £28 million and £10 million respectively in 1850 to £71 million and £26 million twenty years later.

Standing guard behind these exports were the great industries themselves, feeding each other and the home population, as well as the export trade, expanding vigorously, and reorganizing their plant to meet the demand for their goods. Alongside them were the English financiers relentlessly extending their control over England and Europe. 'Since the Franco-Prussian War, we have become to a much larger extent than before the Bankers of Europe', Walter Bagehot wrote exultantly in 1870. 'The German Government, as is well known, keeps its account (and a very valuable one it must be) at the London Joint Stock Bank.'[2] Perhaps, had he wished, he could have given details of other governments, crowned heads and distinguished personages who did the same. Certainly there was good reason for Bagehot's jubilation, for England in 1870 was still ahead of her rivals in the industrial race, and London the financial centre of something approaching a world economy.

English agriculture, too—no doubt to the pleasure and confusion of those 'uncountry gentlemen' whom Byron castigated earlier in the century—took advantage of the international situation to share in the general prosperity. In the sixties, Russia was recovering from the Crimean War and freeing her serfs; Germany was fighting Denmark and Austria as a preliminary to unification, while the United States was engaged

---

[1] *Royal Commission on Trade Unions* (1868–9, XXXIX), Question 10,696, quoted by J. H. Clapham, *An Economic History of Modern Britain, Vol. II, 1850–1886* (Cambridge, 1952), pp. 248–9.

[2] *Lombard Street*, in Mrs. Russell Barrington (ed.), *The Works and Life of Walter Bagehot* (1915), VI, 20, 188.

in a war to decide whether there should be one union or two. English farmers benefited by their competitors' preoccupation. They also took advantage of the fact that English railways had widened the home market, and new farming techniques made it possible to meet the new demand from home and abroad. As early as 1859 a visiting Frenchman could observe, somewhat jealously, that Britain's cattle were far superior, and that English farmers sold twice as much milk as the French and got twice the French price for it,[1] while thirty years later, in spite of a great deal of rural distress in the seventies, an English onlooker, partisan certainly, could describe enthusiastically how the English farmer 'has learnt the use of reaping and mowing machines, each of which can do the work of ten men; of steam ploughs . . . which do the labour of ten men and twenty horses; of steam machines . . . for threshing corn, cutting straw and hay, and similar purposes.'[2]

The years between 1850 and the middle seventies were, indeed, a glittering age, even though the cotton famine in 1862–63 and a financial panic in 1867 gave warning of what was later to come.

In view of this imposing panoply of prosperity, it was no wonder that so many of the Victorians were well satisfied with what they had become, and that their faith in progress was based on the confident expectation that in the future they would become more like themselves than ever. Their zest sometimes sprang from enthusiasm for sheer size and quantity—bigger population, more tons of coal, longer lines of railroads—which Matthew Arnold satirized in *Culture and Anarchy*, but more often it was an excited tribute to that mastery over the physical universe which had compelled Wordsworth earlier to confess that he rejoiced,

> Measuring the force of those gigantic powers
> That, by the thinking mind, have been compelled
> To serve the will of feeble-bodied man.[3]

This idea was floating at the surface of Edwin P. Hood's

---

[1] L. G. Lavergne, *The Rural Economy of England, Scotland and Ireland*, pp. 31, 34–35, quoted by Clapham, *op. cit.*, p. 277.

[2] T. H. S. Escott, *England. Its People, Polity and Pursuits* (1885), p. 180.

[3] *Excursion*, Book 8, in Thomas Hutchinson (ed.), *The Poetical Works of Wordsworth* (Oxford, 1946 ed.), p. 877.

mind, too, when, in the year of the Great Exhibition, he wrote that 'within the last half century, there have been performed upon our island, unquestionably the most prodigious feats of human industry and skill witnessed in any age or time or in any nation of the earth',[1] and certainly the sense of power engendered by these material achievements reinforced the Victorians' glorification of work as the supreme virtue, and their arraignment of idleness as a repudiation of the mission to serve, through one's calling, both God and society.

But even in this period of prosperity from the 1850's to the mid-seventies, the opportunity to enjoy the fruits of man's mastery over the physical universe was limited to a landed gentry, saved by the grudging concessions of 1832, and the middle classes of great bankers, financiers and merchants, professional men, farmers and tradesmen who had cleaved a way to economic and political power. The men and women who composed the working classes remained outside the prosperity and political pale. A large proportion were 'the denizens in Darkest England', as General Booth was later to call them. For them he was to demand 'the standard of the London Cab Horse'. 'These are the two points of the Cab Horse's Charter', said he. 'When he is down he is helped up, and while he lives he has food, shelter and work. That, although a humble standard, is at present absolutely unattainable by millions—literally by millions—of our fellow men and women in this country. Can the Cab Horse Charter be gained for human beings? I answer yes, the Cab Horse Standard can be attained on the Cab Horse terms.'[2]

This contrast between the prosperity of the few and the poverty of the millions—particularly in London—could not fail to strike the chroniclers of the period. Gustave Doré and Blanchard Jerrold, for example, have left us a vivid account of a nineteenth-century 'pilgrimage' through London. 'The two Pilgrims . . . have belted London with their footprints', they confessed. 'We are pilgrims, wanderers, gipsy-loiterers in the great world of London—not historians of the ancient port and capital.'[3] Their description, as 'a touch and go chronicle', of

[1] Edwin P. Hood, *The Age and its Architects, Ten Chapters on the English People in Relation to the Times* (1850) (1852), p. 138.
[2] *In Darkest England and the Way Out* (1890), pp. 18, 19, 20.
[3] *London, a Pilgrimage* (1872), pp. xi–xii, 1.

their excursions in and around London is far too modest, for, gifted with a rapacious curiosity, all-seeing eyes, and an ability to nail down on paper their impressions of things seen and heard, they have given us a series of literary snapshots of London in the mid-nineteenth century. Workaday London, London at play, London life on the docks in the East End, in the City and in the market-places, London charities and London industries— all are raw material for the author's pen and the painter's sketch book. And always their pen and brush dwell upon the contrasts between London's wealth and London's poverty. 'If the silent highway to London shows one of the city's brilliant and imposing sides', they write, 'the shores of the Thames expose its poverty . . . London abounds in startling contrasts. These stately arcades of the Royal Exchange . . . are but a few minutes' walk from the Market—the Exchange—of rags!'[1] Whether by design or innocence, the two pilgrims did not discern the same menace in this situation as did an unknown Englishman describing 'Charity and Pauperism' in 1869. 'There are contrasts in the streets that are rather unpleasant to contemplate', he wrote. '. . . We see in a shop window French pears at we know not how many guineas a dozen, and on the other side of the pavement is a living heap of rags, filth and dirt, representing so much explosive social material.'[2]

Observations such as these were by no means new in the 1860's. Engels had already published (in 1845) the German edition of *The Condition of the Working Class in England* which made an exposé of conditions in industrial towns which, the author claimed, had been so devised that poverty was always removed from the sight of 'the happier classes'. 'True, poverty often dwells in hidden alleys close to the palaces of the rich', he wrote, 'but, in general, a separate territory has been assigned to it, where, removed from the sight of the happier classes, it may struggle along as it can.' Manchester, he added more specifically, 'is peculiarly built so that a person may live in it for years, and go in and out daily without coming into contact with a working-people's quarter or even with workers'.[3] Again,

[1] *Ibid.*, pp. 16, 116, 122.
[2] An unsigned article on 'Charity and Pauperism', in *The Saturday Review*, Vol. 27, No. 690 (16 January 1869), p. 73.
[3] *The Condition of the Working Class*, printed in Karl Marx and Frederick Engels, *On Britain* (Moscow, 1953), pp. 59, 79.

many observations, oblique, but no less indignant, had been made upon English poverty. Novelists such as Charlotte Brontë and Mrs. Gaskell had already described the dank, drab drudgery of life in the early factory towns; Disraeli, in moments free from duties of parliament, had used a novelist's pen to warn his countrymen of the existence of 'the Two Nations', while Charles Dickens had already earned from Macaulay the abusive half-truth of 'sullen socialism' to describe the creation of Scrooge as a personification of selfishness in men, Gradgrind as selfishness in a system, and Podsnap as complacency in both. Likewise Ruskin and Carlyle had stepped beyond conventional limits of literary criticism to denounce a sweltering industrialism which crushed men's bodies and spirits, and Christian Socialists, such as Charles Kingsley, had sought to scourge Englishmen into taking action to remedy the conditions in great towns 'which recruit those very dangerous classes from the class which ought to be, and is still, in spite of our folly, England's strength and England's glory'.[1] That these critics spoke truly, if hotly, of Victorian society was proved by the official reports of a long series of Royal Commissions and Committees of Enquiry which, beginning in the eighteenth century, reached a peak in the 1830's, 1840's and 1850's as the Victorian conscience was stabbed into action.[2]

Considering this interest displayed in poverty, it is surprising that there is so little accurate knowledge of its extent. Statistics there are in plenty to show that the numbers of 'vagrom men' apprehended by nineteenth-century Dogberrys seemed to be growing steadily during certain decades. In the sixties the number of times vagrants were relieved increased from 1,542,000 in 1860 to 7,020,000 in 1869.[3] Through sober statistics of London deaths occurring in certain years 'upon which a Coroner's Inquest has been holden and Verdicts of Starvation or Accelerated by Privation, has been returned', the reader can

[1] 'Great Cities and their Influence for Good and Evil', in *Sanitary and Social Lectures and Essays* (1889), p. 206.

[2] It has been claimed, however, that these Blue Books give a one-sided, often exaggerated, and sometimes inaccurate view of conditions in England at the time. See F. A. Hayek (ed.), *Capitalism and the Historians* (1954), particularly Essays 4 and 5.

[3] *Report on the Departmental Committee on Vagrancy* (1906), Cd. 2852, Vol. I, Appendix VI, p. 33.

feel the intensity of the problem of poverty. The Return for 1868 and 1869 placed the number of deaths at 50. These included Ann Weeton, a widow of 64, who was receiving outdoor relief of 2s. 6d. a week and a quartern loaf, who had been offered admission into a workhouse because of illness, but had refused to go, and the verdict on whose death was 'exhaustion through want'. The death of Sarah Ann Sampson, aged 2 months, daughter of Thomas Sampson, a tin man, produced a verdict of 'atrophy from want of proper food'; the death of Sarah Mills, aged 43 years, wife of a hawker, a verdict of 'starvation', the death of a man known as McSherry 'exhaustion from want of food', and the death of a female child, Elizabeth Margaret Wilkins, aged 2 years, illegitimate daughter of a professional singer, a verdict of 'mesenteric disease from want of food'.[1]

But although there was fragmentary information of this kind, it was not until Charles Booth in 1892 published the first of his seventeen volumes of *Life and Labour of the People of London* that the full story of the city's poverty was known. Surveys of one kind and another had been made in England before Booth's time. As early as 1796, Sir Thomas Bernard, in founding 'The Society for Bettering the Conditions and Increasing the Comforts of the Poor', had called to fellow philanthropists to 'make inquiry into all that concerns the poor and the promotion of their happiness, a science. 'Let us', he said, 'investigate practically and upon system.'[2] The following year, Sir Frederic Morton Eden, one of those professional nosey parkers to whom history owes so much, had published under the title, *The State of the Poor*, a great dossier of detailed and disquieting facts on poverty and the administration of the Poor Law in England. Again in 1851, Henry Mayhew, a journalist of genius, claiming that people in London were as little known as pygmies in Africa, set out to wander through the streets and note the qualities of people. The result was four volumes of *London Labour and the London Poor* in which he described the various street occupations he observed, presented interesting tables showing numbers of persons, wages, criminal statistics and

[1] *Returns of the Number of Deaths in the Metropolitan Districts in the Years 1868, 1869 and 1870* (July 1871), Cd. No. 348, pp. 4–6.
[2] Rev. J. Baker, *Life of Sir T. Bernard*, I, pp. ii, iii, 2, quoted by B. Kirkman Gray, *A History of English Philanthropy* (1905), p. 279.

housing, and recorded life-histories and conversations he had heard from street-sellers, coster mongers, match-girls, cabmen, rat-catchers, chimney-sweeps, mudlarks and scavengers.[1] But it remained for Booth to make what Beatrice Webb called 'the grand inquest into the conditions of life and labour of the four million inhabitants of the richest city in the world.' 'Prior to this enquiry', she wrote, 'neither the individualist nor the socialist could state with any approach to accuracy what exactly was the condition of the people of Great Britain'.[2] She might have added that never again could they avoid precise statistics.

Like his predecessors, Bernard and Eden, Booth was a man of means who used a private fortune for a public purpose, but coming ninety years after them, he worked in different circumstances. The problem of poverty and the approach to it had changed, and the techniques of social research improved. Eden's starting-point, as he tells us, had been the misery caused by bad harvests and the exceptionally high prices of 1794 and 1795.[3] For Booth it was a new evil—urban squalor produced by increasing industrialization. Both Bernard and Eden had taken as their subject, 'The Poor'. The term was descriptive, not of a condition of society, but of the character of a group of people. It suggested a rigidly stratified society in which the poor would always be present. Booth took the subject of 'Poverty', which indicated a very different approach, and by establishing what he called his 'double method' for testing the condition of people —by 'surveying' them first, street by street, family by family, in their homes, and then at work, trade by trade, in their factories, warehouses and shops—he achieved the double object of high-lighting the contrasts between wealth and poverty and emphasizing the variety of working conditions. But not only had the problem and approach changed; research techniques also had improved. Eden wrote before the first population census in 1801, and, apart from a travelling investigator, relied upon the local squire or clergyman to supply him with information about the administration of the poor law and the conditions of the labouring poor. Booth, on the other hand, had at his

[1] See Peter Quennell (ed.), *Mayhew's London, being Selections from 'London Labour and the London Poor'* (1949).

[2] *My Apprenticeship* (1950 ed.), p. 186.

[3] A. G. L. Rogers (ed.), *The State of the Poor. A History of the Labouring Classes in England with Parochial Reports* (1928), p. xvii.

disposal the published and unpublished material of the Census of 1881, afterwards corrected and amplified by the more detailed Census of 1891, and a fleet of school attendance officers to be dispatched to collect information from all corners of London. With these aids at hand, Booth invented the social survey, making it a piece of apparatus indispensable to succeeding generations of social scientists.

Only one of Booth's statistics has retained its original vividness. In the London of the 1890's, he discovered, 30·7 per cent of the inhabitants lived at or below the level of bare subsistence. These 1,292,737 people fell within Booth's categories of 'poor' and 'very poor'. 'The divisions . . . are necessarily arbitrary', he explained. '. . . My "poor" may be described as living under a struggle to obtain the necessaries of life and make both ends meet; while the "very poor" live in a state of chronic want.'[1] Booth's remedy was for the State to raise Class B, the 'very poor', outside 'the daily struggle for existence', not only to eliminate the distress of 'those who are not competent to provide for themselves', but also to make it easier for 'the true working classes' to secure a larger share of national wealth. 'My idea', he said, 'is to make the dual system, Socialism in the arms of Individualism, under which we already live, more efficient by extending somewhat the sphere of the former and making the division of function more distinct.'[2]

It was obvious that Booth's approach to—and solution for— the problem of poverty was new to the nineteenth century. He had made a scientific investigation not of 'the poor' but of 'poverty'. The extent of poverty he had found so startling that it was obvious that the existing methods for handling it were entirely inadequate. A new solution was necessary; the State itself, he said, must 'nurse the helpless and incompetent as we in our own families nurse the old, the young and the sick'.[3] Poverty, in other words, was not pre-ordained, part of a 'natural' order, or proof of individual aberration. It was not to be exorcized by incantations on thrift and self-help. It was human, explicable, and removable, and if the existing methods for dealing with it were inadequate, unsuitable or desultory, the State itself must step into the role of provider. To Bernard's

[1] *Life and Labour of the People of London* (1892), I, 33, II, 21.
[2] *Ibid.*, I, 154, 165, 167. [3] *Ibid.*, p. 165.

unspoken claim that the poor must always be with us, Booth had countered by asking why there should be so much poverty. It remained now for Lord Beveridge, on the results of social surveys made between 1928 and 1937, to state categorically that want in the England of 1942 was 'needless'.[1]

That the existence of this poverty, and the social discontent that it engendered, spelt danger to the State was clearly realized. For all its imposing strength, Victorian society, particularly in the period before 1850, was shot through with the fear that one day the masses would overthrow the existing order and confiscate private property. The note of warning had been sounded in Burke's *Reflections on the French Revolution*. At the conclusion of the Napoleonic Wars it had echoed through the speeches of Canning, who obviously saw a Jacobin hiding behind every political bush. 'The festal blazes of the war are at an end', he had told the House of Commons in 1817. '. . . We must take care that during this cold and cheerless twilight the spoiler and the assassin do not break in and destroy.'[2] This fear of social revolution grew as the franchise was liberalized, for democracy carried emotional connotations much like those of communism today. 'The last time I saw Southey', Carlyle reminisced in 1881, '. . . we sat on the sofa together; our talk was long and earnest; topic ultimately the usual one, steady approach of democracy, with revolution (probably explosive) and a finis incomputable to man; steady decay of all morality, political, social, individual . . . and noble England would have to collapse in shapeless ruin, whether for ever or not none of us could know.'[3] William Cobbett, a powerful figure in the movement which brought about the Reform Bill of 1832, expressed a similar aversion to universal suffrage. 'I have witnessed its effects too attentively and with too much disgust', he said, 'ever to think of it with approbation.'[4] A liberal such as Macaulay viewed with dark suspicion Chartist demands for economic reform in political disguise. 'My firm conviction', he said, 'is that, in our country, universal suffrage is incompatible . . . with all forms of government . . . that it is incompatible with

[1] *Social Insurance and Allied Services. Report by Sir William Beveridge* (1942), Cd. 6404, para. 445, p. 165.

[2] Speech of 29 January 1817, *Hansard*, Vol. XXXV, col. 135.

[3] J. A. Froude (ed.), *Reminiscences by Thomas Carlyle* (1881), II, 326–7.

[4] J. M. Cobbett (ed.), *Political Works of W. Cobbett* (1835), VIII, 51.

property, and . . . consequently incompatible with civilization';
to grant the demands of 'The People's Charter' 'will be to
plunder every man in the kingdom who has a good coat on his
back and a good roof over his head'.[1] As was to be expected,
the Reform Bill of 1867 produced the same kind of agitated
comment. Lord Cranborne (afterwards Lord Salisbury) had
long 'entertained a firm conviction that we were going to the
dogs'; Carlyle thought 'the tug of revolution struggle may be
even *near* for poor England', while Disraeli, attacking the Bill
of 1866, prophesied the 'rule of mobs in great towns and the
sway of turbulent multitudes'.[2] (This morbid thought, though,
did not prevent him from carrying a Reform Bill the following
year.)

Behind these purely political arguments there usually lay a
profound suspicion of the working classes. Robert Lowe, for
example, who, in the House of Commons, opposed the Reform
Bill with passionate intensity, often spoke as though every
working man was a terrorist in trade union clothing. To grant
the franchise to the working classes, he said, would mean that
political power would be used in the interests of crude class
domination. 'The working men of England', he said, 'finding
themselves in a full majority of the whole constituency, will
wake to a full sense of their power. They will say, "We can do
better for ourselves. Don't let us any longer be cajoled at
elections. Let us set up shop for ourselves."'[3] The constitution
would then be swamped by numbers and society itself rent apart.

This suspicion of the working classes was not confined to
politicians seeking to turn back the political tide. It was also
reflected in the discussion of humbler subjects in contemporary
journals and newspapers. In *The Contemporary Review* in 1866,
one correspondent, Benjamin Shaw, exhorted men to take more
interest generally in the works of benevolence. The arguments
Shaw used were familiar ones at the time. 'The working
classes', he explained, 'are growing daily in power and influence,
socially and politically. And as yet the vast gap which severs

[1] Lady Trevelyan (ed.), *The Works of Lord Macaulay* (1875), VIII, 221, 222.
[2] Contemporary quotations taken from O. F. Christie, *The Transition from Aristocracy, 1832–1867* (1927), p. 257.
[3] Speech on the Reform Bill of 1866 (13 March), *Hansard*, 3 s. Vol. CLXXXII, col. 144–63, in G. M. Young and W. D. Handcock (eds.), *English Historical Documents*, XII (1), 1833–74 (1956), 163.

them from the classes above them is not bridged over—in the eyes of some among us it seems to be widening. Is this a matter to be looked on with unconcern?'[1] The same note of alarm was sounded in the columns of *The Saturday Review* when in 1870 it reported the first meeting of the Society for Organising Charitable Relief and Repressing Mendicity. The reporter drew attention to the increasing number of the working classes receding into pauperism, and commented glumly, 'That such a state of things is healthy or free from danger no one will contend. Indeed it is full of danger.'[2]

How, then, was this menacing poverty dealt with? Charles Booth's suggestion of what was, in effect, a Welfare State, even though it was made at a time when the Social Democratic Federation and the Fabian Society had softened many minds to the idea of social change, was not generally acceptable. The majority of Booth's countrymen preferred their individualism unlaced with socialism. Certainly this was an ideal increasingly difficult to attain. Throughout the nineteenth century the State had been forced to intervene in economic activities in order to alleviate the worst stresses and strains of the Industrial Revolution. In the field of industrial welfare, for example, the government had taken its first step in 1802 by passing the Health and Morals of Apprentices Act to limit hours of work of apprentices in cotton mills. From this tentative, almost surreptitious beginning, the State had gradually extended its sphere of operation. Then, having admitted the principle that intervention was justified to protect the worker against the worst results of industrial capitalism, the State had to consider the further questions of which workers were to be protected and what kind of protection they should get. At first the State intervened only on behalf of children and women. Men were considered to be strong enough to make a satisfactory contract with their employers without State protection, and it was only in exceptional circumstances that intervention between employer and employee was justified. In the case of coal miners (in 1850) and sailors (in 1875), justification was made on the grounds of men's

[1] 'Is there room for works of mercy in a busy London life?' *The Contemporary Review*, III (September–December, 1866), 18.

[2] 'The Organisation of Charity', *The Saturday Review*, Vol. 29, No. 753 2 April 1870), p. 442.

helplessness once they left terra firma to traverse the sea or descend into the bowels of the earth. As for the kind of protection needed, three aspects of modern industry called for attention—at what age should a person be allowed to work? for how long? and under what conditions? For many years, industrial regulation was concerned with these aspects, but later, another question arose—could the State regulate payment for work?—and yet another, what was to happen to the worker who, through accident, sickness, old age, or unemployment, was not able to work? In answering these questions, and putting the answers into operation, there was gradually built up in England an industrial code which, by the first decade of the twentieth century, not only covered hours and conditions of work, but was being extended to the fields of industrial unemployment and social insurance.

Again, in the field of education, the State had been forced to make educational provision for the growing numbers of children able to survive the dangers of the first year of life. The first reaction of the State had been against popular education. Davies Giddy, opposing Samuel Whitbread's Education Bill of 1807, warned the House that education would teach 'the labouring classes of the poor' to 'despise their lot in life', 'render them fractious and refractory' and 'insolent to their superiors'.[1] Fifty years later, however, the ruling class had begun to realize that a little education, far from being dangerous, could offer protection against social revolution. 'The uneducated state of the "lower orders"', proclaimed Andrew Ure, '. . . is the dark den of incendiarism and misrule . . . which, if not cleared out, will give birth ere long to disastrous eruptions in every other province'.[2] Especially after the Reform Bill of 1867 did reasoning such as Ure's carry weight, so that the State which in 1833 had grudgingly granted £20,000 to education for building purposes only, by 1870 was prepared to pass an Education Act to provide a system of public education to supplement the existing voluntary system.

In the field of public health, too, the same process was at

[1] Debate on Whitbread's Education Bill of 1807, quoted by M. G. Jones, *The Charity School Movement. A Study of 18th Century Puritanism in Action* (Cambridge, 1938), p. 327.
[2] *Philosophy of Manufactures* (1861 ed.), p. 404.

work. Originally regarded as a means of protecting the rich against infection, public health had gradually broadened its objectives. The sheer magnitude of the problem of maintaining health in the new industrial towns had forced the government to intervene, and a series of Public Health Acts from 1848 to 1875 empowered central and local authorities to provide environmental and personal services to safeguard public health.

In these and other fields, then, the government had stepped in, at first tentatively and then with increasing insistence, to lay down rules for the protection of its citizens. But always these laws were passed in the face of intense opposition, and even those most concerned to get them on the statute book often felt it necessary to apologize for them. Shaftesbury, for example, agreed to undertake his work of promoting factory legislation only on condition 'that there should be a careful abstinence from all approach to questions of wages and capital; the labour of children and young persons should alone be touched',[1] while Southwood Smith and Chadwick, who together laid the foundations of the Public Health laws, were disciples of Bentham who, at first, accepted the principle of *laisser-faire*. Thus in spite of the thickening statute book, it was still generally believed that the adult citizen should be left free to make what use he liked of his own capacities, and that any attempt on the part of the State to interfere with this freedom must sap individual, and eventually national, strength. Only as a last resort must the State intervene. 'State benevolence', Shaftesbury warned, 'is a melancholy system that tends to debase a large mass of the people to the condition of the nursery, where the children look to the father and mother, and do nothing for themselves.'[2]

This prevailing distrust of State intervention not only led to a rejection of Booth's plan for a Welfare State. It also influenced the theory and practice of Poor Relief which was one of the traditional methods of dealing with the problems of poverty.

English poor law in Elizabethan days had been something more than a means of relieving destitution and suppressing

[1] Quoted by Gertrude Williams, *The State and the Standard of Living* (1936), p. 2.

[2] 'The Dwellings of the Poor' (1883), in Michael Goodwin (ed.), *Nineteenth Century Opinion. An Anthology of Extracts from 'The Nineteenth Century', 1877–1901* (Penguin Books, 1951), p. 75.

vagrancy. The Poor Law of 1601, designed to deal with the residue of unemployment after constructive measures to create work had been put into operation, had been part of a network of social security. But by 1722 the workhouse test had been introduced, and 'the right to existence' replaced by 'the right to work'. Later at Speenhamland an attempt was made to fix a living wage, to be made up out of parish rates. This had proved ruinous. Annual expenditure on the relief of destitution rose from £2 million in 1784 to £6½ million in 1813, and to nearly £8 million in 1818. This, to a generation unaccustomed to public expenditure, was a stupendous sum. By the 1830's all the arguments against the existing poor law had been marshalled, and the parliamentary stage set for the Act of 1834. Cutting costs, one would gather, was far less important a consideration than saving the pauper from the detrimental effects of a life of ease. 'You will find the pauper tormented with the worst ills of wealth', proclaimed the Lord Chancellor during the debate on the Poor Law Amendment Act of 1834, '(he is) listless and unsettled . . . needy yet pampered . . . ill fed, yet irritable and nervous. Oh! monstrous progeny of this unnatural system, which has matured in the squalid recesses of the workhouse the worst ills that haunt the palace and make the pauper the victim of those imaginary maladies which render wealthy idleness less happy than laborious poverty'.[1] 'Parish allowance', he summed up, 'is far worse than any dole of private charity, because it is more likely to be abused . . . more certain in its nature . . . better known . . . (and) approaches in the mind of the poor, to the idea of a right.'[2]

Behind these words, and the Poor Law Act of 1834 which put them into practice, there lay a system of thought new in the nineteenth century. It was believed that the public relief of destitution, financed out of taxation, as distinct from the alms of the charitable, must have a demoralizing effect on the recipient. It sapped his initiative, degraded his character, and encouraged him to be thriftless and dependent. Moreover, by raising wages above the level of mere subsistence, such relief encouraged the poor to multiply their numbers, and the wage

[1] Debate on the Poor Law Amendment Act of 1834, *Hansard*, 3rd. s. Vol. XXV, col. 231.
[2] *Ibid.*, col. 222.

17

increase was nullified. This Malthusian law was reinforced by Ricardo's Wages Fund doctrine, popularized, though later retracted, by John Stuart Mill, which claimed that all wages, rates, taxes, and even alms, were paid out of a fixed wage-fund. What was levied in Poor Rate was merely abstracted from what would otherwise have been paid out in wages. Thus in the long run, it was against the interests of the poor to give them either poor relief or alms, because it diminished the Wages Fund. And finally, the whole system of relief was a foolish interference with a 'natural' order of society. This, it was assumed, included all laws relating to the private appropriation and protection of property, but excluded all collective provision for the citizens at large, whether in the form of a State Poor Law, or Factory Acts, public health administration or free education. All these arguments led to the same conclusion—that relief of the poor from public funds should ultimately be abolished, but pending this, should be restricted to an ever-diminishing number of recipients. This could be achieved by limiting all relief to the maintenance of workhouses regulated by boards of guardians according to the principle of 'less eligibility'. This 'grand discovery of a commercial age', as R. H. Tawney called it, 'that relief might be so administered as not merely to relieve, but also to deter'[1] was incorporated into the Act of 1834. Thus did the ruling class seek to drive the poor out of their poverty, or failing this, to leave them to live as best they could.

There was, however, an alternative to the Poor Law. Over the centuries the rich, prompted by sympathy, guilt, fear or a love of power, have given of their abundance to the poor. Ideas of philanthropy have varied at different times, for although the giving a man does is personal, it is influenced, not only by the size of his pocket, but by the gods he worships, the tribe to which he belongs, and the form of government under which he lives. Thus while philanthropy's general aim to relieve different kinds of social distress remains the same at different periods, the objects, scope, methods and content of philanthropic action change as the social context changes. 'I have given bread to the hungry man', proclaimed the Book of the Dead, 'and water to him that was athirst, and apparel to the naked man, and a ferry boat to him that had no boat. I have made propitiatory

---

[1] *Religion and the Rise of Capitalism* (Pelican ed., 1948), p. 268.

offerings and given cakes to the gods.'[1] Five thousand years later Elizabeth I of England might agree that the necessity to give cakes to the gods had passed, but saw nothing strange in including among appropriate charitable uses 'the repair of bridges, ports, havens, causeways, churches, sea-haunts and highways'.[2] Patrick Colquhoun, by arguing that Charity was not only a social responsibility but also a prerequisite of social decorum and peace, could extend the range of philanthropy to include the police function,[3] and Robert Nelson, addressing in 1715 'Persons of Quality and Estate' on 'Ways and Methods of doing Good', could earnestly include in his list of Charities not only schools, missionaries, hospitals and religious societies, but also ways by which decayed tradesmen could be helped 'without any very great expense', poor distressed housekeepers assisted, and young women convinced of their folly.[4]

Particularly have the scope and content of philanthropic action varied in more recent times. In the eighteenth century, for example, when state intervention was at a minimum, philanthropy concerned itself with a much wider range of subjects than it does today. Reform of prisons and lunatic asylums, the care of orphans, the provision of schools and the abolition of slavery were considered to be grist to the philanthropic mill no less than the care of the poor, the aged and the sick, and different methods were evolved to meet these different needs. Sometimes philanthropy imported ideas from the world of business. Hospital charities, such as Westminster, St. George's, the London and Middlesex Hospitals which were established in London during the first half of the eighteenth century, were financed by voluntary associations organized along joint stock lines. Charity schools, too, used the principle of the trading company. Sometimes philanthropy evolved its own methods. John Howard, for example, writing his *State of the Prisons* in 1777 in order to shame the nation into a sense of responsibility, was using the method of agitation which, in the eighteenth century, was something of a novelty. Wilberforce adopted similar tactics to present to his countrymen, inside and outside parliament, the

[1] E. A. Wallis Budge (tr.), *The Papyrus of Ani* (New York, 1913), p. 587.
[2] 43 Eliz., c. 4, quoted by B. Kirkman Gray, *op. cit.*, p. 36.
[3] *Police of the Metropolis* (1800), quoted by B. Kirkman Gray, *op. cit.*, pp. 281–2.
[4] *An Address to Persons of Quality and Estate, Ways and Methods of Doing Good*, pp. 191, 189, quoted by B. Kirkman Gray, *op. cit.*, pp. 94–95.

case for the abolition of slavery. In the nineteenth century, however, as State Intervention eddied out into various fields, the scope of philanthropy became narrower and its methods more limited. In some fields, such as education, private philanthropy receded as charity schools gave way to State schools; in other fields, such as the care of the aged and the sick, the State and philanthropy began to fence off their respective spheres of operation, to forge links of the most various kinds between them, and to work, sometimes as allies, sometimes as enemies, on the common task of shoring up the system of social security. At present the field of voluntary action, which is today's version of the nineteenth century's philanthropy, is still shrinking before the encroachment of the Welfare State. Nevertheless the voluntary organisation still has an important role to play. Not only have many State services grown out of voluntary services, but there are fields better served by voluntary organisations than by the State. Today's greater emphasis on what has been called 'the enrichment of normal life',[1] rather than on the relief of material distress, suggests that where the handling of human needs and problems requires a special degree of tact and understanding, a voluntary agency can sometimes provide more individual attention than the impersonal, and often more inflexible, State agency. Lord Beveridge recognized this fact when, having presented his report on what the State can and should do to achieve a system of social security, he felt obliged to write a sequel in 1948 on *Voluntary Action* to emphasize what the individual can and should do independently of the State. 'Voluntary action', he said, 'is needed to do things which the State should not do—in the giving of advice, or in organizing the use of leisure. It is needed to do things which the State is most unlikely to do. It is needed to pioneer ahead of the State and make experiments.'[2] But not only can voluntary action repair the deficiencies of the State; it has a positive service to render in the democratic cause. As the Bishop of Sheffield pointed out in the House of Lords in June 1949, voluntary action, whether for philanthropic ends or mutual aid, is one way 'of checking the natural bias of the Welfare State towards

[1] Henry A. Mess, 'What is Voluntary Social Service?' in Gertrude Williams (ed.), *Voluntary Social Services since 1918* (1947), p. 2.

[2] *Voluntary Action. A Report on Methods of Social Advance* (1948), pp. 301–2.

totalitarianism'.[1] 'The voluntary spirit is the very life-blood of democracy', added Lord Pakenham, '. . . . democracy without voluntary exertion and voluntary idealism loses its soul.'[2]

Judged by this criterion, the 'democracy' which existed in England during the second half of the nineteenth century had certainly not lost its soul. Just at the time when Booth's survey was proving the inadequacy of philanthropy in handling mass poverty, private and organized charity was at its zenith in London. Philanthropic individuals and associations were inspired by a number of motives. In a society politically conservative, fearful both of collectivism and democracy, it was natural that greater emphasis should be placed upon philanthropy and mutual understanding than upon drastic forms of social change. An emotional sympathy for the underdog, whether the underdog was an oppressed nationality, class or individual, was reinforced by religious exhortations to work hard and be charitable. Charity was commended on several grounds. First there was a genuine desire to improve the conditions of the poor. Sometimes this desire was bound up with religious beliefs, but more often it was part of a current of thought which placed greater value on the love of man than on the service of God. Beatrice Webb has drawn attention to this trend in mid-Victorian thought and feeling. 'There was the current belief in the scientific method', she wrote, 'and added to this belief in science was the consciousness of a new motive; the transference of the emotion of self-sacrificing service from God to man.' It was in the middle decades of the nineteenth century, she suggested, that in England 'the impulse of self-subordinating service was transferred, consciously and overtly, from God to man'.[3] Frederick A. Maxse was aware of this new motive, too, when in a letter to the Reverend Henry Solly, he commended Solly's work which was to result in the creation of the Charity Organisation Society, and mused, 'I wonder when the necessity will be seen of teaching men to be good for the sake of *this* world'.[4]

Being good for good's sake, as well as God's, was a means of

---

[1] Speech in the House of Lords on 22 June 1949, during a debate on 'Voluntary Action for Social Progress', 163. H.L. Deb, s 5, c. 105.

[2] *Ibid.*, col. 119.   [3] *Op. cit.*, pp. 112, 123.

[4] Letter from Frederick A. Maxse, undated, probably 1868 or 1869, in *The Solly Collection* (in possession of the London School of Economics and Political Science, University of London), Vol. IX, Section 10b, item 1, contd., J 191-2.

assuaging that sense of personal guilt which lay at the base of so much of the humanitarianism of the Victorian period. C. S. Loch, who devoted himself to the cause of Charity Organisation from 1875 until illness drove him into retirement in 1913, was obviously oppressed by a sense of guilt that his own lot in life was so fortunate. 'A young man', he confessed in later life, 'is stirred to interest himself in general or public charity, by some vague regret that the lives of others, as he judges from the contrast with his own, are sunless and sad.'[1] Edward Denison often spoke as though the work he did during his short life, first as a 'settler' in London's East End and then as a Member of Parliament for Newark, was an expiation of the sin of being born, as the son of a bishop, into comfortable surroundings. From his self-chosen lodgings at 49 Philpot Street, he went forth to champion the poor, nurse the sick, scourge local authorities into action, and build, endow and teach in a school. 'My plan is the only really practicable one', he explained in 1867, 'and as I have both means, time and inclination, I should be a thief and murderer if I withheld what I so evidently owe.'[2] When many Lochs and many Denisons felt this way, individual guilt-complexes combined to produce what Beatrice Webb called a 'class consciousness of sin',[3] born of the realization that an industrial organisation which brought riches to the few failed to provide a decent livelihood for the many. How to close this menacing gap between classes was a problem very much in the forefront of the Victorian mind. Charity, properly organized, appeared to many as a solution more acceptable than reform of the social system. 'Since the beginning of this century the gulf between rich and poor has become fearfully wide', Sir Charles Trevelyan announced in 1870 to a Conference of the Society for Organising Charitable Relief and Repressing Mendicity, 'The proposal is to . . . knit all classes together in the bonds of mutual help and good will. Everything else would follow from this'.[4] But the beneficial effects of charity were not confined to the comfortable classes. If it were properly organized, charity

---

[1] 'The Charities of Church and Chapel', in *Charity Organisation Review*, Vol. VIII, No. 89 (May 1892), p. 168. Afterwards cited as *C.O. Review*.

[2] Sir Baldwyn Leighton (ed.), *Letters and Other Writings of the Late Edward Denison, M.P. for Newark* (1872), p. 48.   [3] *Op. cit.*, p. 157.

[4] *Address on the Systematic Visitation of the Poor in their own homes an indispensable basis of an effective System of Charity* (1870), p. 7.

could benefit the recipient by strengthening his character and making him self-supporting. 'Charity is a social regenerator', Loch explained in 1884. '. . . We have to use Charity to create the power of self-help.'[1]

Considering this belief in the benefits of philanthropy, it was not surprising that in England charities had increased in number and variety. Particularly was this so in London during the first half of the nineteenth century. Sampson Low, Junior, who, in 1861, made a survey of the number and income of the charities in existence, estimated that in 1861 there were 640 institutions, of which 279 had been founded between 1800 and 1850, and 144 between 1850 and 1860. The annual aggregate income of these institutions he placed at nearly £2½ million.[2] This latter figure is misleadingly low, because it does not include private charity in the form of individual gifts and special subscriptions for deserving objects. These, considering the number of contemporary Trimmers and Cheerybles, must have been quite considerable. Even so, it is obvious from Low's estimates that the income of charities in London exceeded the provision made from the public funds for the relief of distress. Low's survey revealed not only the number and wealth of London's private charities, but also their variety. His list included not only institutions with clearly definable objects such as hospitals, infirmaries, penitentiaries, almshouses, asylums for orphan children, and Bible and Home Missionary Societies, but also organisations with less specific aims such as the twelve listed 'for the Preservation of Life, Health and Public Morals' and the six for 'Protestant Dissenting Ministers'. In this diverse world of charity, there was no attempt to co-ordinate the efforts of different organisations or to evolve any general principles to guide them in their work. 'These charities', as Loch was later to complain, 'stand, one by one, isolated like light-houses; but unfortunately not, like light-houses, placed with care precisely on those points of the dangerous coastline of pauperism, where their lights will save from shipwreck the greatest number of distressed passers-by.'[3] This lack of co-operation among

[1] 'The Future of Charity', *Charity Organisation Reporter*, Vol. XIII, No. 551 (27 September 1884), pp. 320, 321. Afterwards cited as *C.O. Reporter*.

[2] *The Charities of London in 1861* (1862), Table, Preface, pp. vii–xi.

[3] 'Some necessary reforms in charitable work', *C.O. Reporter*, Vol. XI, No. 436 (13 July 1882), p. 211.

London's charitable organisations led to the further abuse of giving indiscriminately to all who applied, without any attempt to investigate the actual needs of each case, either to find out whether aid was being received from some other quarter, or to decide the kind and amount of help it was necessary to give. It was to correct these and similar abuses that Charity Organisation was born, to evolve, with the Poor Law and ordinary philanthropy, a third method of dealing with the poverty which existed in the midst of Victorian plenty.

This, then, is the background against which the Charity Organisation Society—or as it was called in 1869, the Society for Organising Charitable Relief and Repressing Mendicity— has to be viewed. It is necessary now to take a closer look at the work of the C.O.S., because it was within the framework of this Society, more than of any other, that social case work was evolved, to become the first and most highly developed of the three methods of social work. Not only did the Society hammer out a philosophy and a technique to guide its own friendly visitors and social workers in their daily task, but through the early establishment of a training school, later to become the Department of Social Science and Administration at the London School of Economics, the Society had a tremendous influence on the development of social work in England. And when, as will be shown later, the philosophy and practice of Charity Organisation were transplanted in 1877 to the United States, the influence of the Society began to spread beyond the home border.

II

<hr>

The C.O.S. and Social
Casework

<hr>

Aʟᴛʜᴏᴜɢʜ the origin of the Charity Organisation Society, as one of its early members remarked, is 'as undiscoverable as the sources of the Nile'[1] and much controversy has raged around the question of who can claim to be its founders,[2] the conditions which provoked the Society into existence in 1869 are beyond dispute. Especially in London, private charities, offering as they did immediate, easy, short-run solutions to the problems of poverty, had spawned to such an extent that many believed the

[1] Quoted by W. A. Bailward, *The Charity Organisation Society. A Historical Sketch, 1869–1906* (1935 ed.), p. 2.

[2] Different versions of how the C.O.S. originated are contained in Helen Bosanquet, *Social Work in London, 1869–1912: A History of the C.O.S.* (1914), Chapter I; Charles B. P. Bosanquet, *The History and Mode of Operation of the C.O.S.* (1874); Thomas Hawksley, *Objections to 'The History' of the Society* (1874); W. M. Wilkinson, *A Contribution towards the History of the C.O.S.* (1875); W. M. Hicks, *A Contribution towards the History of the Origin of the C.O.S. with Suggestions on Reports, Balance Sheets and Audit of Charity Accounts* (Soho, 1875); Sartor Minor, *Philanthropic Tailoring and Historical Cobbling* (1875); C. S. Loch, *Charity Organisation* (1892), Chapter I; and *The Solly Collection* (in possession of the London School of Economics and Political Science, University of London), Vol. X, Section 10c, J 325–J 346, especially a letter from Joseph Dare to the Rev. Henry Solly, dated 11 July 1892 (J 325–6), in which he objects to Loch's account of the origin of the C.O.S., and another letter, dated 15 November 1892 (J 341–3), in which he protests against 'the extraordinary story in the *C.O. Review* entitled "The Origin of the London C.O.S."'

poor had become pauperized as a result. Octavia Hill, whose experiments in housing management and training workers so profoundly influenced succeeding generations of social workers, was convinced that this was so. 'I am quite awed when I think what our impatient charity is doing to the poor of London', she told a captive audience at Fulham, 'Men who should hold up their heads as self-respecting fathers of families, learning to sing like beggars in the streets—all because we give pennies.'[1] 'Charity . . . is a frightful evil', agreed Edward Denison. '. . . The gigantic subscription lists which are vaunted as signs of our benevolence, are monuments of our indifference.'[2] 'Charity . . . infects the people like a silent working pestilence',[3] added Loch, '(It has) become an endowment to the hypocrite and a laughing stock to the cynic.'[4]

Certainly London's charitable scene lent weight to these harsh judgments. Private charities were numerous, diverse, unco-ordinated and competitive. Moreover, they were incurious about their applicants and issued soup, doles, coal-tickets, blankets and alms to all who asked, without any attempt to investigate the actual needs of each case to find out whether aid was being received from some other quarter, or to decide the kind and amount of help it was necessary to give. But not only was Charity pauperizing the poor; it was also proving an expense to the rich. Statisticians, in bud or in bloom, had begun counting the cost. When Sampson Low, Junior, made his survey of the number and income of London charities in 1861, his estimates showed that the income of private charities exceeded the provision made from the public funds for the relief of distress. The total poor-rates expended in 1857 ('which is a fair average') in the Metropolitan District, he placed at £1,425,063 as against the aggregate income of charities of £2,441,967.[5] A decade later, the figures had increased. Thomas Hawksley in 1869 estimated that 'seven millions sterling a year' were

---

[1] 'The C.O.S. A Paper read at the meeting of the Fulham and Hammersmith Charity Organisation Society Committee, February, 1 1889, at Fulham Palace', *C.O.S. Occasional Paper*, First Series, No. 15, p. 25.

[2] Sir Baldwyn Leighton (ed.), *Letters and Other Writings of the Late Edward Denison, M.P. for Newark* (1872), p. 103.

[3] 'Some Necessary Reforms in Charitable Work, Part I', *C.O. Reporter*, Vol. XI, No. 434 (29 June 1882), p. 196.

[4] C.O.S., *Thirteenth Annual Report*, 1882, p. 20.

[5] *The Charities of London* (1862), pp. 86, xi. See above, p. 23.

contributed by the charities and poor rates in London alone.[1]
This, as one commentator later pointed out, was an amount 'that
would keep in idleness one in eight persons of the whole population of the metropolis'.[2]

It is no wonder, then, that Loch, interpreting Charity in the
older, tender sense of 'Caritas', denounced this indiscriminate
almsgiving as 'a voluntary . . . insufficient . . . wasteful . . .
self-imposed tax on the rich',[3] and that he and many others
came to the mistaken conclusion that Charity was the cause of
the problem it sought to solve. 'The charities of England, in
extent, variety and amount are something perfectly stupendous',
wrote one lady in 1853. '. . . There is scarcely a conceivable
form of human want or wretchedness for which a special provision has not been made.'[4] The writer was obviously assuming
that what she called this 'noxious Charity' was the root cause
of poverty, and that if only Charity were beneficent, better
organized and more wisely administered, society would be re-
stored to a state of pristine prosperity. 'Destitution, and the
charity which so largely causes it', she wrote, '. . . (are) temporary evils, which will pass away together, so soon as true
benevolence, under the guidance of wisdom, shall have brought
back society into its normal condition of sanity and sound-
ness.'[5]

It was with the idea of co-ordinating the efforts of charitable
organizations in London and of formulating some general
principles to guide them in their work, that the Society for
Organising Charitable Relief and Repressing Mendicity met
for the first time in Willis's Rooms in March 1870. Members
of the nobility were well to the fore in the Council, so much so
that Mr. Verey, a Guardian of St. Marylebone, was goaded into
saying, only half in fun, that 'he was afraid this association
would fail like a good many others. There were too many lords
and noble gentlemen attached to it'.[6] The Earl of Derby, who

[1] Thomas Hawksley, *The Charities of London and Some Errors of their Administration with Suggestions for an Improved System of Private and Official Charitable
Relief* (1869), p. 7.

[2] Sartor Minor, *op. cit.*, p. 3.

[3] *How to Help Cases of Distress* (1883), p. 7.

[4] Katherine S. Sterling, *Charity, Noxious and Beneficent* (1853), p. 6.

[5] *Ibid.*, p. 29.

[6] *Meeting of the Society for Organising Charitable Relief and Repressing Mendicity.
Held at Willis's Rooms on March 30th, 1870* (Printed for the Society, 1870), p. 15.

was in the chair, opened the meeting by proclaiming that although there was no want of wealth in London, pauperism was increasing more rapidly than either charity or wealth. 'It admits, to my mind, of only one explanation', he said. 'By want of proper supervision and control, by excessive laxity, and absence of discrimination between the deserving and the undeserving, we are pauperizing, year by year, an increasing number of our people.'[1] The Bishop of Winchester echoed these remarks. 'I do believe, really', he said, 'that misplaced charity is one of the greatest evils of the present day. . . . It has not only had a bad effect upon the giver, but the result is calamitous to the deserving poor.'[2] There was only one solution. 'The numerous local charities of London', Lord Derby announced, 'should be made to co-operate instead of competing, and . . . all of them, as far as may be, should be brought into co-operation with the agents through whom the Poor Law is administered.'[3]

The main aims of the Society were expressed in the title. By 'organising charitable relief' according to certain well-defined principles the Society hoped to introduce order into the chaos of London's philanthropic organizations and to reduce the incidence of pauperism. By 'repressing mendicity', and hence treating only cases deemed deserving of help, the Society aimed not only at reducing unnecessary expenditure, but at using Charity as a means of increasing the moral stature of the individual and society. Charity given indiscriminately and thoughtlessly demoralized; it encouraged habits of thriftlessness and dependence and these, the Society considered, were a root cause of poverty and pauperism. True Charity, administered according to certain principles, could encourage independence, strengthen character, and help to preserve the family as the fundamental unit of society. This was the ideal of Charity Organisation to which the members of the Society pledged themselves in 1870.

The chief vendor of these principles was the vivid, dynamic Charles Stewart Loch, who, appointed Secretary of the C.O.S. in 1875, piloted the Society through the next thirty-eight years until illness forced him to retire. Today Loch suffers the fate of many men who have become so completely identified with the cause they serve that it is impossible to see them apart from it.

[1] *Ibid.*, pp. 5–6. [2] *Ibid.*, p. 23. [3] *Ibid.*, p. 9.

Attention becomes limited to one particular aspect of their lives and personalities, and if, for any reason, the cause becomes suspect, superseded or ignored, the man, too, suffers the same fate. Loch and the C.O.S. have become so identified. When *The Times* came to write Loch's obituary in 1923, it summed up his work by saying, 'He made the C.O.S.; he was the C.O.S.[1]' During the years of his Secretaryship, when the Society wielded its greatest influence, Loch was the magnet which drew charity organizers and social workers from all corners of the United Kingdom and the world to seek advice and inspiration. 'Mr. Charles Loch—that busiest and most capable of men', enthused Professor E. E. Morris,[2] who established the first Australian Charity Organisation Society in Melbourne in 1887. 'There is not a family social worker in America today', wrote Mary E. Richmond, doyen of American social work, 'not a social case worker of any sort, in fact—who does not owe him a heavy debt.'[3] 'It was what Mr. Loch was, even more than what he said or did', related a colleague, 'that left so grateful an impression on his fellow-workers.'[4] 'Mr. Charles Stewart Loch is one of the most surprising facts of the present day', summed up the editor of the *Oxford Magazine* in 1905 when Loch was given the honorary degree of D.C.L. 'Here is a man with no official position, no letters after his name, not even a ribbon, whose name is known everywhere, whose influence is felt everywhere.'[5] Today, however, mainly owing to profound changes in social conditions and in ways of thought, many of Loch's ideas have been ignored or discredited. His dislike of State old age pensions, for instance, sounds strange to ears attuned to the language of the Beveridge Report; some of his writings, too, breathe a class-consciousness galling to a generation more embarrassed about class-distinctions than his own; and even his favourite term, 'Charity', which he once declared

[1] *The Times*, 25 January 1923, p. 13.

[2] *Charity Organisation Societies in England and the U.S. A Paper read at a Meeting of the Council of the Melbourne C.O.S. held at the Town Hall on Wednesday, March 26, 1890* (Melbourne, 1890), p. 9.

[3] Joanna C. Colcord (ed.) *The Long View. Papers and Addresses of Mary E. Richmond* (New York, 1930), pp. 559–60.

[4] F. Morris, in 'The Reporter: Proceedings of the (C.O.S.) Council', *C.O. Review* (New Series), Vol. XXXVI, No. 215 (November 1914), p. 348.

[5] 'C. S. Loch: An Appreciation', *C.O. Review* (N.S.), Vol. XVIII, No. 104 (August 1905), p. 103.

he would not barter for a dozen 'Social Welfares',[1] now has emotional connotations universally disliked. And yet there is so much sense and wisdom in what he believed, and so clearly do his writings reveal the theoretical foundations on which early concepts of social work were built, that it is worth examining his ideas a little more closely.

In the first place, the motives which led Loch in 1875 to identify himself with the Charity Organisation Movement, rather than to continue the studies which would eventually have led him to the Bar, were well understood and shared by many of his contemporaries engaged in this and similar kinds of welfare work. Personal letters at this time to his friend, Charles P. B. Bosanquet, who was resigning the Secretaryship of the C.O.S., and to his fiancée, Sophia Peters,[2] reveal a deep indecision. Strongly idealistic, preoccupied with the usual worries of a young man about to marry and support a wife, not wishing to become a lawyer, toying with the idea of entering the Church, Loch was obviously casting around for work which would not only give him an income, but which would engage his mind and heart and use his talents and energy to the full. That he chose Charity Organisation is not surprising. His social conscience had already been stirred into life, mainly by a sense of guilt born of 'some vague regret' that the lives of others, judged by his own, were 'sunless and sad'.[3] Combined with this sense of guilt, there was a desire for action, in which he could play a part, to set the world right. 'Primarily we were drawn to work of this kind by the sight or thought of individual suffering', he confessed in 1898. 'A young man thought the world awry and waiting for him to set it straight, so he dreamed of Utopias and tried crude experiments, which had failed again and again.'[4] But more important than either a sense of guilt or a desire for action was Loch's strong instinct for service. Charity Organisation must have seemed to him a means whereby he could serve

[1] In reply to discussion on a paper, 'The Programme of Charity Organisation', *C.O. Review* (N.S.), Vol. XXVIII, No. 163 (July 1910), p. 71.

[2] No biography of Loch has yet been written. For these and other biographical details, the writer is indebted to Mrs. R. B. Mowat, daughter of Sir Charles Loch, who kindly allowed her to read Loch's diary and many of his family papers.

[3] 'The Charities of Church and Chapel', *C.O. Review*, Vol. VIII, No. 89 (May 1892), p. 168. See above, p. 22.

[4] A discussion of Bernard Bosanquet ,'Idealism in Social Work', in *C.O. Review* (N.S.), Vol. III, No. 15 (March, 1898), pp. 166–7.

—not God, though he was deeply religious as his Diary[1] and poetry[2] reveal—but his fellow men. In this he was typical of his age. Had he lived fifty years earlier, he probably would have become a clergyman, but since it was in 1875 that he was faced with the decision of what to do with his life, he was influenced by a current of thought in England which placed greater value on the love of man than on the service of God. Loch was influenced by this trend in mid-Victorian thought and feeling to the extent that he made his decision to serve his fellow men as a charity organizer rather than as a clergyman, and to devote his life to creating what he called 'a Church of Charity'[3] rather than to serving a sect of a church. 'If Charity is to fulfil her mission', he said, 'she can not suffer herself to be made either the servant or the nurse of even the most vigorous sectarianism.'[4]

That Loch is an example of what Beatrice Webb called 'the religion of humanity'[5] can be seen in his own account, written many years later, of why he joined the C.O.S. It is worth quoting at some length. 'If I were asked why I joined the Society', he wrote in 1904,

> I should answer that through its work and growth I hoped that some day there would be formed a large association of persons drawn from all churches and classes who, disagreeing in much, would find in charity a common purpose and a new unity. That, it seemed to me, was 'worth anything'. Such an organisation, I thought, could do more than Parliament, or preaching, or books, or pamphleteering. These, indeed, without the other, seemed likely to effect but small results. But such an organization might bring to bear on the removal and prevention of evils a combined force that would far exceed in weight and influence any yet existing. It could make legislation effective, could see that it was enforced. Apart from all legislative interference and with the use of means and influences more far-reaching it could renew and discipline the life of the people by a nobler, more devoted, more scientific religious charity. It

[1] Unpublished *Diary of Charles Stewart Loch, 1876–1892*, in the possession of Mrs. R. B. Mowat.

[2] *Things Within* (Oxford, 1922). This is a volume of poems which Loch wrote at intervals during his life, and published the year before his death 'for friends who would care to know me better'.

[3] 'The Development of Charity Organisation', *C.O. Review* (N.S.), Vol. XV, No. 86 (February 1904), p. 68.

[4] 'The Future of Charity', *C.O. Reporter*, Vol. XIII, No. 551 (27 September 1884), p. 321.

[5] *My Apprenticeship* (1950 ed.), p. 124.

could turn to account all that newer knowledge would bring to the help of charity. It could eventually provide out of all classes and sects a great army of friendly and by degrees well-trained workers. It could help us to realise in society the religion of charity without the sectarianism of religion.[1]

These, then, were the motives which prompted Loch to identify himself with Charity Organisation—an eagerness for action to allay a sense of guilt born of the realization that so many of his countrymen lived lives of hardship and hopelessness, a desire to serve his fellow men, and a conviction that this could best be done outside the Church, if only to flee the horrors of sectarianism.[2]

Strengthened by these beliefs, Loch set out to 'sell' the principles of Charity Organisation. 'There is a theory of Charity', he proclaimed, 'a theory that is like the map of a land . . . through which we can not make our way without disaster if we have not learnt where are its hills and valleys, and where its paths and passes.'[3] This theory of Charity he preached and popularized. In the annual reports of the C.O.S., in papers, signed and unsigned, in the Society's *Reporter* and *Review*, in letters to *The Times*, in pamphlets and in articles in learned journals, he expounded the principles of Charity with evangelical fervour. Often he was so defensive that even today his writings splutter with rage. The charge that the C.O.S. was solely a relief organization, or that it was concerned mainly with the detection of fraud ('a useful watch-dog to bark at imposters', fumed Loch[4]), or that people starved while in-quiries were being made always put him in war-like mood, but in calmer moments, his exposition of his philosophy of Charity has both eloquence and grace.

Loch began from the premise that the individual should make provision against what he called 'the ordinary contingencies of life'. Unless the individual maintained himself and his family,

---

[1] 'The Development of Charity Organisation', *op. cit.*, pp. 67–68.

[2] Cf. L. E. Elliott Binns' comment: 'It may be pointed out that some of those who gave themselves up to social work did so as a way of escape from the difficulties which they felt in regard to Christianity as a doctrinal system.' (*English Thought, 1860–1900. The Theological Aspect* (1956), p. 281.)

[3] 'The Growth of Medical Charities', *C.O. Review* (N.S.), Vol. IV, No. 23 (November 1898), p. 240.

[4] 'The Development of Charity Organisation', *op. cit.*, p. 65.

both the individual and society would suffer. The productive power of the community would be sterilized, and the individual demoralized. The individual, Loch explained, is

> originative and productive. If he cease to originate and produce, he must as a rule succumb, unless someone makes good to him the deficiency that results from his barrenness of production. In that case he is, socially speaking, a slave, a bad economic bargain. To shift the responsibility of maintenance from the individual to the State is to sterilise the productive power of the community as a whole, and also to impose on the State . . . so heavy a liability . . . as may greatly hamper, if not almost ruin, it. It is also to demoralize the individual. No social system of rewards and punishment . . . will be a substitute for the influence of the social law by which energy, honesty, and ability have their own reward, and failure in these things carries with it its own penalty.[1]

Into this economic framework, Loch fitted his principles of Charity. First, he said, no work of charity is complete which does not place the person benefited in self-dependence. Second, all means of pressure must be brought to bear upon the individual to help or force him into being self-dependent. Fear of destitution, a sense of shame, the influence of relatives, the threat of disfranchisement on the receipt of poor relief—these were the weapons to be used. Third, the family was to be considered as a whole; otherwise the strongest social bond would be weakened. Family obligations—the care of the young and the aged, help in sickness and in trouble—should be borne as far as possible by the family. Fourth, a thorough knowledge was necessary, both of the circumstances of the persons seeking relief and of the means of helping them; and fifth, relief, to effect a cure—as distinct from placing the applicant in a position of self-help—should be adequate in kind and quantity.[2]

In promulgating these principles, Loch was obviously making certain assumptions about human nature and society, assumptions which were more acceptable to his generation than to our own. First, he was assuming that, with certain rare exceptions, 'self-dependence' was possible for all men, and that if they failed to attain it, the fault lay in themselves, and not in any external

---

[1] 'Manufacturing a New Pauperism', *The Nineteenth Century*, Vol. XXXVII, No. 218 (April 1895), pp. 698–9.
[2] *How to Help Cases of Distress*, pp. 6, 8–9.

causes. The possibility that the fault could lie, wholly or in part, in the economic set-up of society did not enter the collective mind of the C.O.S. To them, character, not circumstance, was the explanation of failure.

This calm assumption that all was well with the economic and social organization of society and that there could be, would be, and should be no change in it, had several interesting results. In the first place, it led many C.O.S. supporters to deny that social conditions could ever be responsible for individual failure. 'But what if the social conditions will not permit them to meet the responsibility (of family)?' asked Helen Bosanquet, surprised. 'It is a vain and idle hypothesis. The social conditions *will* permit them; for their very effort to do so will make them steady and efficient workers, whose services will be valued by the community, and will be supplemented by the help of the young people who will grow up in such a family as theirs will be.'[1]

In the second place, the assumption that all was well with the economic and social organization of society led the C.O.S. grossly to under-rate the extent of the poverty with which they or the State had to deal. This is revealed most clearly in some of the asides which crop up in C.O.S. literature. For example, the Annual Report for 1894–95, discussing the training of volunteers, remarked that 'Charity (is) not the business of the upper classes only, nor even of that two-thirds of the population which many group as belonging to other than the working classes.'[2] This extraordinary claim that only one-third of England's population could be described as belonging to the working classes was voiced at a time when Charles Booth was making the survey which led him to conclude that 30·7 per cent of the inhabitants of London lived at or below the level of subsistence.

The second assumption which Loch was making in expounding his principles of Charity was that it was both necessary and desirable that State intervention be kept to an absolute minimum. The role of the State was to be limited to maintaining a Poor Law, based on the principles of 1834, to deal with those cases which were regarded as ineligible for private charity

[1] *The Strength of the People. A Study in Social Economics* (1903 ed.), p. 208.
[2] C.O.S., *Twenty-Seventh Annual Report. 1894–95*, p. 43.

either because the applicants were thriftless, given to drink, or leading immoral lives, or because their poverty was chronic and hence beyond the means of private charity to deal with effectively. If, for any reason, it was considered that an applicant for relief would not respond to the bracing qualities of private charity, he was to be handed over to the Poor Law. 'Poor relief', said Loch, 'is for those who, for some reason or other, are defaulters in the contract of social obligation. They do not maintain themselves. They throw the fulfilment of their obligation on others—on the State or on members of the community',[1] and because they were defaulters, they deserved the harsh treatment meted out to them by Poor Law Guardians reared on the principles of 1834.

Third, Loch's exposition of his theory of Charity—in particular his claim that the Poor Law and the voluntary agency each had its own clientele and methods—was based on the assumption that there was some means by which the 'deserving' poor could be separated from the 'undeserving'.

C.O.S. attempts to hammer out this concept of the 'deserving' began soon after the Society was established. When the first number of the *Charity Organisation Reporter* appeared in 1872, it was obvious that a heated debate on the subject had been going on in C.O.S. circles for some time. 'There is a good deal of difference of opinion as to the meaning of the word, "deserving",' J. R. Hollond was reported to have confessed to a meeting of representatives of Country Societies. 'To my mind it ought to include providence, or some attempt at it, and attendance of children at school.'[2] Ten years later the argument was still raging. 'A "deserving" poor person is one who does not impose on the benevolence of the rich, and is respectable', announced an editorial in 1882. 'It is by no means a condition of his desert that he should have made some provision for the future or for sickness.'[3] This marked inability to decide what constituted a deserving cause was responsible for a good deal of latitude in the application of the concept. When, for example,

[1] 'Solidarity Considered as a Test of Social Condition in England', *C.O. Review* (N.S.), Vol. XXVI, No. 154 (October 1909), p. 263.
[2] 'The Principles of Charitable Relief', *C.O. Reporter*, Vol. I, No. 11 (27 March 1872), p. 62.
[3] Editorial on 'Deserving Cases', *C.O. Reporter*, Vol. XI, No. 411 (19 January 1882), p. 15.

a circular was issued in 1878 to the District Committees seeking information on what they would consider to be conditions of eligibility for a pension, there was a great variety of answers, ranging from that of the District Committee of Poplar which, frowning upon any kind of pension, laid down such stringent conditions of eligibility that few would qualify, to that of the District Committee of Hampstead which admitted that 'good character' should always be considered 'but should not be pressed too far in the case of persons who have grown up under circumstances unfavourable to the exercise of this virtue'.[1]

In 1878, the Society made a gallant attempt to settle the question once and for all. Arising out of a letter which Loch wrote on behalf of the Council to Mr. Francis Peek, who had placed £1,000 at the disposal of the London C.O.S. to help them to deal with School Board cases referred to them by the Divisional Committee of the Board, the Council published its *Principles of Decision*. In this it declared:

> When . . . a District Committee has to decide upon any particular case, the questions it has to ask are:
> 1. What is the cause of the distress? . . .
> 3. . . . what effect will charitable relief have upon that cause?
> 4. . . . should charity deal with the cause or should it be left to the sterner treatment of the Poor Law?[2]

It then proceeded to lay down 'Suggestions' for dealing with certain cases such as the children of the family seeking aid, deserted wives or widows, and husbands unable to support their families. The principles which emerged from these suggestions were that each case was to be considered, not as isolated but as related to the general problems of poverty and pauperism; that if there had been wilful thriftlessness, it was as a rule wrong to assist; and that every case found after enquiry to be deserving should be assisted if the assistance was likely to improve permanently the condition of the recipient.[3] But, as though uneasy at laying down principles even as nebulous as these, the Society kept stressing the need for flexibility in their application 'We only urge', ran an editorial in 1883, 'that while

[1] *Digest of Answers to Questions Addressed to the District Committees of the C.O.S. on the Treatment of Deserving Permanent Cases of Distress, June, 1879* (1879), pp. 17, 25–27.
[2] 'Principles of Decision', *C.O. Paper*, No. 5, p. 2.   [3] *Ibid.*, p. 4.

keeping steadily and firmly to what have been found to be the best working principles, we should be careful not to forget their limitations, and above all, not to dogmatize on what may after all be an open question.'[1] Three years later, the C.O.S. came to terms with the inevitable. In its table of cases dealt with, it changed the title of 'undeserving' to 'not likely to benefit'; in 1887, it went further, and substituted the non-committal 'not assisted'.

Working on these principles, loosely defined and flexibly applied, the Society dealt with cases of distress brought to their notice. The Society stressed the fact that it was best to work on 'the special cases system'—that is, to raise the necessary money for each case separately instead of dispensing it from a fund previously collected—for, as Loch pointed out, a committee that can relieve from a general fund is tempted to neglect the principles of Charity Organisation. Because the money for relief was at hand, there was little incentive to take the trouble of writing letters to interest people in the case; reliance on a general fund had a tendency to make relief inadequate; the committee might be tempted to grant a small sum when a large one should be procured. And finally, he argued, 'every good report on a case is an education in charity organisation; every case, therefore, relieved from the general fund of the Committee is an opportunity lost'.[2] Accordingly, the Society aimed to raise help separately for each case. In its Central Office, it kept a 'Golden Book' to record the names of whose who would be willing to be referred to occasionally when a 'heavy' case had to be dealt with by one of the District Committees. On at least one occasion this Golden Book assumed human powers, for in June 1878 a letter, signed 'Golden Book', found its way to the editor of the *Charity Organisation Review*. 'I have now been for some time in actual existence', it complained softly, 'but I am leading an idle and useless life.'[3] Since the Golden Book often failed to arouse a response, personal letters were written to known philanthropists, details of cases deemed worthy of aid were printed in the Annual Reports, and advertisements, asking for a

---

[1] *C.O. Reporter*, Vol. XII, No. 477 (26 April, 1883) p. 133.
[2] 'Secretary's Report on Visits to District Committees, December, 1880', *C.O. Reporter*, Vol. XI, No. 417 (2 March 1882), p. 61.
[3] *C.O. Reporter*, Vol. VII, No. 262 (20 June 1879), p. 119.

particular sum in each case, appeared regularly in the Society's newspaper. Once money was raised, assistance was given in suitable form.

The amount and kind of help can be gauged from the figures of cases decided upon by the District Committees in 1872.

Class I: Dismissed as:

Not requiring relief	1,037
Ineligible	2,273
Undeserving	1,240
Giving false address	360
Class Total:	4,910

Class II: Referred to:

The Poor Law	1,413
District Agencies	1,645
Private Persons	1,157
Charitable institutions	469
Class Total:	4,684

Class III: Assisted by:

Grants	3,293
Loans	1,039
Employment	391
Letters to Hospitals	435
Labour Register	623
Class Total:	5,780

Grand Total:	15,374[1]

Behind these sober statistics, there lay, not only a story of hard work and devoted endeavour, but the set of assumptions which the C.O.S. and their fellow welfare workers made, consciously and unconsciously, about the nature of society and human behaviour. That the social order was unalterable, and the division between rich and poor should continue, was taken for granted. The assumption that poverty was a problem of individual character and its waywardness, rather than a problem of industrial and economic organisation, was shown by C.O.S. attempts to distinguish between the deserving poor who should be rewarded and the undeserving who should be turned

[1] C.O.S., *Fourth Annual Report, 1873*, Table, p. 2.

away. The belief that human beings, under the stress of poverty, would lie, cheat and prefer parasitism to work was shown by the numbers of cases found suitable only for dismissal or transference to the Poor Law. That there was also hope of reform, human nature being malleable and hence subject to improvement, was also shown by the type of help most frequently given. 'It is the economic competence of the individual . . . which forms the best antidote against pauperism',[1] the C.O.S. announced, and accordingly hand-tailored its help to increase competence. Certain cases were referred to the appropriate charitable quarters. Grants were made to set a man on his feet, and loans to tide him over certain emergencies such as sickness. Employment relief was granted only very reluctantly and in exceptional cases, for it was believed that if an agency, or worse still, the State, gave relief in any form to a man who could work for a living, it would drive him into idleness. 'Some classes of workmen have to expect periodical want of employment', the Society declared in 1879, 'In these cases it is unwise to give charitable assistance except by loan and on a prospect of work being forthcoming at an early date'.[2] State public works, especially, were frowned upon. Loch issued grim warnings against 'the State as caterer-in-chief for its citizens',[3] while as late as 1905, the Society sternly denounced the Unemployed Workmen Act on the grounds that 'What is called the problem of unemployment cannot be solved by the artificial provision of work with relief more or less disguised as wages'.[4]

The type of assistance of which the Society approved was individual, personal, temporary and reformatory. A single woman, a dressmaker, laid low for a year by sickness, would be granted a loan of £1 'to complete sum required for purchase of sewing machine', and would repay the loan at one shilling a week.[5] A young man, an iron chipper, who had 'broken down in his work' would be sent to a Convalescent Home at Ramsgate to recover, the costs being shared by the C.O.S. and 'two single

---

[1] C.O.S., *Thirty-Ninth Annual Report, 1906–1907*, p. 3.

[2] C.O.S., *Tenth Annual Report, 1879*, p. 25.

[3] Arthur Clay (ed.), *A Great Ideal and its Champion. Papers and Addresses by the Late Sir Charles Stewart Loch* (1923), p. 221.

[4] C.O.S., *Thirty-Eighth Annual Report, 1905–1906*, p. 7.

[5] C.O.S., *Annual Reports of the Council of the District Committees, 1883–1884*, Report of Battersea Committee, p. 158.

brothers . . . in receipt of good wages'.[1] Parents of a boy of thirteen, who had lost a knee-cap through accident, would be granted a sum of money so that they could complete the purchase of a surgical boot for him.[2] A widow with four young children to support, removed from the parish of her birth and hence unable to get out-door relief, would be given 'a laundry business, with a mangle and other necessaries, in a small cottage', and her youngest child, who was ailing, sent to hospital.[3] Another widow would be given training as an ironer so that she could do laundry work to support herself and her four young children.[4] A garrulous old lady sent by the Board of Guardians, with the message, 'Before making a pauper of me, the gentleman said I was to come to see you', would be given a weekly pension of 7 shillings, solicited from friends, old employers and a nephew, because at seventy-six, it was granted, she was too old to work to support herself.[5] A labourer, with a wife and three children, unable to get work, would be given £5 'for necessary outfit and expenses' before he migrated to America at the expense of his sister who lived there,[6] while at a later date, the Society, in more frivolous mood, might advance £19 10s. 0d. to a 'very poor, thin, shabby, young man, thoroughly down on his luck' for the purchase of 'drums and other instruments such as are used in jazz bands'.[7]

Of course, many an appeal for assistance was unsuccessful, either because the District Committee handling the case considered it should be dealt with by the Poor Law or some other agency, or because the applicant had been found wanting in some respect. 'Case 1,123 was ineligible', the Brixton Committee sternly announced in 1884, 'and illustrates how inclined many are to run to charity for help, instead of themselves "putting by for a rainy day". A man, 36 years of age, earning 34s. a week, paying 4s. 6d. a week for rent, and having only

---

[1] Report of Fulham and Hammersmith Committee, *ibid.*, p. 59.
[2] Report of City of London Committee, *ibid.*, p. 113.
[3] 'Principles of Decision', *op. cit.*, p. 8.
[4] 'The Work of the District Committees. A Paper read by Miss Pickton, an Honorary Secretary of the Paddington Committee, at a Special Meeting of the Council of the C.O.S., March 23, 1896', *Occasional Paper*, First Series, No. 58, p. 271.　　　　　　　　　　　　　　　[5] *Ibid.*, pp. 270–1.
[6] C.O.S., *Annual Reports of the Council of the District Committees, 1883–1884*, Report of the Kensington Committee, p. 53.
[7] C.O.S., *Fifty-Seventh Annual Report, 1926*, p. 9.

his wife and one child to keep, applied for a convalescent letter for his child, stating that he could not afford anything towards sending her to a Home, as he was greatly in debt. It was proved that he had only five weeks out of work, during the last twelve months.'[1]

The principles on which individual cases were decided were stated in formal fashion[2] for use by the Society's workers, and advertised widely so that all prospective clients would know exactly where they stood. Form No. 28, which was the Society's *Notice to Persons Applying for Assistance*, must have deterred many, for it barked out the conditions on which the Society gave help.

1. The Society desires to help those persons who are doing all they can to help themselves, and to whom temporary assistance is likely to prove a lasting benefit.

2. No assistance should be looked for without full information being given in order that the Committee may be able to judge:

(1) Whether the applicant ought to be helped by charity.

(2) What is the best way of helping them. . . .

3. Persons wishing to be assisted by Loans must find satisfactory security, such as that of respectable householders. . . . Loans have to be paid back by regular instalments.

(4) Persons who have thrown themselves out of employment through their own fault ought not to count upon being helped by charity.

5. Persons of drunken, immoral or idle habits can not expect to be assisted unless they can satisfy the Committee that they are really trying to reform.

6. The Society does not, unless under exceptional circumstances, give or obtain help for the payment of back rent or of funeral expenses. But when help of this sort is asked for, there may be other and better ways of assisting.

7. Assistance will not, as a rule, be given in addition to a Parish Allowance.

By Order,

C.O.S.

.................Committee.[3]

---

[1] C.O.S., *Annual Reports of the Council of the District Committees. 1883–1884*, Report of the Brixton Committee, p. 149.

[2] 'Principles of Decision', *op. cit.*

[3] *Form No. 28. Notice to Persons Applying for Assistance*, included in collection of *C.O.S. Forms, Papers, Investigation Tickets, Bye-laws, Almanack, etc. 1877–90*, in the possession of the Family Welfare Association (formerly C.O.S.), Denison House, London.

Other forms and notices, too, were drawn up and circulated, for from the beginning, the Central Office did its best to encourage and to help the District Committees to follow a system with all of its cases. The first publications of the C.O.S. in 1870 were on the organization of district charities, house-to-house visiting, and included six *District Committee Papers* containing model bye-laws, forms, and statements of principles.[1] In addition, the Central Office supplied many kinds of forms—for making loans, for demanding repayments, for requesting information from a previous employer whose name was given as a reference by an applicant, for sending information to secretaries of District Committees and Country Societies, and for revision of pensions. It also issued Visitors' Reports, application forms, Decision Books and Record Books, with spaces for entering such details of the applicant as occupation, previous addresses, the condition of his house and neighbourhood, names and ages of all his family, his debts including articles in pawn, his past and present earnings, the cause of distress, whether any friends or relatives could help him, his personal character, his state of health, how he was subsisting, and the kind of assistance asked for and given.[2] In addition, the Society, with didactic intent, unleashed a spate of *Occasional Papers*, which not only explained the principles and practice of Charity Organisation, but instructed the Society's workers in the arts of district visiting and case work. As Loch stressed, 'Good casework is the first condition of organisation', and the Society could expect cooperation only if it proved that its work was 'better on every point' than that of other agencies.[3] Moreover, by keeping these written, uniform, confidential records of each case, as Octavia Hill pointed out, some unity of action could be achieved and and the privacy of the poor maintained.[4] And since the books of reference at the Central Office also included accounts of 'cases of Imposters', cut from leading newspapers and alphabetically

[1] Contained in two C.O.S. collections, entitled *District Committee Papers, etc.* and *C.O.S. Pamphlets, 1870–82*, in the possession of the F.W.A., London.

[2] Contained in two collections of C.O.S. documents, *C.O.S. Forms, Papers, Investigation Tickets, Bye-laws, Almanack, etc., 1877–90*, and *C.O. Papers, 1898*, in the possession of the F.W.A.

[3] 'Secretary's Report on Visits to District Committees, December, 1880', *C.O. Reporter*, Vol. XI, No. 414 (9 February 1882), p. 40.

[4] 'The Work of Volunteers in the Organisation of Charity' (from *Macmillan's Magazine*, October 1872) included in *C.O.S. Pamphlets, Leaflets, 1884*, p. 12.

indexed,[1] there was little likelihood that the Society would be easily hoodwinked into giving relief to what they considered undeserving cases. Detection of fraud, for all Loch's protestations to the contrary, was an important part of the Society's work, and was a bait which attracted many followers to the C.O.S. banner. 'I joined this Society because I saw that it was really engaged in . . . the detection . . . of fraud in connection with charity', said the Earl of Shaftesbury. '. . . I congratulate you upon the establishment of a Society . . . which . . . acts so promptly in exposing the imposter.'[2] 'I do not think it is possible to overrate the services which the C.O.S. has rendered in detecting and exposing this kind of rascality', echoed Lord Derby[3] at a later date, while in 1878, a prominent member of the Society, Mr. Alsagar Hay Hill, could, without a flicker of a smile, recommend that the name of the Mendicity Sub-Committee be changed to that of the Inquiry Sub-Committee.[4]

In appealing to individuals and agencies to support those cases which thorough investigation proved to be worthy, the C.O.S. relied on the effect of case histories given in full. Here is a typical case from Newington in 1883.

9552: W.S. is a hawker of clothes-horses, which he makes himself. In March, 1883, he applied to the Relieving Officer, and was by him referred to the Committee for assistance to buy stock. He had formerly cleared 20s. or 30s. a week, but illness, succeeding a slack time, had brought him very low, and, having run out of stock, he was unable to pursue his calling. He had been compelled to part with his horse and cart, and had pawned many of his things; and he owed 8s. for rent. He was thirty-six years of age, and had a wife and ten children, the eldest of whom was a boy of twelve. Inquiry showed him to be a man of respectable character, and the Committee thinking that he would do his best to recover his position, gave temporary assistance to take the family off the parish, obtained £1 from the Society for the Relief of Distress to provide him with stock, and allowed him 4s. a week for two months for the hire of a donkey and cart. When in the middle of June, the family were left to support

[1] *C.O. Paper*, No. 8, p. 7.

[2] 'The Opinions of Several Experienced Men, expressed at the late Annual Meeting in reference to the Operations of the C.O.S.', undated, possibly 1876, p. 1. Included in collection of *C.O.S. Papers, etc.*

[3] In a letter of apology for absence from annual C.O.S. meeting on 22 March 1888, *C.O. Review*, Vol. IV, No. 41 (May 1888), p. 199.

[4] *C.O. Reporter*, Vol. VIII, No. 276 (14 November 1878), p. 193.

themselves, the total expenditure on the case amounted to £3 16s. Shortly afterwards, S. applied for a loan to enable him to purchase his donkey and cart, but this the Committee were not, as yet, prepared to grant. In January, S. was visited at his home. He stated that he had, in spite of a fire, by which he lost tools and stock, maintained himself and family to the present time. He was now earning on an average 24s. a week, and had no debts. He had previously been advised to join a Friendly Society, but this, he stated, he had not yet been able to do, as the hire of his donkey and cart—3s. 6d. a week—absorbed the whole margin of his earnings. Wishing to enable him to make provision against a recurrence of sickness, the Committee now have it in contemplation to purchase the donkey and cart, and, conditionally on his joining a Friendly Society, to let them out to him on the present terms until he has paid in hire their full value, when, if it is found that he has kept up his club payments, they will become his property.[1]

Thus, after investigation of a case of distress, did the C.O.S. seek to administer aid.

Of course, casework, with its concomitants of the interview, the visit, the investigation and the case committee, did not spring Minerva-like from the collective brain of the C.O.S. There were many antecedents on which the Society could draw for its principles and practices. A student in pursuit of what Marc Bloch calls 'the demon of origins'[2] could find much to interest him in the work of St. Vincent de Paul, who, in the France of 1617, established what was known as 'Ladies of Charity'. These were groups of well-to-do women, who, under the spell of St. Vincent, looked beyond their own cushioned existence, and visited the poor in their homes to nurse the sick and bring food and clothes to the needy. But the volunteer work of leisured women was uncertain, so in 1633 St. Vincent founded the famous organisation, 'The Sisters of Charity', recruited from peasant country girls, who sallied forth from their cloister to attend the sick, the dying, the prisoner and the poor. Rules were devised to guard against indiscriminate giving; a case, before it was visited, had to be 'passed' by the treasurer, and St. Vincent was careful to divide the poor into categories according to whether they were fully or partially self-supporting.

---

[1] C.O.S. *Fifteenth Annual Report, 1882–1883*, p. 45.
[2] *The Historian's Craft* (Manchester, 1954), p. 31.

Other sources on which English, and later American, Charity Organisation could and did draw for some of their techniques and ideas were the late eighteenth-century Hamburg scheme of poor relief, with its well-organized system of district visiting; Count Rumford's charitable work in Bavaria with its emphasis on self-dependence, strict book-keeping and publicity of accounts; the use of the district conference made, in the 1830's, by Frederick Ozanam and Sylvain Bailly to guide and help the friendly visitors of their newly created Society of St. Vincent de Paul; and the work of the Elberfeld system in Germany in the 1850's, with its emphasis on individualization in the case of the poor and the importance of records and comparative statistics.[1]

But perhaps of all the precursors of the Charity Organisation movement, few had greater influence than Dr. Thomas Chalmers, the great Presbyterian leader, who, in the Glasgow parish of St. John's in the short period from 1819 to 1823, devised a scheme for meeting the problem of poverty which anticipated in many ways the work of the C.O.S. later on in the century.[2]

The Poor Law, Chalmers claimed, is like the rod of Aaron, whereby 'if it once make its appearance amongst them, all the divinations of all the wise men will be swallowed up and brought to nothing'. Pauperism—the reliance in whole or in part on poor relief or alms—should be abolished, and a thoughtful, considered charity, which took cognizance of the effects of its gifts upon the recipient, should be encouraged. Only then would what Chalmers called the 'Four Fountains', 'now frozen or locked up by the hand of legislation', be free to do their beneficent work. 'The first and by far the most productive of these

[1] For further detail, see Frank Dekker Watson, *The Charity Organisation Movement in the United States. A Study in American Philanthropy* (New York, 1922), Chapter II.

[2] It is misleading, though, to claim, as A. F. Young and E. T. Ashton do, that the C.O.S. 'was in direct line of descent from Chalmers'. (*British Social Work in the Nineteenth Century* (1956), p. 113). For example, C. S. Loch, while acknowledging the fact that Charity Organisation 'has gradually worked out its system on lines more and more similar to those that Dr. Chalmers advised', stated specifically that '. . . when the C.O.S. was established in London . . . I should doubt if the fundamental conceptions of Dr. Chalmers were then appreciated.' ('Dr. Chalmers and Charity Organisation', *C.O. Review* (N.S.), Vol. II, No. 8. (August, 1897), pp. 69, 73.)

[3] N. Masterman (ed.) *Chalmers on Charity. A Selection of Passages and Scenes to illustrate the Social Teaching and Practical Work of Thomas Chalmers, D.D.* (1900), p. 25.

fountains, is situated among the habits and economies of the people themselves,' he wrote.

> It is impossible but that an established system of pauperism must induce a great relaxation on the frugality and provident habits of our labouring classes . . .
> The second Fountain which pauperism has a tendency to shut, and which its abolition would re-open, is the kindness of relatives . . .
> A third Fountain, on which pauperism has set one of its strongest seals . . . is the sympathy of the wealthier for the poorer class of society.
> But there is another Fountain, that we hold to be greatly more productive than the last . . . the sympathy of the poor for one another.[1]

While having no faith in systems—'either the potato system, or the cow system, or the cottage system or the village system of Mr. Owen, or any one system of miraculous achievement'— Chalmers yet inaugurated a scheme in Glasgow which was to influence social work in England during an important phase of its development. The poor of Glasgow were clamouring for the introduction of a system of public relief. This demand Chalmers opposed. 'Nothing can be more natural', he explained, '. . . than that the care thus taken of each man by the legislature should lessen his own care of himself.[2] Although he failed in this fight against the introduction of out-door relief into Glasgow, he did succeed in getting permission to abolish it in the parish of St. John, which the Glasgow Town Council specially created in one of the poorest parts of the town so that he could try out his scheme of voluntary relief for the poor. The parish, consisting of 10,000 people, was divided into twenty-five districts, each in charge of a deacon who had some fifty families to look after. It was the deacon's task to investigate the circumstances of each individual who came to him for help. 'He who seeks another's bounty', Chalmers claimed, 'shall also submit to another's scrutiny'. After that, the deacon was to see what 'natural resources' could be mobilized to solve the particular problem of poverty.[3] Every attempt must be made to allow the Four Fountains to flow. Only if these failed, was public relief to be granted.

---

[1] *Ibid.*, pp. 59, 61, 65, 67. [2] *Ibid.*, pp., 223, 59–60. [3] *Ibid.*, pp. 247, 300.

It was obvious that Chalmers was expecting a great deal from his voluntary visitors who were to garner from applicants for relief such information about their family circumstances, their history and even their personalities as would help the deacon to act wisely and well. Where these visitors were to come from never worried Chalmers, for he assumed that there would always be a 'thoroughly natural' inequality in society and that the rich would be a reservoir from which to draw friendly visitors. 'For the best construction of a social edifice', he said, 'we would have a king upon the throne—not rising like a giant among pygmies or as an unsupported May pole in the midst of a level population; but borne up by a splendid aristocracy and a gradation of ranks shelving downwards to the basement of society.' Drawn from this favoured class, the visitor should have 'the taste and inclinations of a thorough localist', be prepared to enter upon 'a territory' in which 'he will feel a kind of property in families', and, moreover, be trained to 'stand forth', not 'in the general aspect of an almoner, but rather in the general aspect of a friend'.[1]

It was in this emphasis on the necessity to select and train voluntary visitors to understand and handle effectively all applications for relief, as well as in his emphasis on the evils of promiscuous and sentimental giving, that Chalmers made his most important contribution to nineteenth-century social work. And the practical application of his ideas in St. John's Parish influenced the poor relief system which was established in the Rhine city of Elberfeld in 1853, as well as the many casework societies, such as the Metropolitan Board of Guardians, the Central Relief Society and the Metropolitan Visiting and Relief Association, which were established in London in the mid-nineteenth century.[2]

Long before 1869, therefore, many of the C.O.S. precepts were being propounded and practised. It remained for the Society to codify these techniques, to transmit them from one worker to another, and, in doing so, to lay the foundation for a profession of social work with its own discipline and its own code of ethics.

---

[1] *Ibid.*, pp. 166, 168, 254, 241.
[2] For further detail of these societies, see A. F. Young and E. T. Ashton, *op. cit.*, Chapters 4 and 5.

In codifying techniques, and in keeping written records of cases so that each could be known and studied individually, the Society was acting in accordance with the mid-Victorian belief in the scientific method. Many writers of the '70's and '80's referred to 'our modern God Science',[1] and certainly, considering the material achievements which had resulted from worship at the God's shrine, there was reason for respect. Now came an attempt to apply scientific principles to human affairs. 'Among the many characteristics of a remarkable age', proclaimed the Reverend Henry Solly, 'not the least noteworthy is the rise and progress of Social Science. Practically speaking, this is the science of doing good and preventing evil in our social system.'[2] This 'new policy', agreed Edward Denison, 'aims at utilizing . . . the great stores of knowledge . . . which the mental activity of the last half century has created and accumulated . . . to diminish the sufferings and to increase the happiness of humanity at large'.[3] 'If we wish to improve the condition of the poor', added Loch, 'we must adopt scientific measures'.[4]

It is obvious from these remarks that the men and women who were in, or hovering on the fringes of, the C.O.S., did not underestimate the importance of their work. The C.O.S. to them was not just another voluntary organisation. It was to be the means to a better society based on what Shakespeare called 'degree', a society where each man had his station and used it to serve his neighbours; and if in this society a residue of misfortune remained, an all-beneficent Charity marshalled the philanthropic resources of the community to deal with it.

That the early social workers saw the world in this way is shown in their analysis of the problems they saw to be solved and the urgency they attached to their solution. First of all, even though they under-estimated the extent of the poverty with which they had to deal, they were well aware of its social danger. 'Every householder in Belgravia and Pimlico', a C.O.S. leaflet warned its readers in 1883, 'is in danger from a

---

[1] Ellice Hopkins, 'Social Wreckage', *The Contemporary Review*, XLIV (July 1883), p. 98.

[2] *The Solly Collection*, Vol. IX, Section 10 (*a*) Item 9; a paper on 'Social Science and Organised Philanthropy', J 81.

[3] Sir Baldwyn Leighton (ed.), *op. cit.*, pp. 167–8.

[4] 'The School of Sociology', p. 1, included in C.O.S. collection, *C. S. Loch. Pamphlets*.

wide bordering hem of a poor population.'[1] Across the border of Scotland, the fear was voiced even more bluntly. 'It is unsafe to have amongst us', said one observer, 'an ever-increasing number of starving, desperate men.'[2]

Two elements in this situation seem to have struck the social worker very forcibly. The first was the existence of class divisions so deep that not only had the rich and the poor little, if any, knowledge of each other, but the poor were removed from the beneficent influence of contact with the rich. T. H. S. Escott, speaking grandiloquently of 'Social Citizenship as a moral growth of Victorian England' might claim that 'the class fusion born of class sympathy . . . was in steady process of evolution',[3] but to less optimistic observers this was far from the truth. 'Each class is extraordinarily ignorant of other classes',[4] Loch wrote worriedly in 1897, while Octavia Hill in 1877 felt obliged gently to reprimand a meeting of district visitors and clergy for thinking of the poor as a race apart. 'Depend upon it', she said, 'if we thought of the poor primarily as husbands, wives, sons and daughters, members of households, as we are ourselves, instead of contemplating them as a different class, we should recognize better how the house training and high ideal of home duty was our best preparation for work among them.'[5]

In view of this separation of classes, it was thought that if the rich and poor could be brought together, both would benefit. 'The rich, in seeing something of the distresses of the poor', explained the C.O.S., 'will have forced upon their minds the responsibility attaching to wealth and leisure. . . The poor will . . . have the comfortable assurance that if the day of exceptional adversity should come, they will not be left to encounter it without a friend.'[6] Sometimes this idea was pushed

---

[1] A C.O.S. leaflet entitled *Ostriches in Belgravia*, p. 1, included in a collection of *C.O.S. Pamphlets, Leaflets, 1883*, in possession of F.W.A.

[2] *How to Relieve the Poor of Edinburgh and other Great Cities without Increasing Pauperism. A Tried, Economical and Successful Plan* (Edinburgh, 1867), p. 9.

[3] *Social Transformations of the Victorian Age. A Survey of Court and Country* (1897), chapter heading for Chapter VI, and p. 75.

[4] 'The Growth and Wants of Charity Organisations', *C.O. Review* (N.S.), Vol. II, No. 11 (November 1897), p. 244.

[5] *Our Common Land and other Short Essays* (1877), p. 25.

[6] *Personal Visitation of the Poor. Report of a Sub-Committee of the Council of the C.O.S. on the Visitation of the Poor in Connection with the C.O.S.* (1877), pp. 1, 2.

further, and 'settlements' of what Edward Denison called 'residents of a better class' were advocated or made in the poorest and most densely populated working class districts, so that they could 'give a push to a struggling energy . . . guide aspiring intelligence . . . or break the fall of unavoidable misfortune'.[1] As will be shown later, these settlements, unknown to themselves, were to become a source of social group work, which is one of the three main methods of social work.

The second element in this situation which struck the early social worker was the moral degradation which attended poverty in so many cases. No one reading the writings of the reformers of the period can miss the horror they felt, not at the poverty, but at the degradation of their fellow beings.[2] Octavia Hill, for instance, revisiting her childhood home in Russell Square in London, described her youthful despair as she gazed from the windows. 'There', she wrote, 'the first knowledge of misery and poverty came to me, the first real feeling of poverty for ourselves. . . . There . . . I had sat and watched, through the great windows, the London poor pass in rain and fog. There I sat and cried . . . at the remembrance of Tottenham Court Road on Saturday night, with its haggard faces.'[3] Likewise Beatrice Webb described her horror of 'the slums of great cities, stagnant pools of deteriorated men and women . . . demoralizing their children and all new-comers, and perpetually dragging down each other into ever lower depths of mendicancy, sickness and vice'.[4]

As a product of this mid-Victorian world where poverty entailed moral degradation and both constituted a danger to peace, social work played a dual role of social sedative and 'regenerator'. As a social sedative, it served to damp down social discontent by stressing the duties which the rich owed to the poor ('a sense of citizenship',[5] as Loch called it), while denying the fact that the poor had the social rights of a citizen. By making its concessions to the alleviation of poverty, it helped, not only to recreate that 'sense of membership in social

---

[1] Sir Baldwyn Leighton (ed.), op. cit., p. 8.
[2] Una M. Cormack, 'Developments in Case Work', in A. F. C. Bourdillon (ed.), Voluntary Social Services (1945), p. 89.
[3] Quoted by E. Moberley Bell, Octavia Hill, A Biography (1943), p. 19.
[4] Op. cit., pp. 172–3.
[5] Charity Organisation, p. 9.

life'[1] on which Loch set such store and which had been lost in the scrambling world of industrialism, but to eliminate the danger of social revolution. As one writer on Charity Organisation remarked in 1870, self-sacrifice on the part of the rich 'has its material or political uses. . . . A more kindly sentiment grows up which insensibly leavens the intercourse of classes, and softens, if it does not prevent, the threatened collision between them'.[2]

In its second role of 'regenerator', social work played a more positive, constructive part. The pauperism which was the main concern of the early social workers was regarded not merely as poverty to be relieved, but as moral degradation to be cured. Hence the individual rather than his environment was the focus of attention, and emphasis was placed on rescuing character. How to ferret out, beneath the surface of dependence, apathy, and hopelessness, some elements of character and will-power which could be utilized to bring the poor back to be self-respecting members of society—this was conceived to be the problem of the nineteenth-century caseworker. 'In the deep souls of those even who appear the worst', wrote Octavia Hill, 'there is a spark of nobleness.'[3] 'Charity is a social regenerator', added Loch, '. . . she has to support new desires; to revive old instincts; to keep alive family affection . . . to preserve the humane in man. We have to use Charity to create the power of self help'.[4]

In pursuing this aim 'to preserve the humane in man', the nineteenth-century social worker evolved many principles which still form an essential part of the modern theory and practice of social casework. Although she was more concerned with the economic problems of her clients, and much of her 'treatment' consisted of supplying financial and material assistance, in her aim to help individuals to attain strength to meet their problems, she was at one with her modern counterpart. Certainly she used a different language. Whereas a modern social worker often speaks of 'instinctual drives' and 'early experiences', of

[1] *The Ethics of Charity*, p. 2, included in C.O.S. Collection of *Miscellaneous Papers of C.O.S.*
[2] 'The Organisation of Charity, II,' *The Saturday Review*, Vol. 29, No. 754 (9 April 1870), p. 477.
[3] C. Edmund Maurice (ed.), *Life of Octavia Hill as told in her Letters* (1913), p. 61.
[4] 'The Future of Charity', *op. cit.*, pp. 320, 321.

'super-ego strengths' and 'unconscious influences', Octavia Hill stressed the necessity for 'knowledge of character' and divided her clients into 'deserving' and 'undeserving'. But the idea of developing a healthier, happier personality and of using the worker-client relationship to stimulate the client to want to change is common to both generations, even though in the nineteenth century it was expressed in terms of friendship and neighbourliness which assumed a kind of society which had already passed away. 'Our ideal must be to promote the happy, natural intercourse of neighbours',[1] said Octavia Hill. 'Only when face meets face, and heart meets heart; only in the settled link with those who are old friends . . . is (there) more opportunity . . . to grow and to shine.'[2] Likewise, although she spoke of the need for 'knowledge of character', it was obvious that she used the term in a very elastic sense to include the inner life and past experiences of the individual. 'By knowledge of character', she told the Social Science Association in 1869,

> more is meant than whether a man is a drunkard or a woman dishonest, it means knowledge of the passions, hopes and history of people; where the temptation will touch them, what is the little scheme they have made of their own lives, or would make, if they had encouragement; what training long past phases of their lives may have afforded; how to move, touch, teach them. Our memories and our hopes are more truly factors of our lives than we often remember.[3]

Again, although she sometimes seemed more concerned with the psychological boons which her good deeds could bring to herself and her fellow workers than with the welfare of her clients,[4] it was obvious that in her work as a whole, she placed the same emphasis on the worth and dignity of each individual as one of 'God's children'[5] as her modern counterpart does,

---

[1] *Our Common Land and other Short Essays*, p. 26.

[2] 'Our Dealings with the Poor', *The Nineteenth Century*, Vol. XXX, No. 174 (August 1891), p. 169.

[3] 'The Importance of Aiding the Poor without Almsgiving', in C. E. Maurice (ed.), *op, cit.*, pp. 257–8.

[4] E.g. '. . . unite the loving kindness of the friend to the control of the landlord, and, whether by gradual improvement of court, or wise management of block, you will rule a little kingdom in righteousness.' ('A Few Words to Fresh Workers', *The Nineteenth Century*, Vol. XXVI, No. 151 (September, 1889), p. 459.)

[5] C. E. Maurice (ed.), *op. cit.*, pp. 161, 111.

stressing the necessity to respect his right to self-determination. 'It is essential to remember', she said, 'that each man has his own view of his life, and must be free to fulfil it; that in many ways he is a far better judge of it than we, as he has lived through and felt what we have only seen. Our work is rather to bring him to the point of considering and to the spirit of judging rightly, than to consider and judge for him.'[1]

That this casework, with its assumed knowledge of human society and behaviour, entailed special qualities and qualifications in friendly visitors was very early realized. Inefficient, tactless or sectarian workers were likely to earn the criticism of friends and the opprobrium of critics. In 1877 speculation was rife about 'the injury which these lady-brigades from the West End would do the East'.[2] One clergyman complained bitterly that since personal work among the poor was inadequate, unorganized and often tainted with religious prejudice and partisanship, his parish might go unvisited, 'then there was a swoop of rival charitable eagles from all sorts of religious quarters to settle on the body'.[3] Later, another asked severely whether this was 'the only field of human action in which . . . good intentions take the place of training',[4] while Loch announced that since Charity was 'the work of the social physician', it was to the interest of the community that it 'should not be entrusted to novices or to dilletanti or to quacks'.[5]

As a result of this agitation, the C.O.S. in 1896 instituted for its visitors and social workers a scheme of training through lectures and practical work. The first ideas about training social workers stemmed from several sources, including the work of Octavia Hill, who, beginning her plan of rent-collecting in 1864, soon found it necessary to delegate some of the work to others. Perceiving the need for some kind of apprenticeship training, she began teaching new recruits her methods of helping the poor. The problem, as she saw it, was 'how to unite the fresh, loving, spontaneous, individual sympathy with the quiet,

---

[1] Quoted in a footnote by T. S. Simey, *Principles of Social Administration* (Oxford, 1937), pp. 157–8.
[2] Mr. Alsager Hay Hill, in *C.O. Reporter*, Vol. VI, No. 205 (15 February 1877), p. 27.
[3] Rev. M. S. Walrond, *ibid.*, p. 26.
[4] N. Masterton, *C.O. Review*, Vol. IV, No. 41 (May 1888), p. 188.
[5] *The Charities Register and Digest* (1895), p. x.

grave, sustained and instructed spirit of the trained worker'.[1]
At the same time, Margaret Sewell, Warden of the Women's
University Settlement in Southwark, began teaching her voluntary workers through the medium of group instruction in
lectures and classes. In 1890, the two schemes joined hands,
and volunteers, as well as paid workers, were trained for both
settlement work and rent-collecting through lectures at the
Settlement and field work in both sectors. The C.O.S., too,
through its District Committees, had also begun training
workers by setting them tasks to do under supervision in the
district offices. As early as 1894 Mrs. Dunn Gardner had
stressed the necessity for more systematic training and suggested practical measures.[2] Shortly afterwards a scheme of
training through lectures and practical work was instituted.
This, as the need for it became greater, suffered a sea-change.
In 1903 it became the School of Sociology with E. J. Urwick as
lecturer and tutor to the sixteen students enrolled. This school
had only a brief life under the C.O.S. wing, because in 1912,
owing mainly to lack of financial support, it amalgamated with
the London School of Economics to become the Department of
Social Science and Administration.[3]

Thus it can be seen that social casework, beginning as a bye-
product of the work of the C.O.S., changed quite considerably
during the first three decades of its history. By the end of the
century, it had broken free from many of its Lady Bountiful
traditions. Originally based on the concept of Charity, it had
evolved from a set of rules to guide volunteers in their work as
friendly visitors of the poor into a philosophy which embodied
many of the principles of modern casework and a technique
which could be transmitted by education and training from one
generation of social workers to another. But in spite of this,
social casework was still very much the product of nineteenth-
century individualism. Because it had originated and developed
within the framework of an organisation wedded to a certain
social philosophy, social casework inherited a set of assumptions

[1] 'Trained Workers for the Poor', *The Nineteenth Century*, Vol. XXXIII,
No. 191 (January 1893), p. 36.
[2] 'The Training of Volunteers', *C.O. Review*, Vol. XI, No. 120 (January 1895),
pp. 2–6.
[3] For further detail, see Marjorie J. Smith, *Professional Education for Social
Work in Britain* (1952).

about the nature of human society and its organisation which belonged to the nineteenth century rather than the twentieth. Particularly in the days when the C.O.S. engaged in its long-drawn out struggle with socialism, there was a tendency for social casework always to be identified with the Society's political and social philosophy. That there was justification for this might be inferred from the Society's annual report for 1927, which was entitled 'Bolshevism and its only true antidote: being the 58th Annual Report of the Council' and which claimed that 'the only real antidote to Bolshevism is good casework'.[1] This identification of casework with a conservative political ideology has proved a handicap. On the one hand, it has often retarded recognition of the value of casework as a method of helping individuals to live more effectively, and on the other, it has made more difficult the task of adapting social casework to the changed conditions of this modern age.

Social work, then, has inherited the inadequacies as well as the achievements of the particular period in which it was born. How to overcome the one and to use the other has been a problem which has engaged the attention of social workers almost since the inception of their craft.

[1] C.O.S., *Fifty-Eighth Annual Report, 1927*, p. 1.

III

◇◇

Social Group Work and Community
Organisation in 19th-Century England

◇◇

SOCIAL casework today has two companions, social group work and community organisation. Although there is a core of precepts, principles and practice which is common to all three methods of social work, there are also differences in content and emphasis which distinguish them from one another. Whereas social casework is preoccupied with the individual per se, group work, as its name suggests, is concerned with the group of individuals as the working unit, while community organisation aims to mobilize the resources of the community to meet human needs. Especially in the United States since the 1920's, when community organisation began to grow into a profession and group work to draw strength from developments in group dynamics and cultural anthropology, social workers have been busily trying to define and demarcate the two newest divisions of their craft. But even though they are more introspective and loquacious than their counterparts elsewhere, American social workers have often found it difficult to formulate precise definitions and to draw hard and fast lines between group work and community organisation on the one hand, and community organisation and social reform (or 'social action') on the other. As late as 1956, Gertrude Wilson, herself a definition-maker for her craft,[1] could deplore the fact that social group work was 'a label for a catchall of functions',[2] and later, in '58, one of her colleagues felt obliged to explain that the scope and nature of community organisation was not distinct or clear-cut because it was a young and developing specialization 'still in the struggle of professionalization'.[3] Considering, then, the difficulty of precise definition and demarcation, one can sympathize with the modern Monsieur Jourdain who merrily confessed that in England he had been doing something with energy and enthusiasm for a number of years 'which he now found to be group work'.[4]

Although it was only in the twentieth century that social group work and community organisation began to assume professional garb, the pattern was chosen and the cloth cut at a much earlier date. The present principles and practices of social group work were foreshadowed in the daily round of the many groups such as the Friendly Societies, the youth organizations, the Ragged Schools, and especially the Settlements, which Victorian England fashioned to the varying hour, while community organisation, like social casework, originated within the shell of the Charity Organisation Society, and expressed a divergence within the Society which mirrored one of the conflicts on the wider stage of Victorian society.

Within the C.O.S. there were two distinct trends in theory and practice, one leading towards individualization and social casework, the other to 'socialization' and community organisation.

[1] E.g. she describes social group work 'as a process and a method through which group life is affected by a worker who consciously directs the interacting process toward the accomplishment of goals which in our country are conceived in a democratic frame of reference'. (Gertrude Wilson and Gladys Ryland, *Social Group Work Practice* (Boston, 1949), p. 61.)

[2] 'Social Group Work Theory and Practice', *The Social Welfare Forum, 1956. Proceedings of the Eighty-Third National Conference of Social Work* (St. Louis, Missouri, 1956), p. 158. Afterwards cited as *N.C.S.W.*

[3] Genevieve W. Carter, 'Social Work Community Organisation Methods and Processes' in Walter A. Friedlander (ed.), *Concepts and Methods of Social Work* (Englewood Cliffs, N.J., 1958), p. 219. In spite of this philosophy of despair, however, Community Organisation has been defined as 'the process by which people of communities, as individual citizens or as representatives of groups, join together to determine social welfare needs, plan ways of meeting them, and mobilize the necessary resources'. (*Social Work Year Book, 1954* (New York, 1954), p. 121.)

[4] Mr. A. Roberton, Governor of the North Sea Camp, in a discussion on group work. *Report of the Association of (English) Social Workers of a Conference on the Social Worker and the Group Approach* (28–29 May 1954), p. 24.

A social philosophy which regarded poverty as a problem of individual character and its waywardness tended to absolve the social order of any responsibility for the conditions which reduced individuals to destitution. It placed its hope of better things in the change of heart in the individual to be effected through skilful use of the relationship between the friendly visitor and the visited. 'My hope is not in change of circumstances, not in schemes or systems',[1] confided Octavia Hill. 'Alleviation of distress may be systematically arranged by Society, but I am satisfied that without strong personal influence no radical cure of those who have fallen low can be effected.'[2] The implication was clear. If social evils existed at all, they were due to human weakness.

But an awakened social conscience coupled with some comprehension of the economic and social order gave pause to this comforting proposition, and compelled attention to some of the factors which lay outside the individual which could feasibly be the source of social suffering and discontent. Sometimes this attention was based on rather fragmentary knowledge, but now and then it did tend to move the spotlight from 'internal' to 'external' causes and to promote some analysis of the social order as well as of the individual. Sometimes, of course, this social analysis seemed to be undertaken for the express purpose of unearthing evidence to reinforce existing beliefs. C. S. Loch, on one occasion, was so intent upon proving that Charles Booth's scheme for an old age pension of five shillings a week would pauperize those unfortunate enough to receive it, that he could quote Giffen's figures of the jagged distribution of income between the various classes without once realizing their significance,[3] while Helen Bosanquet, reviewing the reasons why a man might not be able to meet his family obligations, could scoff at the idea that social conditions could ever be responsible for individual failure.[4]

[1] 'Our Dealings with the Poor,' *The Nineteenth Century*, Vol. XXX, No. 174 (August 1891), p. 169.

[2] 'The Importance of Aiding the Poor without Almsgiving. An address to the Social Science Association, 1869', printed in Henrietta G. Barnett, *Canon Barnett. His Life, Work and Friends* (1919), I, 29.

[3] 'Pauperism and Old Age Pensions. A Paper read at the Poor Law Conference for the South Wales District, May, 1892', printed in Bernard Bosanquet (ed.), *Aspects of the Social Problem* (1895), pp. 126–66. See especially pp. 158–61.

[4] *The Strength of the People. A Study in Social Economics* (1903), p. 208.

But there were others in the field of social work who followed where their studies led. Edward Denison, for example, hotly denounced what he conceived to be the social evils of his time— an urban population which had become redundant and demoralized, the lack of a due balance between agricultural and manufacturing industry, a political and industrial structure 'ingeniously framed to keep the bulk of the people in a state of serfage', pauperism and crime which were 'social ulcers' so malignant 'as to demand instant surgical treatment'—and in denouncing these evils, he was led to deplore 'the contented ignorance of the true causes of our economic derangement', and to resolve to seek them out for himself.[1] 'The problems of the time are social', he decided, 'and to social problems must the mind of the Legislature be bent for some time to come.'[2] Likewise General Booth, trumpeting his call for 'a Social Lifeboat Brigade', turned his eyes to the social system to explain why, in spite of the well-meaning efforts of philanthropists, 'a perfect quagmire of Human Sludge'[3] still remained, and Canon Barnett, adherent of a 'practicable' if limited Socialism, foresaw the day when victims of the social system would seek recompense for their suffering. 'The most dangerous symptom of the disease of society is not the ragged sleeper on the doorstep, but the ill-paid and unemployed worker', he warned, '. . . by and by it will perhaps be seen that what neighbours need is not the crumbs which fall from the table, but a seat at the board.'[4]

Sentiments such as these must have influenced quite profoundly the friendly visitors and social workers of the C.O.S. In 1893, for instance, we find Miss H. Dendy, District Secretary

[1] Sir Baldwyn Leighton (ed.), *Letters and Other Writings of the Late Edward Denison, M.P. for Newark*, pp. 156, 158, 153, 194, 110.

[2] *Ibid.*, p. 67. It should be pointed out, however, that Denison also disapproved of 'that vortex of public works which leads inevitably to the bottomless pit of Communism' (*ibid*, p. 114) and described as 'the fatal Communistic element pervading our Poor Laws' the legal right which permitted the allegedly improvident and worthless to be maintained out of the earnings of the industrious. (*Ibid.*, pp. 137–8.)

[3] '"Let things alone", the laws of supply and demand, and all the rest of the excuses by which those who stand on firm ground salve their consciences when they leave their brother to sink, how do they look when we apply them to actual loss of life at sea. . . . We want a Social Lifeboat Institution, a Social Lifeboat Brigade, to snatch from the abyss those who, if left to themselves will perish as miserably as the crew of the ship that founders in mid-ocean.' (*In Darkest England and the Way Out* (1890), pp. 43, 73.)   [4] H. O. Barnett, *op. cit.*, II, 271, 270.

of the Shoreditch Committee, stressing the necessity to know the past history of 'cases', and obviously aware of the influence which social factors had upon her clients' behaviour. 'Human beings cannot be treated as simple units', she said. '. . . the man with his character such as his temperament and surroundings have made it, can only act within the limits of the community of which he is a fraction.'[1]

This divergence, inside and outside the C.O.S. fold, between those who pointed the finger of criticism at the individual and those who directed it towards the social system led to a dual approach to the problems which social work tried to solve. On the one hand, C.O.S. visitors continued to give an individualized service to those who sought material or spiritual first-aid, accepting them as they were, granting aid to tide them over their difficulties, and working on their strengths to make them once again self-supporting members of society. At the same time, they began to advocate changes within the existing framework of society which would produce less devastating effects upon the individual.

Right from its inception, the Society had one eye cocked to its casework, the other to the wider questions affecting the conditions of the poorer classes in London. The *First Annual Report* had declared that the daily experience of the District Committees 'shows that the great questions of Sanitary Improvement, Emigration, Education, Provident Societies, Improved Dwellings for the Poor, and other collateral subjects must at an early date engage their most earnest attention',[2] and in accordance with this cinemascopic vision of its task, the C.O.S. combined casework with an active campaign for the improvement of social conditions. It co-operated with Octavia Hill in her campaign for better housing. It set in motion Sanitary Aid committees to prevent the spread of infectious diseases. It organized a body of more than five hundred voluntary health visitors, and in 1886 inaugurated a project for visiting sick and crippled children out of which was to grow the Invalid Children's Aid Association. A little later a School

---

[1] *Thorough Charity. A Paper read at the First Meeting of the Charity Organisation Conference, London, 15 May, 1893* (1893), p. 4.

[2] Quoted by Helen Bosanquet, *Social Work in London, 1869 to 1912. A History of the C.O.S.* (1914), pp. 28–29.

Children's Care Committee and the first tuberculosis dispensary were established, to be later taken over by the London City Council. Likewise the Society undertook work for the blind and mentally defective, played an important part in the reform of medical charities, and with the appointment in 1895 of one of its District Committee secretaries, Miss Stewart, as almoner at the Royal Free Hospital, it initiated the hospital social service so familiar to us today.

Considering this many-sided activity on behalf of the community, it is no wonder that Canon Barnett applauded the destruction of what his wife called 'the walls of degrading and crippling environment',[1] and Octavia Hill on one occasion exclaimed 'Neighbourhood! Oh yes, it has strong claims—some of the best possible'.[2] These were verbal acknowledgement that the individual was influenced by factors external to himself, and that if the social worker was to help her clients to live more effective lives, she must not only take cognizance of the forces at work in society, but also mobilize community resources to meet human needs. This was the conviction which prompted these early experiments in social action. From them the later theory and practice of community organisation were to stem.

In seeking the nineteenth-century beginnings of social group work, one must look beyond the C.O.S. to the many groups, societies, associations and clubs which the Victorians fashioned for their own delight. 'This age may have its faults', said one lady in 1884, 'but it is not a lazy age', and to prove it, she extolled the work of the Society of Parochial Mission Women who plotted to improve, via soap, thrift and sanitation, 'the very lowest and least thrifty among the wives and mothers of the poorest class'.[3] Again, the Dowager Countess of Shrewsbury, applauding the aim of the Girls' Friendly Society to bind together 'ladies as Associates and working girls and young women as Members', explained that the advantage offered to members was 'to make virtue easier, and to act as a fence between them and the pitfalls of vice',[4] while Mrs. Barnett

[1] H. O. Barnett, *op. cit.*, I, 76.

[2] *Our Common Land and Other Short Essays* (1877), p. 71.

[3] Maud C. Hamilton, 'Mission Women', *The Nineteenth Century*, Vol. XVI, No. 94 (December 1884), pp. 984, 985.

[4] 'Prevention', *The Nineteenth Century*, Vol. XVIII, No. 106 (December 1885), pp. 957, 958.

exhorted the lady visitors of the Metropolitan Association for Befriending Young Servants to counsel the girls on behaviour and dress and to direct their minds from lovers to the wholesome reading of monthly periodicals. 'It is not like girls of our own class whose ignorance about sin we foster for fear of losing their innocence', she explained. 'The girls, alas! many of them with naturally coarse minds . . . are conversant already with all the terrible facts of life'.[1] There were other societies, too, which aimed to preserve youthful virtue or salvage the fallen, to inculcate Christian principles and to build up character.

Forming these clubs and associations was often a formidable task, not only because so many boys and girls of the new Machine Age had drifted from ancient family, neighbourhood or village moorings, but also because society itself placidly accepted the fact that for many there was no fate worse than childhood. William Pitt had publicly stressed the advantages of 'early employing (children) in such branches of manufacture as they are capable to execute',[2] and by the early nineteenth century child labour was geared to serve the needs of industrialism. So much was the institution of child labour taken for granted, that even the gentle Charles Lamb could voice sentimental delight in meeting a chimney sweep. 'Not a grown sweeper', he hastened to say, '. . . but one of those tender novices blooming through their first nigritude',[3] and some of Lamb's countrymen, even less squeamish than he, could argue that the chimneys of England's stately homes were far more important than its children. '. . . it is a thing impossible to do away with our climbing boys', the United Society of Master Chimney Sweepers were told at their first annual dinner in 1886. 'For instance, look at the Duke of York's fifty-one new chimnies. Let me ask any one of you in company, is it possible a machine could be poked up any one of them?'[4] The nineteenth century, even though it had its protagonists of youth, still had need of Jane Addams to give warning to its Chicagos that they were creating a society which wasted the young and that, in caring

---

[1] *The Work of Lady Visitors. Written for the Council of the Metropolitan Association for Befriending Young Servants* (1880), pp. 6, 10–11.

[2] Debate on Whitbread's Minimum Wage Bill, 1795–6, in Bland, Brown and Tawney (eds.), *English Economic History. Select Documents* (1937), p. 563.

[3] 'The Praise of Chimney Sweepers', in *Essays of Elia* (Oxford, 1951), p. 157.

[4] William Hone, *The Everyday Book* (1827), II, 620–1.

more for the products the young manufactured, they had denied youth's immemorial ability to reaffirm the charm of existence.[1]

In view of the widespread attitude towards children in the nineteenth century, one can appreciate the work done by the various youth clubs which began to make their appearance in the early part of the century. The Y.M.C.A. was founded in 1844, the Boys' Brigade, the Y.W.C.A. and various 'boys' clubs' in the 1850's,[2] while the Boy Scout and Girl Guide movements did not appear until the early twentieth century, when Lord Baden-Powell, finished with war in South Africa, could turn his mind to boys' camps in Brownsea Island and his pen to the romance of woodcraft and nature lore and the advantages of self-education for citizenship.[3]

It was not only the young, suddenly presented with more leisure to squander or to invest, who were organized into groups. There were many others as well. Friendly Societies, creatures of brotherly feeling and mutual aid, had long been a feature of English society. Defoe in 1696 had devoted a chapter to them in his 'Essay on Projects', using the term as something well understood by his readers, while George Rose in 1793 had shepherded through parliament 'An Act for the Encouragement and Relief of Friendly Societies'. These societies—as well as meeting a three-fold desire for security in sickness, a lump sum to spend at a future date, and avoidance of a pauper funeral— were social clubs for members, and since their objects did not constitute a threat to the existing order, Friendly Societies were regarded as desirable. It was only in the period from 1799 to 1824, when the outlawed trade unions made a retreat to fight behind the friendly benefits line, that society looked askance at some of them. Suspicions were soon allayed, however, for the objects of Friendly Societies were very much in accordance with Victorian injunctions to be thrifty and self-reliant.

Similarly, the Sunday School and the Ragged School, both based on a stern desire to protect property as well as to inculcate Christian knowledge, may have contributed, by example if not by theorizing, to the common stock of social workers' ideas. Taking pains not to compete with the 'British', 'Foreign' or

---

[1] *The Spirit of Youth and the City Streets* (New York, 1909).

[2] For further detail, see W. McG. Eagar, *Making Men. The History of Boys' Clubs and Related Movements in Great Britain* (1953).

[3] See Lord R. Baden-Powell, *Scouting for Boys* (1930).

'National' Schools in their task of transmitting as much of
the three R's as a commercially-minded middle class considered
necessary, both the Sunday and the Ragged School aimed to
'save' possibly unregenerate youth. Particularly in the case of
the Ragged School, the aim was child-care, rather than learning,
and often this led teacher and taught into fields more akin to
social work than to education.

But the institution which, unknown to itself, contributed
most to the theory and practice of social group work was
undoubtedly the Settlement. The first Settlement, Toynbee
Hall, was established by Canon Barnett in 1884, and within a
few years it was joined by Oxford House in Bethnal Green, the
Women's University Settlement at Southwark, Mansfield
House in Canning Town, the Bermondsey Settlement founded
by J. Scott Lidgett, and Newman House. When Charles Booth
in 1903 directed his surveyors' eyes to the Settlement scene, he
found there were 'now about a dozen Settlements in London',
four of them with special buildings, equipped with lecture halls,
class-rooms, club-rooms and gymnasia as well as rooms for residents, and all fulfilling their role of 'residential club with a purpose', the purpose being the social, moral or religious improvement of the neighbourhood in which the club was established.[1]

Inspiration for founding these Settlements came mainly
from religion, for in spite of such corrosive forces as Charles
Darwin, industrialism and a host of honest doubters, Christianity
still held its own. Even if intellectual doubts were not completely dispelled, there were many who echoed Canon Ainger's
sentiments and found them sufficient.

> With eager knife that oft has sliced
> At Gentile gloss or Jewish fable,
> Before the crowd you lay the Christ
> Upon the Lecture table.

> From bondage to the old beliefs
> You say our rescue must begin—
> But *I*—want refuge from my griefs,
> And saving from my sin.[2]

[1] *Life and Labour of the People in London. Third Series. Religious Influences*,
VII (1903), pp. 377, 377–8.

[2] Quoted by L. E. Elliott-Binns. *English Thought, 1860–1900. The Theological
Aspect* (1956), p. 365.

But although the religious motive was always present and many of the Settlements were sectarian, sometimes, as in the case of the Passmore Edwards and the Women's University Settlements, the founders sternly rejected sectarian bias and evangelical intent. The main emphasis was on creating what Octavia Hill called 'a solemn sense of relationship'[1] between the rich and the poor. It was believed that the estrangement between classes would be brought to an end only when the educated and the well-to-do went among the poor, and became Jacob in Esau's need.[2]

The philosophy which lay behind the Settlement movement was nowhere better expressed than by W. Moore Ede in 1896 when he discussed the attitude the Church should take to the social problems of town life. 'The dwellers in the East End of our towns', he said,

> will not be converted by missionaries and tracts sent by dwellers in the West End. The dwellers in the West End must go to the dwellers in the East themselves, share with the East those pleasures which give interest and delight to the dwellers in the West, and make up the fulness of their life. When the dwellers in the West go thus to the dwellers in the East they will be themselves converted, for they will have turned to Christ and accepted His yoke of personal service, and the dwellers in the East, recognizing the true helpfulness of the Christian life, will be converted too.[3]

The idea that dwellers in East and West should live side by side as neighbours was by no means new. Prior to 1884, when the movement took shape as a University Settlement, the purposes of Settlements had been defined by a succession of thinkers and workers. As early as 1850, Frederick Denison Maurice, in founding his Working Men's College, had dwelt upon the advantages of true human fellowship between the more educated and the less educated, the value of knowledge for its own sake, and the duty of all men to fulfil their functions in the social

[1] 'The Work of Volunteers in the Organisation of Charity' (from *Macmillan's Magazine*, October 1872). Included in collection of *C.O.S. Pamphlets, Leaflets, 1884*, p. 14.

[2] Rev. Brooke Lambert, 'The Outcast Poor: Esau's Cry', *The Contemporary Review*, XLIV (December 1883), pp. 916–23, and 'Jacob's Answer to Esau's Cry', *The Contemporary Review*, XLVI (September 1884), pp. 373–82.

[3] *The Attitude of the Church to Some of the Social Problems of Town Life*, pp. 102–3, quoted in K. S. Inglis, *The Churches and the Working Classes in Victorian England*, to be published in this Series.

order. Five years later, he was uttering the same sentiments with regards to women.[1] Again, Edward Denison in 1867 had become the first 'settler' in London's East End, and two years later, he and several others, including John Ruskin, met to discuss the possibility of doing something for the poor. At this meeting, it has been claimed,[2] the idea of a University Settlement was born.

That Cam and Isis should be summoned to this important undertaking of healing the breach between the classes was not surprising. Although few would go as far as William Garnett who claimed in 1887 that 'the old universities must be regarded as the property of the nation . . . in which every Englishman has a share',[3] the universities, especially through their extension work,[4] were beginning to lose something of their stubbornly aristocratic character. In addition, they were, in the '80's, an intellectual furnace in which new ideas were forged and old ones recast. 'The old Universities are no longer sleepy institutions outside the broad current of the national life', reminisced Alfred Milner in 1894, '. . . any new movement of thought at the Universities in these days rapidly finds an echo in the press and in public opinion'.[5] Furthermore, around the men in the Universities there was an aura of darkling discontent. Canon Barnett himself, seeking to explain the response to his call for Settlements, drew attention to this. 'They were conscious of something wrong underneath modern progress', he said, 'they realized that free trade, reform bills, philanthropic activity and missions had made neither health nor wealth. They were drawn to do something for the poor.'[6]

It is not surprising, then, that Canon Barnett—a product of Oxford and, while vicar of St. Jude's, plying back and forth

[1] 'Plan of a Female College for the Help of the Rich and the Poor', in *Lectures to Ladies on Practical Subjects* (1855).

[2] By Rev. Brooke Lambert, 'Jacob's Answer to Esau's Cry', *op. cit.*, p. 377. Mrs. Barnett, however, claims that the idea was her husband's. (*Canon Barnett. His Life, Work and Friends*, I, 308–9).

[3] 'University Education for the People', *The Contemporary Review*, LII (November 1887), p. 644.

[4] See J. Churton Collins, 'The Universities in Contact with the People', *The Nineteenth Century*, Vol. XXVI, No. 152 (October 1889), pp. 561–83.

[5] 'Reminiscence', printed in Arnold Toynbee, *Lectures on the Industrial Revolution of the Eighteenth Century* (1920), p. xxv.

[6] S. A. Barnett, in W. H. Reason (ed.), *University and Social Settlements.* (*Social Questions of Today*) (1898), p. 12.

between Oxford and Whitechapel—should have concluded that 'the poverty of life' which he saw in the East End of London, could best be removed 'by contact with those who possess the means of higher life'. 'Friendship is the channel by which the knowledge—the joys—the faith—the hope which belong to one class may pass to all classes', he said. '. . . . residence among the poor is . . . a simple way in which Oxford men may serve their generation.'[1]

Accordingly, the premises next to St. Jude's Vicarage were bought for £6,250, a Committee formed, an Oxford Fellow induced to give a £1,000 donation, and Toynbee Hall, with rooms for sixteen men, a classroom for three hundred students, and dining, conversation and drawing rooms, was given a local habitation and a name.

The name of the first Settlement was as significant as its local habitation. Arnold Toynbee, besides possessing the rare gift of opening the young minds which came to him at Oxford where he spent most of his short life, embodied many of the ideals and self-imposed limitations of the new movement. Playing an active part in the religious and social causes of his day, he was, simultaneously or consecutively, University don, Poor Law Guardian, Co-operator and Church Reformer, and participator in or spectator of Friendly Societies, trade unions, and any movements likely to promote better housing, open spaces, free libraries and municipal Socialism. But although he may have flirted with the left-wing movements of his day, his social philosophy had much more in common with Andrew Carnegie's call to his fellow millionaire to become 'the mere trustee and agent for his poorer brethren'[2] than with Karl Marx's manifesto to the revolutionaries of 1848. Toynbee, like Canon Barnett and his followers, was interested in social harmony, not economic equality. Like Canon Barnett, who accepted a 'practicable' Socialism which he thought could be put into operation without revolution, redistribution of income, increase in taxation and political parties,[3] Toynbee foresaw no changes in

---

[1] *Canon Barnett. His Life, Work and Friends*, I, 307.

[2] 'The Advantages of Poverty' (from *The Nineteenth Century*, March 1891), reprinted in Andrew Carnegie, *The Gospel of Wealth and other Timely Essays* (1901), p. 15.

[3] 'Practicable Socialism', *The Nineteenth Century*, Vol. XIII, No. 74 (April 1883), pp. 554–60.

the social structure. He put his faith in the belief that Robber Barons could be turned by exhortation into Robin Hoods. It was because there had been a ruling aristocracy in England, he argued, that 'we have had a great Socialist programme carried out'; therefore, it was safe to trust the capitalists 'to use their wealth . . . as a great national trust and not for selfish purposes'. 'We do not hesitate', said he, 'to unite the advocacy of social reform with an appeal to the various classes who compose society to perform those duties without which all social reform must be merely delusive.'[1]

Herein lay the appeal of Settlements. At most they aimed to mitigate class conflict, not to touch the economic and social order. As Booth remarked, '. . . they have given a new form to the practice of neighbourliness, and have thus made for social solidarity',[2] while a later observer, obviously soured by his experience of American Settlements, suggested that the residents seemed bent on reaching down to help the poor climb not quite up to the level of their benefactors.[3]

This was not to say that the settlers themselves could learn nothing from their experience. Settlements were designed, not only to bring culture and light into the hard, hopeless lives of the East End, but to deepen the University man's understanding of the poor and their problems. T. H. S. Escott saw the Settlement as a 'social education for the West End club-man'.[4] At a later date, Lord Beveridge, an ex-warden of Toynbee Hall, applauded it as 'a school of post-graduate education in humanity'. 'Such places', he wrote to his mother, 'represent simply a protest against the sin of taking things for granted',[5] while Canon Barnett saw Toynbee Hall not only as 'a centre of education, a mission, a centre of social effort', but also as 'a club house . . . occupied by men who do citizen's duty in the neighbourhood'[6] while pursuing their own occupations in the universities, law, civil service, church or elsewhere.

---

[1] 'Are Radicals Socialists?' in *Lectures on the Industrial Revolution of the Eighteenth Century*, pp. 231, 237.

[2] *Op. cit.*, p. 381.

[3] Malcolm Cowley, *Exile's Return. A Literary Odyssey of the 1920's* (New York, 1951), p. 34.

[4] *Social Transformations of the Victorian Age* (1897), p. 128.

[5] *Power and Influence* (1953), pp. 29, 30.

[6] *Towards Social Reform* (1909), pp. 262-3.

Doing citizen's duty in the neighbourhood was expansible, for it was difficult to draw the line between philanthropic and political activity. Just by reading the lists of Toynbee Hall's debaters and their subjects, one can see what an active interest the residents took in the questions of the day. Ben Tillett visited the Settlement at the height of the Dock Strike of 1889 to speak on 'The Future of the Dockers' Union', and three years later Tom Mann followed him with a paper on 'Docks and Dockers'. Beatrice Potter, mariée Webb, delivered her views on 'Sweating' in 1891 and in 1896 Sir Edward Grey gave his on 'British Foreign Policy'. 'Shall we Abolish the London School Board?' asked the Fabian Edward R. Pease in 1903, while later the same year, George Bernard Shaw was certain 'That the Working Classes are Useless, Dangerous and Ought to be Abolished'.[1]

But civic activity at Toynbee Hall was not confined to discourse and debate. Mrs. Barnett herself, flanked by three of the most civic-minded of her residents, interviewed the managing body of Bryant and May's during the Match Girls' Strike of 1888, while Canon Barnett always stressed the necessity for residents to take up some citizen's duty—on public boards or in clubs, as school managers or children's playmates, in social movements or as clergymen—which would bring them into contact with others and put them in a position both to learn and to teach.[2]

When the Settlement idea was transferred to American soil,[3] the whole concept of 'Neighbourhood' was broadened out to include all aspects of neighbourhood and community welfare, and agitation for better sanitation, education, recreational facilities, housing and industrial relations resulted not only in local improvements in these fields, but also remedial legislation. For example, at Hull House in Chicago and later at the Henry Street Settlement, in New York, Florence Kelley, Secretary of the National Consumers' League, combined protests against industrial exploitation with practical proposals which provided the framework for labour laws and factory inspection, while

[1] *Canon Barnett. His Life, Work and Friends*, I, 370–1.   [2] *Ibid.*, II, 65, 93.
[3] The Neighborhood Guild was established in New York by Stanton Coit and Charles B. Stover in 1886 and Hull House in Chicago by Jane Addams and Ellen Gates Starr in 1889. These were followed by many other Settlements in different parts of the country.

Lilian D. Wald, making forays from the Henry Street Settlement, laid the foundation of the federal Children's Bureau which was to be manned by Julia C. Lathrop and later Grace Abbott, both of whom were residents of Hull House.

It is obvious, then, that the Settlement played a part in the social reform movements of its day. But it was in the realm of group work theory and practice that, unbeknown to itself, the Settlement, and especially Toynbee Hall, made its most important contribution to social work. For in reading Mrs. Barnett's description of the daily round at Toynbee Hall, one can hear the articulate audible voice of the social group work past.

Canon Barnett and his wife began by accepting, wholly or in part, the principles laid down by the C.O.S. and its caseworkers. Today such principles, labelled 'the worth, integrity and dignity of the individual', 'relationship' and 'self-determination', would be regarded as generic principles common to all branches of social work, but in the nineteenth century they were couched in simpler tongue. The Barnetts believed that they must treat each case individually, study it in its family setting, and seek to exert 'friendly' or 'neighbourly' influence to help the distressed one solve his problem. 'We must deal with the people as individuals', Mrs. Barnett explained, 'being content to speak, not to the thousands, but to ones and twos; we must become the friend, the intimate of a few; we must lead them up . . . until we attain the higher ground whence glimpses can be caught of the . . . land of spiritual life'.[1] Accordingly, the Canon and his wife lived by the precept of 'one by one', three words which, embroidered by one friend and framed by another, always hung in their drawing-room at Toynbee Hall. The individuality of each human being was worthy of reverence, for were not all 'the children of your Father Who is in Heaven'? '"One by one" is the phrase which best expresses our method', wrote the Canon, 'and "the raising of the buried life" is that which best expresses our end. . . . Our real work lies below these classes, systems, and entertainments, as our real object is far beyond the success which is measured by numbers and comfort.'[2]

[1] 'Passionless Reformers', in Rev. and Mrs. S. A. Barnett, *Practicable Socialism: Essays on Social Reform* (1888), p. 54.

[2] *Canon Barnett. His Life, Work and Friends,* I, 184; II, 233; I, 320.

How much freedom the client was allowed in determining the ways and means of raising the buried life is problematical, for the degree of self-determination permitted varied quite considerably from one case to another. Sometimes Mrs. Barnett spoke as though she expected her clients to be swift in all obedience, so that one might muse whether it was she who was the model for J. R. Green's savage satire which portrayed the social worker as a dictatorial busybody who retreated only before the Sister of Mercy or the Deaconess.[1] Mrs. Barnett's authoritarianism[2] may have been due to her strong sense of responsibility for the agony of the world,[3] or it may have been due to the fact that she shared, if somewhat reluctantly, her husband's view that all misery was the result of wrong-doing and that to relieve it without reforming the character which had caused it, 'was but to interrupt God's methods of teaching mankind'. '. . . my husband', she explained, 'thought that . . . like wise physicians, we must bear to inflict suffering if it were necessary to effect a cure.'[4]

This rather forbidding philsophy was softened, fortunately, in a variety of ways. That many cases needing most help would be regarded as ineligible Mrs. Barnett was astute enough to realize and kindly enough to deplore.[5] Likewise Canon Barnett was saved from degenerating into dictatorship, if not didacticism, by his love and respect for all human beings and his insistence that it was impertinent to judge who was 'deserving' and who

---

[1] 'The District Visitor', in *Stray Studies from England and Italy* (1892), pp. 269–282.

[2] E.g. apropos of advising lady visitors of the Metropolitan Association for Befriending Young Servants on the proper way of dealing with relations, she said, '(The girl's) mother, however undesirable, is her mother still, and we dare not break lightly the divinely ordained relationship' (*The Work of Lady Visitors*, p. 11) —which sounds as though she would be quite prepared to break the relationship, divinely ordained or not, if she considered it necessary.

[3] E.g. 'Which of us having once seen a Whitechapel Street at five o'clock on an August afternoon, and realising all it means, besides physical discomfort, can go and enjoy afternoon tea daintily spread on the shady lawn, and not ask himself difficult questions about his own responsibility—while one man has so much and another so little?' (*What has the C.O.S. to do with Social Reform? A Paper read at the Meeting of the C.O.S., Kensington Vestry Hall, February 23, 1884, p.* 7.)

[4] *Canon Barnett. His Life, Work and Friends*, II, 230; I, 202.

[5] E.g. 'And why is it (a C.O.S. case) ineligible?' she asked on one occasion. 'Because the Committee think that money will do the family no good . . . and yet not one of us could say that this family did not need help.' (*What has the C.O.S. to do with Social Reform?*, pp. 4, 5.)

was not,[1] that investigation was undertaken not to find out the applicant's deserts but to discover the best means of helping him,[2] and that once the information was obtained, it must be treated as strictly confidential.[3] Furthermore, since he was convinced that it was only through his clients' active participation[4] that the desired results could be obtained, he sought to stimulate initiative in the people who came to him and to strengthen their capacity to make decisions and to keep to them.

These ideals were shared by the leaders of other Settlements, too. In 1892, we find Miss Sewell, Warden of the Women's University Settlement in Southwark, explaining her beliefs to fellow workers at Bristol. 'Surely our business is not to try and force people—a vain task—into our moulds', she said, 'but to take their ideal, even if it is not so high as we think it should be, and, setting it before us, seek to help them to realize all that is best in it.'[5]

But Canon Barnett went further than this. He realized that this aim to make stronger a person's strength could often be better achieved within a group, where the pursuit of a common goal created a sense of purpose, where fellowship spelt comfort, and numbers imposed the discipline of co-operation. This was clearly shown in his explanation of the objects of his brainchild. 'An association of persons with different opinions and different tastes', he wrote, 'its unity is that of variety; its methods are spiritual rather than material; it aims at permeation rather than conversion; and its trust is in friends linked to friends rather than in organization.'[6] The qualifications which he once said he would like to find in the Warden of his future Settlement might be more exacting than those advertised for a

---

[1] E.g. 'Who is to be judge of character? Who is to say that A shall have relief and B go into an Infirmary, that C is to be treated as if he were an honoured guest and D as if he were a criminal?' (*Canon Barnett. His Life, Work and Friends*, I, 202.)

[2] E.g. 'When some one comes begging, I . . . send him to a Charity Organisation Society, who investigates the case, not so much with a view of finding out the applicant's deserts as to show us, from his past life, the best means of helping him in the present.' (*Ibid.*, p. 83.)

[3] E.g. 'The secrets and sorrows of a man's life are his own . . . and not for public use.' (*Ibid*, p. 203.)

[4] E.g. 'Inquiries into social conditions . . . show that little can be done *for* which is not done *with* the people.' (*Ibid.*, p. 307.)

[5] 'The Conditions of Effectual Work among the Poor', *C.O.S. Occasional Papers*, First Series, No. 41, p. 168.

[6] *Canon Barnett. His Life, Work and Friends*, I, 311–12.

group leader today, but descriptions which we have of his con-
tacts with the men at Toynbee Hall show that, although he spoke
a different tongue, he was, in fact, using methods which made
him the occupational ancestor of the modern group worker. The
'half hours in the study' during which he would try to find what
he called the 'Christed' self of those who came to him were to
some men, his wife tells us, 'made sacred by revelations of their
own potentialities'.[1] Likewise the classes he formed at Toynbee
Hall, ranging in subject from literature to life-saving and from
citizenship to carving, the many clubs, the 'reading parties',
the 'Monday evening discussions'—even the children's 'play
classes'[2]—were, in effect, essays in group work. For the
Canon's care to make each man feel that he could make a worth-
while contribution to the group, whether the group was a club,
a class in a schoolroom, a conversazione or one of Mrs. Barnett's
'At Homes', was part of a policy to use group relationships to
unleash a man's capabilities, to give him a feeling of self-worth,
and to strengthen him to play a vital role in society at large.
'What do we do at Toynbee Hall?' he asked on one occasion.

> I should say that . . . we learn much; we unlearn more. We have
> too . . . the opportunity not merely of enlarging our sympathies . . .
> but of building up a new system of relationship side by side with
> our old, . . . forming around the Hall a new world of student-
> friends and guest-friends, acting and reacting on one another, by
> whose means refinement and knowledge may pass electrically as
> from friend to friend, and not professionally as from tutor to
> pupil.[3]

This statement, an anticipation of our twentieth-century science
of 'group dynamics', expresses the underlying aim of all the
varied activities carried on within Toynbee Hall.

These, then, were the nineteenth-century groups from which
social group work derived. Varied as they were, they still had a
common denominator. Their existence was based on the realization that, faced with the demoralizing hugeness of the modern
industrial state, men and women often laboured under a sense
of disability, for they felt that, having lost social control, they
stood alone and unprotected. Groups, consciously organized
around selected interests, could compensate for this sense of loss.

[1] *Ibid.*, II, 40.
[2] *Ibid.*, I, 330–1, 356, 327; II, 62–63; I, 288.   [3] *Ibid.*, I, 322.

Within the broader framework of the State, they could recreate that sense of intimate purpose which had once belonged to the village of an earlier age. In their activities, sensitively fashioned as the occasion demanded, there lay potentialities for developing emotionally sound personalities and satisfying social relationships. This was the idea from which social group work stemmed, and in giving it corporate life, the nineteenth century made its contribution to later theory and practice.

PART TWO

Lady Bountiful in the New World

IV

◇◆

Poverty and Oysters
in the U.S.A.

◇◆

ALTHOUGH Charity Organisation and the Settlement began in England, their metamorphosis into modern social work took place mainly in the United States. Ideas and concepts, preached and practised in the Old World, were transplanted to the New, where subjected to different influences and interpretations, they suffered a sea change into something richer than had prevailed in England. Thus transformed, these ideas and concepts were transmitted in the twentieth century back to the land of their origin to enrich the theory and practice of social work from which they had sprung.

That the United States in the mid-nineteenth century faced a problem of poverty similar in kind, though not in magnitude, to that which plagued the countries of the Old World came as a shock to many of its inhabitants. America was the land of proverbial plenty. Christopher Columbus, in the very first letter sent from the New World, had enumerated the wealth to be found in what he thought were the Indies, and in the seventeenth and eighteenth centuries there were many in Europe intrepid enough to undertake the six months' sea voyage to the New World to see if he was right. Certainly the incentive to brave known and imagined perils was very strong. There were some in Europe who were politically oppressed; there were others who had to endure religious persecution; many more longed for a life in the New World free from the travail and heavy sorrow which so often oppressed them in the Old. Of these factors the economic was by far the most important, and it induced Europeans to people the New World in the same way as it had earlier led them to discover and explore it. Even the Pilgrim Fathers, on whose collective head admiring historians have insisted upon clapping a halo, seemed much more concerned with the possibility of winning a comfortable livelihood from the American soil than of propagating the true religion;[1] and in the following centuries, there were many who limped after in not so base imitation. Nicholas Cresswell, confessing to his Derbyshire diary that he had 'a number of cogent and substantial, though private reasons that rather oblige me to leave home', wrote on 1 March, 1774 that 'I . . . am this day come to a determined resolution to go into America, be the consequence what it will . . . I am sensible a person with a small fortune may live better and make greater improvements in America than he can possibly do in England', and off he went to find all his hopes fulfilled and, after a journey through the colonies, to conclude that 'this was a paradise on earth for women, the epicure's Elysium, and the very centre of freedom and hospitality'.[2]

Here, then, was a land of opportunity, and during the nineteenth century at least, it was often advertised in Europe with the same zeal and imagination as cigarettes and automobiles are advertised today. Europe was old, America was young. European soil had been farmed for generations, American soil was practically untouched. In Europe land was in the hands of a small class, in America it was available to all and sometimes free. In Europe, there were too many workers after the same job and wages were low and employment precarious. America,

[1] E.g. A contemporary historian, Nathaniel Morton, describing the migration of 'divers godly Christians of our English nation', first to Leyden in Holland (which they found 'would be no place for their Church and Posterity to continue in comfortably'), lists the 'reasons of their removal' to America, giving pride of place to 'the hardness of the country' which forced the Pilgrims 'either to return back to England, or to live very meanly', and putting last on the list, 'the propagation and advancement of the Gospel of the kingdom of Christ'. (Howard J. Hall (ed.), *New Englands Memoriall* (*1669*), (New York, 1937), pp. 1–4.)

[2] *The Journal of Nicholas Cresswell, 1774–1777.* Foreword by Samuel Thornely. (1925), pp. 2, 1, 271–2.

as Benjamin Franklin pointed out in 1783, 'is the Land of Labour'. 'The People have a saying that God Almighty is himself a Mechanic', he wrote, '. . . and he is respected and admired more for the Variety, Ingenuity and Utility of his Handiworks than for the antiquity of his family.'[1] So high a premium was placed on a labour-force that every encouragement was given to increase the size of families. Although an interested government had not yet achieved that refined torture known as a tax on bachelors, circumstances in this new land ensured that a large family was an asset rather than a burden. Even children could earn, and here was some of the best farmland in the world waiting to be developed. The climate and soil were suitable for the production of practically every product of the temperate zone. There were a network of rivers to water fertile valleys, plains on which millions of cattle could graze, and copper, gold, coal, iron and oil awaiting an exploiter. 'The United States possess . . . an advantage over most of the European kingdoms', an earnest clergyman had written in 1795, 'for they . . . seem capable of supplying almost all the productions of the earth.'[2] It is no wonder, then, that with this seeming promise of an easy livelihood for its sons, America became a magnet which attracted people from all parts of the world. And so they came. The migration began with a few people in the early seventeenth century, grew to hundreds, then thousands, until in 1905, 1906 and 1907, more than one million people entered the United States each year.

There is no parallel in modern history to the drama of this swift expansion of a few straggling seaboard colonies into a powerful nation. The trapper, the trader, the rancher and the missionary were indefatigable in blazing a trail across the Continent, to be followed later by the farmer, the industrialist and the manufacturer. Certainly the expansion westward stopped in the 1840's at the 98th meridian, to leap across the Great Plains and the Rockies to the more amenable land of the Pacific coast. But once the frontiersmen had fashioned the tools to subdue this new plains environment, the gap in westward

---

[1] 'Information to those who would remove to America', *Works*, VIII, 603–14 printed in D. S. Muzzey, *Readings in American History* (Boston, 1921), p. 184.

[2] Rev. William Winterbotham, 'An Historical, Geographical, Constitutional and Philosophical View of the American U.S.', III, 287–93, in A. B. Hart, *American History told by Contemporaries* (New York, 1901), III, 66.

expansion could be plugged. By the 1870's this had been done. Deep-drilled wells and windmills mitigated the thirst of the Great Plains even if they could not assuage it; barbed wire solved the fencing problem and symbolized the cutting-up of the open range into stock farms; irrigation and dry-farming methods helped to overcome shortage of water; railroads opened up the country more quickly than the covered wagon had been able to do, and the invention of the six-shooter provided a weapon to wipe out the nomadic, fast-riding Indian who was so much more formidable a foe than his brother to the East. By 1890, the Great Plains had been subdued. The two shambling frontiers—one from the East, the other from the West—had met, and a solid belt of states stretched across the Continent.

By the 1890's, too, the United States had achieved industrial pre-eminence. Between 1860 and 1894 she had leaped to first place among the nations of the world. The value of her manufactures had quintupled, while that of her Old World competitors had not even doubled. In the period from 1849 to 1899, the number of her manufacturing establishments had increased four-fold, the number of wage-earners more than five-fold, the amount of capital invested nineteen-fold, and the value of production thirteen-fold.

It is hard for us to realize that the '60's and '70's knew little of the telephone, the bicycle, the trolley-car, the Linotype machine, the incandescent lamp, the cash register, the fountain pen, the wrist-watch and the phonograph. And yet all these made their general appearance only during the decades from 1870 to 1900. It was in the 1870's that two Milwaukee inventors placed the typewriter on the market, Bell exhibited the instrument he called the telephone, Brush patented the arc lamp, and Ford began his experiments which, in the '90's, were to produce that gasoline motor-car which was so much of a novelty to his contemporaries that he had to chain it to a lamp-post when he left it in a street. Behind the industries which produced these consumption goods, there stood the great iron and steel industry whose production in the period from 1880 to 1900 was to increase by 170 per cent, the slaughtering and meat-packing kingdom ruled over by Armour, Swift and Morris, the foundry and machine shops, and the great lumber mills. These symbolized the new age of Big Business, an age which not only produced more goods more quickly and more cheaply than ever before, but which bred a new kind of salesman who 'sold' a belief in American prosperity and free enterprise as zealously as he sought to sell his goods. Andrew Carnegie was the model. The dedication of his book, *Triumphant Democracy*, was not only a tribute to his adopted land, but a testament of political faith as well.

> To the
> Beloved Republic
> Under whose equal laws I am
> Made the peer of any man, although denied
> Political equality by my native land,
> I dedicate this book
> With an intensity of gratitude
> And admiration which the native-born citizen
> Can neither feel nor understand.[1]

Perhaps the native-born citizen could have felt and understood this gratitude and admiration if he had been in the same fortunate position as Carnegie. For when Carnegie's Steel Company combined in 1901 with its largest rivals to become the U.S. Steel Corporation, the property of the new Corporation was estimated at 676 million dollars, the Carnegie Company received for all its assets 492 million dollars in bonds and stocks, and Carnegie took his share of 225 million dollars in gold bonds.

The same story of heady prosperity was repeated in other spheres—in oil, sugar, coal, lead and other products—with prosperity accompanied by increasing concentration of control into fewer and fewer hands, and, in many cases, a great deal of suffering on the part of workers often too humble, cowed, scattered or polyglot to be easily organized. 'Wages of labour are everywhere falling in the United States and Canada', wrote an English observer in 1844, 'and . . . the condition of the working population is getting worse and worse.'[2] Twenty years later the sewing women of Cincinnati wrote to President Lincoln, 'We are unable to sustain life for the price offered by

---

[1] *Triumphant Democracy, or Fifty Years March of the Republic* (1886).
[2] John Finch, 'Notes of Travel in the United States' (1844), in John R. Commons *et al.* (eds.), *A Documentary History of American Industrial Society* (New York, 1958), VII, 55.

contractors, who fatten on their contracts by grinding immense profits out of the labor of their operatives',[1] while the following year the United Sons of Vulcan, known—mercilessly—as the Puddlers' and Boilers' Union, told the Iron Workers of Great Britain that 'We have a common saying now in this country, that you go to market with money in a basket, and carry home the goods in your pocket.'[2]

Yet in spite of this mounting evidence that American prosperity did not seep through to all ranks of society, there was an extreme reluctance to admit either that the poor formed a class or that poverty was not necessarily the outward and visible sign of moral degradation or an inherited spinelessness. 'In providing for the poor, the dependent, and the vicious', stated the Massachusetts Board of State Charities in 1866, '. . . we must . . . bear in mind that they do not as yet form with us a well marked and persistent class, but a conventional, and, perhaps, only a temporary one. They do not differ from other men, except that, taken as a whole, they inherited less favourable moral tendencies, and less original vigor. Care should be taken that we do not by our treatment transform the conventional class into a real one and a persistent one.'[3]

The American attitude towards poverty which this statement typified was a hybrid of two conflicting points of view. On the one hand, traditional religion had taught that poverty was a fortunate necessity which led the poor into paths of industry and the rich into acts of charity. On the other hand, it was believed equally firmly that in this land of plenty, poverty was an unnecessary misfortune. Because there was work for all, no man willing to work need want. Hence poverty was the punishment meted out to the poor for their indolence, inefficiency or improvidence; or else it was to be interpreted in terms of heredity,[4]

---

[1] *Fincher's Trades' Review* (18 March 1865), p. 2, col. 6, in John R. Commons *et al.* (eds.), *op. cit.*, IX, 72.

[2] *Fincher's Trades' Review* (31 March, 1866), p. 8, col. 1, in John R. Commons *et al.* (eds.), IX, 71.

[3] 'Second Annual Report of Massachusetts Board of State Charities, January, 1866', in Sophonisba P. Breckinridge, *Public Welfare Administration in the United States. Select Documents* (Chicago, 2nd edn. 1938), p. 305.

[4] E.g. Nathan Allen, in 1878, speaking on 'The Prevention of Crime and biruperism', remarked 'the second primary source of pauperism (is) conditions of Path (including the laws of inheritance)'. (*Proceedings of the Fifth Annual Conference of Charities* (Cincinnati, 1878), p. 120.)

intoxicating drink,[1] 'degeneration',[2] partisan politics,[3] or, as in one case, the unrestrained liberty allowed to vagrant and degraded women.[4] Rarely, it seemed, could a student of poverty refrain from projecting his own moral attitudes into an interpretation of poverty's causes. As a result, there were few who saw the social system as a possible source of the trouble. Certainly there was a feeling of guilt that, in the words of Sam Weller, poverty and oysters always seem to go together, and poverty was condemned as 'a rebuke to a people living under constitutional liberty',[5] and as 'a crime against democracy'.[6] But so succulent were the oysters, that the social order which produced them was accepted almost without question and the note of social criticism, when sounded, was quickly silenced. Especially was this so among welfare workers of the period. As a Knight of Labour pointed out in 1890, 'We have always thought it strange that you—men and women of intelligence, with broad minds and open hearts—had never asked yourselves "if there is not something radically wrong in that system which compels men willing to work to stand idle and poverty-stricken in the midst of plenty".'[7]

[1] E.g. Robert Treat Paine, speaking on 'Pauperism in Great Cities: its Four Chief Causes', found the 'four chief causes' to be foul homes, intoxicating drink, neglect of child life, and indiscriminating almsgiving. (John H. Finley (ed.), *The Public Treatment of Pauperism, being a Report of the First Section of the International Congress of Charities, Correction and Philanthropy, June 1893.*) (Baltimore, 1894), pp. 23–58.

[2] E.g. A. G. Warner, *Syllabus of a Course of Ten Lectures on Pauperism given at the University of Wisconsin in October, 1892* (Madison, 1892). See particularly Lecture II, 'Some of the Social Causes and Effects of Individual Degeneration', and Lecture III, 'Personal Causes of Degeneration'. In the latter lecture, Warner remarks: 'In the essentially unfit there is a tendency to extinction through progressive degeneration, unless unwise philanthropy enables them to persist as parasites.' (*Ibid.*, p. 13.)

[3] E.g. 'The fact that our cities have become to a great extent nests of partisan politics, and are governed largely for the benefit of professional politicians rather than the public good, has led to an increase of vice and crime and pauperism in our large cities that is appalling.' ('Report of the Ohio Sub-Committee of the General Committee on the Prevention of Pauperism', *Proceedings of the Sixth Annual Conference of Charities* (Chicago, 1879), p. 39.)

[4] Josephine Shaw Lowell, 'One Means of Preventing Pauperism', *ibid.*, p. 189.

[5] Carroll D. Wright, 'Labor, Pauperism and Crime', *Proceedings of the Fifth Annual Conference of Charities* (Cincinnati, 1878), p. 153.

[6] Hon. S. M. Jones, 'Charity or Justice—Which', *Proceedings of the Twenty-Sixth National Conference of Charities and Correction* (Cincinnati, 1899), p. 157. Afterwards cited as *Proc. N.C.C.C.*

[7] James G. Schonfarber, 'Charity from the Standpoint of Knights of Labor', *Proceedings of the Seventeenth Annual National Conference of Charities and Correction* (Baltimore, 1890), pp. 58–59.

But it was not so strange after all. For most Americans, the cause of poverty lay within the individual, and since America was a land of oysters, poverty, it was believed, was nothing more than a self-inflicted mortification.

This attitude, substantially the same as that which prevailed in Victorian England, had been embodied in the institutions which the early colonists had set up, on the English pattern, to deal with those unable to fend for themselves. The pivot of the system was the local almshouse. Originally intended, as one writer said, as 'comfortable asylums for worthy indigence',[1] it had early become an institution into which were herded the old and the young, the sick and the well, the mentally normal and the mentally deranged, the epileptic, the blind, the alcoholic and the criminal. Inadequately financed and socially scorned, the almshouses had degenerated, as one observer of 1879 complained, into a legalized cesspool or reservoir 'for the reception, and, it may be added, the cultivation of the most repulsive features of our social defects'.[2] As in England, paupers from the almshouses could be farmed out, separately or in families, and children apprenticed to labour-hungry farmers or factory owners. Those who managed to avoid the almshouse received outdoor relief, but only at a price even higher than that paid by their brothers across the sea. Relief was kept at subsistence level and involved loss of civil rights; the names of recipients were placed on the pauper roll which became a public document, and newspapers printed their names and amounts received.

For a number of decades, the almshouses remained local, autonomous, and undifferentiated, but as it became apparent that there were some services too costly and some cases requiring institutional care beyond the capacity of the local unit, state agencies were created to assume responsibility for certain categories of 'the dependent, delinquent and criminal classes', as they were called.[3] Virginia established a State hospital for

---

[1] 'Report of Select Senate Committee to Visit Charitable and Penal Institutions 1857', Breckinridge, *op. cit.*, p. 153.

[2] G. S. Watkins, 'Poor Houses and Jails in the North-Western States', *Proceedings of the Sixth Annual Conference of Charities* (Chicago, 1879), p. 98.

[3] E.g. by George I. Chace, *Proc. 9th N.C.C.C.* (Madison, 1882), p. 20. Contemporary attitudes towards poverty are very clearly revealed in this juxtaposition of words. Cf. also 'charities and correction', 'pauperism, vice and crime', 'labor, pauperism and crime', etc.

the insane in 1773, Kentucky a home for the deaf and dumb in 1822, Ohio a home for the blind in 1837, and Massachusetts one for the juvenile delinquent and the feeble-minded in 1848. Thus public services for the delinquent and the handicapped began on a local plane and expanded outward to the State. There were also attempts, which were to prove abortive, to expand these services still further into the federal sphere. In 1848, Dorothea L. Dix made an appeal to the federal government for a grant of land to support the indigent curable and incurable insane in the United States. 'I ask, for the thirty States of the Union, 5,000,000 acres of land, of the many hundreds of millions of public lands',[1] she said, but her appeal, though couched in eloquent, soaring prose, fell on unresponsive ears. President Pierce, 'compelled to resist the deep sympathies of my own heart', vetoed her Bill on constitutional grounds. 'The question presented', he said severely, '. . . is upon the constitutionality and propriety of the Federal Government assuming to enter into a novel and vast field of legislation, namely, that of providing for the care and support of all those, among the people of the United States, who, by any form of calamity, become fit objects of public philanthropy'.[2] Thus did he sound a note which was to be heard many times in the years to come.

But although the federal goverment remained implacably aloof, state governments found they could not do so. They found, too, that once they assumed responsibility for certain classes, some definite form of organization was necessary. Massachusetts was the first to establish a state-wide organization, creating in 1863 the Massachusetts State Board of Charities. This was a watchdog of the treasury and the law, for it was empowered to inspect, report on and suggest improvements in public charities, particularly reformatories, asylums and almshouses, and, in addition, had the task of enforcing the laws requiring cities and towns to support the paupers settled there. In this way the Board could enforce economy and achieve some degree of control over poor relief whether it was on a state or

[1] 'Memorial of D. L. Dix Praying a Grant of Land for the Relief and Support of the Indigent Curable and Incurable Insane in the United States, June 23, 1848', (U.S. Thirtieth Congress, 1st Sess., 'Senate Miscellaneous Document, No. 150') in Breckinridge, op. cit., pp. 195–221, 221.

[2] 'Extract from Congressional Globe' (Thirty-third Congress, 1st Sess., May 3, 1854, pp. 1061–3), in Breckinridge, op. cit., pp. 222, 224.

local basis. Other states quickly followed this lead, sometimes setting up supervisory boards on the Massachusetts model, sometimes, as in the case of Rhode Island and Wisconsin, boards of control[1] And when, by 1874, it was recognized that these state Boards of Charities had many problems in common and, moreover, that the causes and treatment of social distress could be subjected to scientific enquiry, the first National Conference of Charities and Correction was convened—as a later member reminds us, 'without a typewriter, telephone, trolley car, taxicab, without a recognized social service technique, for it was not yet born'[2] to mark, as Edith Abbott says, the beginning of professional social work in the United States.[3] And thus, modestly, began that system of public social service in the United States which was to continue, equally modestly, until the Great Depression of the 1930's demanded relentless revision of men's ideas of what the State should and should not do.

But although, from the 1860's, the provision of assistance to the poor was being supervised by, if not transferred to, the various state boards of charity or control, there was no liberalizing of the official attitude to the poor and the handicapped. The aim of the state board was to apply business methods to the realm of 'charities and corrections', to increase administrative efficiency, to eliminate waste, and if not to show an annual profit, at least to show a reduction of running costs. '. . . while all the heaven-born, God-given sentiments of humanity may fairly have their scope in operating upon your minds and hearts', said a governor of New York in 1876, '. . . you want, if possible, to unite in your action prudence, caution, frugality and economy of the thorough man of business.'[4] The Governor of Michigan put the matter more bluntly. 'If we can *cure* crime, we make money', he said. 'If we can *cure* pauperism we make money. . . . This . . . is the legitimate field of social science, to prove, so that people may see, that what you claim to be the

---

[1] For further detail, see Frank J. Bruno, *Trends in Social Work 1874–1956* (New York, 1957 ed.), Chapter 4, and the source material collected in Breckinridge, *op. cit.*, pp. 365–426.

[2] Sherman C. Kingsley, 'Presidential Address: Who Needs Social Service?', *Proc. 59th. N.C.S.W.* (Memphis, 1928), p. 3.

[3] *Social Welfare and Professional Education* (Chicago, 1931), p. 82.

[4] Governor Samuel J. Tilden, 'Presidential Address', *Proceedings of the Third Conference of Charities* (Saratoga, 1876), p. 13.

correct theory will save them money.'[1] This was the philosophy which prevailed up till 1917.

Behind these words there lay what has been called an ideology of scarcity,[2] which was in direct contrast to the ideology underlying present-day social security. Transferred from the Poor Laws of England to this land of abundance, the ideology of scarcity persisted till well into the twentieth century. It set great store on public penny-pinching; it assumed that human nature was bad; it took for granted the necessity for a means test to prove destitution, and claimed that, even if a recipient of relief paid the price in humiliation and loss of civil rights, the help granted him must be minimal, local and deterrent. '. . . no human being', said a prominent welfare worker in 1890, 'will work *to provide the means of living for himself* if he can get a living in any other manner agreeable to himself.' She, therefore, recommended that public relief be confined to those proved beyond doubt to be unable to work for a living ('and the way to do this is to provide it under strict rules inside an institution')[3] and went so far as to claim that if there were no relief funds 'to stand as a constant temptation to poor people', there would be very little need of relief at all.[4]

There was ample evidence that these views on public relief were shared by many who professed themselves to be genuinely interested in the welfare of the poor. When, in 1891, public-spirited delegates to the National Conference of Charities and Correction debated the pros and cons of outdoor relief, even those in favour of the system assumed that relief would pauperize the recipient and, worse still, come to be regarded as a right,[5] while those who condemned the system had convinced themselves that it was unnecessary, costly, a temptation to political

---

[1] Governor J. Bagley, 'Presidential Address', *Proceedings of the Conference of Charities* (Detroit, 1875), p. 13.

[2] See, among others, Jessie Bernard, *Social Problems at Mid-Century* (New York, 1957), pp. 27–28.

[3] Josephine Shaw Lowell, 'The Economic and Moral Effects of Public Outdoor Relief', *Proc. 17th N.C.C.C.* (Baltimore, 1890), p. 85.

[4] The Evils of Investigation and Relief' (1898), printed in William Rhinelander Stewart (ed.), *The Philanthropic Work of Josephine Shaw Lowell* (New York, 1911), pp. 216–17.

[5] E.g. 'How easy to think and then say, The State cared for me once, and will again! and so the struggle is given over.' (J. Q. Adams, 'Arguments against Public Outdoor Relief', *Proc. 18th N.C.C.C.* (Indianapolis, 1891), p. 35).

corruption, and tending to separate society into classes, lower wages, foster communism, and excite hostility to the State.[1] 'It is the weak, the lazy and the imposter who demand outdoor relief', Levi L. Barbour summed up, 'and for them we have provided the hospital, the workhouse and the prison'.[2] It was the first duty of a good citizen to provide for his own existence, and if this were impossible, it was hinted darkly, he should be confined to an institution where he would not propagate his species.[3]

But not only were the Poor Law and its philosophy transplanted from the Old World to the New. Charity Organisation, too, was built upon the English ideological pattern, and although it later became adapted to suit American conditions, the fundamental tenets of theory and practice still remained.

Like its English predecessor, American Charity Organisation was largely an urban development. Although the United States was a new country, the slum had early come to stunt the poor, trouble the sensitive, repel the moralist and alarm the comfortable. 'They are not as decent as brutes', declared one clergyman referring to the unfortunate inhabitants of a tenement which he described as 'impregnated with a stench that would poison cattle',[4] while a public-spirited doctor in 1878 gave warning to the world that these conditions constituted a danger to the rich. 'The importance of medical and sanitary work among the poor can hardly be overestimated', he said. 'It is in their squalid dwellings that the poisons are generated

---

[1] Charles R. Henderson, 'Arguments against Public Outdoor Relief', *ibid.*, pp. 39–41.

[2] 'Arguments against Public Outdoor Relief', *ibid.*, p. 42.

[3] E.g. 'It is also generally known that those demanding outdoor relief are . . . members of the lowest (classes). Regardless of all responsibility for it, they bring into the world a race of dependants, physically, morally and mentally deficient. Now, if, when these deficient and delinquent members of the lower classes give evidence that self support is impossible, they are retained in institutions properly regulated, while the individuals are cared for, the propagation of their kind is at least checked.' (*Ibid.*, p. 45.) This was akin to the words by Dr. A. Reynolds of Iowa, who, in 1879, baldly pronounced that '. . . the State should prohibit the marriage of all persons who had, at any time after arriving at the age of eighteen years, been supported in any penal or charitable institution'. ('The Prevention of Pauperism', *Proceedings of the Sixth Annual Conference of Charities* (Chicago, 1879), p. 214.)

[4] Matthew Hale Smith, *Sunshine and Shadow in New York* (1869), p. 366, quoted by Robert H. Bremner, *From the Depths. The Discovery of Poverty in the United States* (New York, 1956), pp. 5–6.

which carry pain and death into the mansions of the rich and the comfortable homes of the middling classes'.[1] Likewise the political as well as the medical danger of the slum was realized. William Ellery Channing, confessing that he needed his work of reform 'to save me from a refined selfishness', could notice 'the present heaving agitation of society', the 'new sense of power in the mass of people', and not be troubled by it. 'I trust in those around me as before', he confided. 'A fear as to the stability of property never crossed my mind.'[2] But there were others who did not feel so safe. Charles Loring Brace, for example, organized the Children's Aid Society of New York and wrote a book to describe his twenty years' work among 'the dangerous classes of New York'. Beware the day, he said, when 'the outcast, vicious, reckless multitude of New York boys, swarming now in every foul alley and low street, come to know their power and *use it!*'[3] while Jacob A. Riis, appealing to the self-interest of the property-owner rather than the sense of justice of the humane, warned his middle-class readers of the danger of the 'tremendous, ever swelling crowd of wage earners which it is our business to house decently'.[4]

Thus the low estate of the city poor was a problem which intermittently engaged American attention, and various palliatives were tried. Many relief societies, for instance, had been formed to deal with it. As in England there were groups to assist persons with particular needs. In Philadelphia a society for 'alleviating the miseries of public prisoners' was formed in 1787; the Massachusetts Charitable Fire Society was founded in 1794, and in the early nineteenth century many organisations were formed for the care of the sick, the hungry, the widowed and the poor. These societies spawned to such an extent that by 1840 there were more than thirty relief-giving societies in the city of New York, while in Philadelphia, by 1878, no fewer than two hundred and seventy voluntary organizations and five hundred and forty seven churches raised more than one and a

---

[1] Dr. Henry B. Wheelwright, 'Medical Outdoor Relief in Massachusetts', *Proceedings of the Fifth Conference of Charities* (Cincinnati, 1878), p. 43.

[2] *Memoir of William Ellery Channing, with extracts from his Correspondence and Manuscripts* (1850), II, 167, 262, 263, 264.

[3] *The Dangerous Classes of New York and Twenty Years Work among Them* (New York, 1872), p. 322.

[4] *How the Other Half Lives. Studies Among the Poor* (1891), p. 282.

half million dollars each year to aid the poor. Occasionally—as in the case of the Association for the Improvement of the Conditions of the Poor, which had been established in New York in 1843—these societies claimed to work in accordance with certain approved maxims such as raising the dependent poor into independence, investigating each case before relief was given, and repressing imposture, but as they were invariably distributors of material relief, this function often superseded all others, and the societies, as one observer remarked in 1893, 'sank into the sea of common almsgiving'.[1]

Common almsgiving, of course, had the same dangers in the New World as it did in the Old. It sapped the foundation of the self-respecting home, as one critic complained, destroyed the best element in true society, lacked the essence of charity, destroyed citizenship 'and those active powers of the human soul that put it in sympathy with the divine ideal', was opposed to the divine order, and in all ways was a crime against society.[2] These disadvantages, combined with the fact that a depression in 1873 threw many out of work, and, worse still, as one contemporary mourned, made 'a heavy draft upon the benevolent',[3] prepared the way for the importation of the philosophy and practice of Charity Organisation from England.

The first Charity Organisation Society in the United States was established at Buffalo in 1877. The influence of the London Society was direct and marked. The Reverend Samuel Gurteen, an English clergyman who had been very active in the London C.O.S., had recently come from England to be assistant minister in St. Paul's Church. Seeing the sore distress around him, he suggested that Buffalo follow London's example, gave a series of sermons on 'Phases of Charity' to popularize the idea, began to systematize the work of his parish guild so that every application for aid was promptly investigated, and soon afterwards, in December 1877, launched the Buffalo Charity Organisation Society. This was to be a centre of intercommunication between

[1] Charles D. Kellogg, 'Charity Organisation in the U.S. Report of the Committee on the History of Charity Organisation,' *Proc. 20th N.C.C.C.* (Chicago, 1893), p. 53.

[2] William F. Slocum, 'The Ideal of the Charity Worker', *The Charities Review. A Journal of Practical Sociology* (published for the C.O.S. of the City of New York), II (November 1892–June 1893), pp. 10–11.

[3] Charles D. Kellogg, *op. cit.*, p. 54.

the various charities and charitable agencies of any given society; it was to investigate thoroughly and without charge the cases of all applicants to the overseer of the poor for official relief, and of all other applicants for charity referred to the Society for enquiry; after this, it was to get from the appropriate charities or individuals suitable and adequate relief for deserving cases, to provide visitors to counsel those needing advice and to procure work for those capable of being wholly or partially self-supporting. The Society stressed that there was to be no proselytism on the part of their agents, no interference with any existing societies, no relief given by the organisation itself except in emergencies, that 'there must be no sentiment in the matter', and, above all, 'no exclusion of any person or body of persons on account of religious creed, politics or nationality'.[1]

During the next five years, many cities followed the Buffalo example.[2] By 1882, in spite of much opposition from long-established charitable institutions, there were twenty-two Charity Organisation Societies in the United States and ten others which had adopted part of the Charity Organisation programme, embracing cities and towns of more than six million people constituting 12 per cent of the total population of the United States. Although practice varied somewhat with local conditions, the early work of these societies was based on the principles of investigation, registration, co-operation and friendly visiting as laid down by the London Society.

That Charity Organisation in the New World should follow so closely the pattern laid down in the Old was not surprising. Not only was there an exchange of ideas and personnel during the formative years, but the whole arcanum of American middle-class beliefs about individual initiative and self reliance in the competitive order closely approximated that of the English middle-class during the same period. American social work, like its English counterpart, was an integral part of the liberal's answer to life under a system of free enterprise. Both began as an attempt to temper the cold wind of capitalism to the shorn lamb of a proletariat whose existence was both a rebuke and a

[1] Rev. S. H. Gurteen, *A Handbook of Charity Organisation* (Buffalo, 1882), pp. 120, 132, 120–1.

[2] For further detail, see Charles D. Kellogg, *op. cit.*, pp. 52–93, and Appendices A and B; and Frank Dekker Watson, *The Charity Organisation Movement in the U.S.* (New York, 1922), Chapters III–VII.

threat to the more fortunate classes, and although in both countries social work changed as the framework of the existing social philosophy changed, the mark of the mint still remained.

Particularly was this so in the field of social casework from 1870, by which time friendly visiting had become a recognized institution,[1] to 1917 when Mary E. Richmond made the first definite formulation in book form of the point of view and method of this new technique.[2] Beginning as a bye-product of nineteenth-century individualism, American social work, even more than its English counterpart, laid stress upon 'individuality'. The doctrine that poverty was due to individual failure, and hence that the poor could be divided into 'deserving' and 'undeserving', was even more acceptable in the United States than in England, for it dove-tailed into the other widely accepted legend that the royal road from log cabin to White House was open to all. Consequently, as early as 1878, the National Conference of Charities was being told that if pauperism was to be eliminated, the history and character of paupers as individuals must be carefully studied and the precise causes and influences that made them such ascertained,[3] while by 1886, the concept of 'individuality' was well and truly crystallized. 'Charitable work, in the best sense, must be done by the individual . . . for the individual', George B. Buzelle told the National Conference. '. . . . Each case is a special case, demanding special diagnosis, keenest differentiation of features and most intense concentration of thought and effort.' As a corollary to this, Buzelle not only implied that poverty was the fault of the poor and could be dealt with only by developing the individual's capacity to adjust himself to his environment, but he went so far as to deny that the poor formed a class with interests separate from, if not antagonistic to, those of other classes. 'The poor, and those in trouble worse than poverty', he explained, 'have not in common any type of physical, intellectual

---

[1] E.g. In the *Proceedings of the First Conference of Charities and Correction* in 1874, the recommendation was made that 'great care . . . should be taken in distributing benefactions, that they only be given after careful house visitation. . . . The proper course is for the fortunate classes to district the poor classes, and visit carefully from house to house finding those who are the truly deserving recipients for charity.' (*Ibid.*, pp. 23–24.)

[2] *Social Diagnosis* (New York, 1917).

[3] Nathan Allen, 'Prevention of Crime and Pauperism,' *Proceedings of the Fifth Annual Conference of Charities* (Cincinnati, 1878), p. 117.

or moral development which would warrant an attempt to group them as a class'.[1] The implication was obvious. No criticism of the social order was worthy and no tinkering with it justified. So strongly entrenched was this belief, that even during the years of depression, when practice made a fool of theory, this note could still be sounded. 'Social work has realized that a program can not make men moral, religious or happy', said Miriam van Waters in 1930. '. . . The true springs of action are in the internal nature of man. Hence the uselessness of programs, particularly those dependent upon State action or force. When they succeed they are no longer needed.'[2]

This school of thought which placed such emphasis upon individuality and all it implied did not, however, hold undisputed sway. At the turn of the century there appeared a new trend of thought which set store on what one of its adherents, Edward T. Devine, called 'conscious social action', and which directed attention from the individual to his environment and the ways in which it could be improved. It 'makes of Charity a type of anticipatory justice', Devine explained, 'which deals not only with individuals who suffer but with social conditions that tend to perpetuate crime, pauperism and degeneracy'.[3] This, of course, challenged the prevailing doctrine that poverty was due to character defect. As a matter of fact, this had never been universally accepted. In the 1830's, for example, Joseph Tuckerman, pastor and missionary to the Boston poor, had shown by deed and word that in seeking the causes of social distress he looked beyond the individual to the social order. 'I have known women, indeed, to be glad to get pantaloons to make for six and a quarter cents per pair who could not, however, by their best industry, make more than two pairs in a day', he said. 'How, then, are they to pay their rent, and to obtain fuel and food?'[4] Similarly, friendly visitors, seeking to make a detached study of the lives and circumstances of families in their charge, found that bad housing, scarcity of

---

[1] 'Individuality in the Work of Charity', *Proc. 13th N.C.C.C.* (St. Paul, Minn., 1886), p. 187.

[2] 'Presidential Address: Philosophical Trends in Modern Social Work', *Proc. 57th N.C.S.W.* (Boston, 1930), p. 19.

[3] *When Social Work was Young* (New York, 1939), pp. 4, 114.

[4] *On the Elevation of the Poor. A Selection from His Reports as Minister at Large in Boston.* Introduction by E. E. Hale (Boston, 1874), p. 83.

work, low wages, and other social conditions outside their clients' control, often accounted for the poverty in which the family lived. Sooner or later, the visitor had to ask, as Mrs. Glendower Evans asked, 'Why are some people rich and others poor?' and to wonder whether the social order itself was the result of forces which could be understood and therefore modified.[1]

These obstinate questionings were to increase from the 1890's onwards. It was inevitable, for instance, that a body such as the National Conference of Charities and Correction, seeking to apply scientific methods to the problems of society, should become concerned with the economic conditions of the age. At first this concern took the form of an intense preoccupation with pauperism rather than poverty, and it was only in the early twentieth century when want had been distinguished from dependency and the concept of poverty extended to include a future insecurity as well as a present insufficiency, that attention became centred on the causes and effects of poverty, and the ways and means of abolishing want were studied as assiduously as the ways and means of relieving distress had been in the past. Or else in the early days of the National Conference, certain facets of the 'economic question' had been selected for study—immigration, child labour, the cost of public charities, the problem of transiency—and although discussion was often cabined and confined within the framework of prevailing prejudice and preconception,[2] it did serve to direct attention to a study of the economic and social order. Therefore, it is not surprising to find a president of the Conference, himself a successful business man, placing responsibility for the economic suffering of society on the unrestrained pursuit of the profit motive—'the foolish and fatal division of affairs of life between business and charity',[3] as he called it—and later, an economist and social worker charging that at the back of evils such as alcoholism, sweated industries and child labour, there lay a

[1] 'Scientific Charity,' *Proc. 16th N.C.C.C.* (San Francisco, 1889), p. 24.

[2] E.g. on the subject of immigration, F. B. Sanborn, admitting that exact statistics were not easy to collect, could say quite dogmatically that 'Now, this whole segment of our people—those of foreign birth or of foreign parentage—furnishes far more than its due proportion of illiteracy, of poverty, insanity, infant mortality, vice and crime.' ('Migration and Immigration', *Proc. 13th N.C.C.C.* (St. Paul, Minn., 1886), pp. 256–7.)

[3] Robert Treat Paine, 'The Empire of Charity', *Proc. 22nd N.C.C.C.* (New Haven, 1895), p. 4.

group which profited by exploitation. It was the duty of the social worker, he said, to *'seek out and to strike effectively at those organized forces of evil, at those particular causes of dependency and intolerable living conditions which are beyond the control of the individuals whom they injure and whom they too often destroy'.*[1] Nor was it surprising that from 1896 the attention of the Conference was increasingly directed towards environmental factors as essential to an understanding of social problems, that since 1910 programmes on economic and social problems have been a regular part of every Conference,[2] and that in 1912 Owen R. Lovejoy, as chairman of the Conference Committee on Standards of Living and Labour, put forth recommendations for a living wage, an eight hour day and other 'minimum requirements of well-being' which were remarkably like the platform of the Progressive Party on which Theodore Roosevelt was defeated.[3] Both platforms reflected the awakening of a popular interest in the social control of economics. Both indicated that the desire to clap a rational democratic harness on to an expanding American industrialism was shared by politician and social worker alike. As Jane Addams pointed out in 1910, two groups of people, the Charitable and the Radical, had gradually come together to unite at last into an effective demand for juster social conditions.[4]

In the light of these developments, many social workers began

[1] Edward T. Devine, 'The Dominant Note of Modern Philanthropy', *Proc. 33rd N.C.C.C.* (Philadelphia, 1906), p. 3.

[2] In 1910, Section IX on 'Occupational Standards' was introduced into Conference *Proceedings*. Paul U. Kellogg, Chairman of the Committee on Occupational Standards, announced, 'While as a National Conference, this body can put forward no platform, the consecutive and co-ordinated discussion of these subjects before its annual session cannot fail more or less to crystallize in men's minds what may be called an industrial program of minimums.' (*Proc. 37th N.C.C.C.* (St Louis, 1910), p. 374.)

[3] E.g. The platform of 'Social Standards for Industry' which the Committee on Standards of Living and Labor laid out included a living wage, eight hour day, safety, health and housing measures, compensation and insurance. (*Proc. 39th N.C.C.C.* (Cleveland, 1912), pp. 388–94.) The Progressive Party, self-described as 'born of the nation's sense of justice', advocated, among other things, the fixing of minimum safety and health standards, effective legislation looking to 'the prevention of industrial accidents, occupational diseases, overwork, involuntary unemployment', minimum female wage, prohibition of child labour, compensation and a system of social insurance 'adapted to American use'. ('The Progressive Party Platform of August 5, 1912', printed in H. S. Commager (ed.), *Documents of American History* (New York, 1958 ed.), II, 253–5.)

[4] 'Charity and Social Justice', *Proc. 37th N.C.C.C.* (St. Louis, 1910), p. 1.

to question some of the tenets of social casework. In 1895 a member of the National Conference of Charities and Correction told his colleagues that although helping individuals one by one was important, Charity Organisation societies must do all they can 'to abolish all conditions which depress, to promote measures which raise men and neighbourhoods and communities',[1] while the president of the Boston Associated Charities went further and asked whether the new Charity Organisation movement had not too long been content to relieve single cases of distress without asking whether there were 'prolific causes permanently at work' to create want, vice, crime, disease and death which could be eradicated. 'If such causes of pauperism exist', he said, 'how vain to waste our energies on single cases of relief when society should aim at removing the prolific sources of all the woe.'[2]

Many social workers agreed, and promptly fashioned deed to word. The foundation for action had already been laid. The Charity Organisation Society, which, along with the county poor house and the settlement, was the social worker's milieu, had already devised schemes to plug the most immediate gaps in the social system. The Buffalo Society, for example, very early added to its work the maintenance of employment bureaux, woodyards, laundries, work rooms, special schools, wayfarers' lodges, loan societies, penny banks, fuel societies, creches, district nursing, sick diet kitchens and an accident hospital, and many other societies followed suit. Now, they began to initiate or take part in movements which, if they did not aim to alter the existing social order, at least sought to mitigate its worst effects. Housing, the prevention of tuberculosis, juvenile probation, legal aid, the care of dependent children, and the publication of philanthropic journals were all considered to be the province of Charity Organisation no less than begging, vagrancy desertion, and non-support. In the first decade of the twentieth century, Charity Organisation began to apply its methods to still other fields of activity and to lay the foundation of what was later to become medical social work and specialized treatment

[1] Jeffrey R. Brackett, 'The Charity Organisation Movement: Its Tendency and Its Duty', *Proc. 22nd N.C.C.C.* (Boston, 1895), p. 84.
[2] Robert Treat Paine, 'Pauperism in Great Cities: Its Four Chief Causes', *op. cit.*, p. 35.

for the handicapped and the inebriate.[1] In addition, spurred on by the demands of such realists as Mary E. Richmond for a 'Training School in Applied Philanthropy'[2] and the example of the New York Charity Organisation Society which as early as 1892 had established an experimental class for its friendly visitors,[3] many societies began to shoulder the responsibility of training their workers.

Thus it was that during the '90's, in America as in England, many men and women employed by charitable institutions began to regard their work as a profession in much the same way as other men regarded law, medicine and theology. Certainly there were many who still spoke as though social work was synonymous with 'friendly uplifting'[4] requiring nothing more than 'warm hearts, cheery spirits and wise thoughts'[5] combined with an ability to deliver homilies on the cheapest kinds of food and the mending of clothes.[6] But there were also a determined few who preached the worth and dignity of the individual, and believed passionately in the social worker's trained skill to use individual, group and community resources to help men and women to lead happier lives. In addition, they were willing to fight to overcome opposition to the paid worker. The fact that many workers accepted payment often incurred the criticism of the rich and the opprobrium of the unthinking. A willingness to work for nothing, it was considered, was the hall-mark of a sincere charity worker. As late as 1898, the Central Council of

[1] For further detail, see Frank Dekker Watson, *op. cit.*, pp. 287–336, 365–406.

[2] See 'The Need of a Training School in Applied Philanthropy', *Proc. 24th N.C.C.C.* (Toronto, Canada, 1897), pp. 181–8, reprinted in Joanna C. Colcord and Ruth Z. S. Mann (eds.), *The Long View. Papers and Addresses of Mary E. Richmond* (New York, 1930), pp. 99–104; and 'The Training of Charity Workers', *The Long View*, pp. 86–98.

[3] See S. E. Tenney, 'The Class for Study of the Friendly Visitors' Work', *The Charities Review*, II (November 1892–June 1893), pp. 58–64 for a description of the twelve weekly classes.

[4] W. J. Breed, 'The Obligations of Personal Work an Aid to Right Structure of Character', *Proc. 19th N.C.C.C.* (Denver, 1892), p. 460.

[5] Rev. Oscar McCulloch, 'Associated Charities', *Proc. 8th N.C.C.C.* (Cleveland, 1880), p. 128.

[6] E.g. 'The visitor ought to be able to give practical advice as to the best and cheapest kinds of food and the wholesome preparation of same. If a woman, the visitor ought to be able to give valuable hints for the making and mending of clothes and as to the proper materials therefor.' (Mrs. Roger Wolcott, 'Friendly Visiting', *Organisation of Charities, being a Report of the Sixth Section of the International Congress of Charities, Correction and Philanthropy* (Chicago, 1893), p. 110.)

the New York City C.O.S., announcing a six weeks' 'Training
School in Practical Charity', warned intending applicants not
to be too interested in money,[1] while in 1901, Edward T.
Devine could still stress the fiction that 'the spirit of charity is
inconsistent with a practice by which paid agents usurp the place
of the charitable individual'.[2] But in spite of a great deal of
feeling against the paid worker, it was becoming increasingly
obvious that in many communities there were not enough
well-to-do and leisured folk who were able to give their time
to friendly visiting, and so, as in England, volunteers unwillingly
retreated to advisory and fund-raising committees, and the
actual casework was left in the hands of paid, trained agents.[3]
Thus sheltered from the bounty of the mutinous, social work
was safe to refine its technique for dealing with the problem of
human distress.

And so from the 'nineties, until the outbreak of war in 1914,
strengthened now by recognition of the necessity for training
as well as good intentions, social work continued what one
speaker called 'the charity of prevention'.[4] Often, it must have
seemed, this programme of social action was carried out at the
expense of casework, with the result that there was sometimes
ill-feeling between the two camps. Miss Richmond felt obliged
in 1915 to defend caseworkers as being 'the champions of social
reform also', to deplore the 'socially mischievous' antagonism
between social worker and social reformer, and to emphasize
the fact that social casework 'came in before and after the mass
movement for any given social reform'.[5] Her words were salu-
tary, for they were a reminder that, although social action and

[1] 'The course, however, will be valuable independently of any opening in this
field, and students entering are asked to do so for the sake of knowledge to be
gained of social conditions in New York City rather than from the hope of securing
immediate employment in the philanthropic field.' (*Charities*, Vol. I, No. 4 (March,
1898), p. 5.)

[2] *The Practice of Charity, Individual, Associated and Organized* (New York,
1901), p. 76.

[3] E.g. There was a 253 per cent. increase in the number of paid workers employed
by the Charity Organisation Societies between 1882 and 1892. Even in 1892, however, there were 3,990 volunteers as against 212 paid workers. (Charles D. Kellogg,
op. cit., Appendix F.)

[4] Charles E. Faulkner, 'Twentieth Century Alignments for the Promotion of
Social Order', *Proc. 27th N.C.C.C.* (Topeka, 1900), p. 9.

[5] 'The Social Caseworkers in a Changing World', *Proc. 42nd N.C.C.C.* (Maryland, 1915), pp. 45, 47.

casework had often been practised separately, they were, in effect, complementary, that although the social work pendulum swung first in one direction, then in another, the oscillation yielded lasting results. Once the social action tide had receded, this was obvious. Casework—in fact, all social work—had been enriched by the current of thought and practice of the preceding period. By focusing attention on the environment, rather than on the individual alone, the adherents of social action had not only underlined the fact that, since poverty and oysters went together in the United States, some modification of the social order was necessary, but they also drew the caseworker's attention to community forces, hitherto overlooked, which had to be taken into account in order to understand individual behaviour. Likewise casework reminded the reformer that although social action was necessary, it could not ensure that the individual was happy, and that if human relationships became marred as a consequence, the difficult, delicate task of adjustment could often be aided by the caseworker's subtle art and understanding.

Thus, if what one writer has called 'the first and moralistic stage'[1] in the development of casework took place in England during the last four decades of the nineteenth century, a second or 'materialistic' phase occurred in the United States from 1900 to the First World War. Whereas in the first period, the caseworker, believing that each man was master of his economic fate, was more concerned with the individual than with his environment, in the second period, the focus of interest was reversed. Attention was now directed to the environment, and the social worker busied herself with the possible ways in which social action, as well as casework, could repair individual failure. A third stage was to dawn in the second decade of the twentieth century when casework again became the centre of interest and an attempt was made to isolate and analyse its main components. This stage was summed up in the work of Mary E. Richmond, who, in her *Social Diagnosis*, published in 1917, made the first definite formulation in book form of the point of view and method of social casework. *Social Diagnosis* is interesting, not only because it is one of the recognized

[1] Una M. Cormack, 'Developments in Case-work', in A. F. C. Bourdillon, *Voluntary Social Services* (1945), p. 101.

landmarks in the history of social work, but because from its eminence, the reader can look fore and aft and see the bases upon which social casework was operating up to 1917, and the differences between Mary E. Richmond's thinking and that of the present time. It is to her work that we must now turn.

V

Social Work takes Stock:
Mary E. Richmond and Social Diagnosis

ALTHOUGH human knowledge owes much to the anonymous many, its greatest debt is to the gifted few. It sometimes happens that one individual, more original or perceptive than his fellows, can make in his field a contribution so rich that he can change the current of men's thought. Karl Marx, seeking in class wars the cause of historical events, drew attention to a view of history which before his time had been sadly neglected. Hitherto historians, hypnotized by the concept of the Great Man, had dwelt with disproportionate fondness in the Senate house of a Pericles, on the prayer mat of a Mahomet, in the Council Chamber of an Elizabeth, or the military tent of a Napoleon. But after Marx had lent his eyes to succeeding generations, there was greater emphasis on social and economic facts and the whole study of history was thereby enriched. Again, Sigmund Freud, in his discovery of the Id's significance, introduced a wholly new factor into human knowledge and revealed a part of reality which many before him had guessed at, but which no one had analysed as convincingly as he did.

Social work, too, in its infant years, produced in the United States a figure to whom modern caseworkers—and in fact, all social workers—acknowledge a profound debt. Mary E. Richmond, born in Belleville, Illinois, in 1861, came almost by chance

101

to the field in which she was to make such a great contribution. After living a lonely, orphaned childhood in Baltimore until 1878, she became in turn a general clerical worker in a publishing firm in New York, and in Baltimore a book-keeper in a stationery store, and later, a general office assistant in a family hotel. In 1889, she was offered a temporary position at fifty dollars a month as an assistant treasurer to the Charity Organisation Society of Baltimore. Knowing nothing about the Society or its work, but with an intuition, perhaps, of what it was to mean to her in the future, she accepted the position, and for the first time found herself in an occupation which not only supplied her with a livelihood, but which engaged her mind and heart and used her energies to the full. Familiarizing herself with the Society's work and concepts, she accepted what she called 'the "thou shalt not's" of our old testament'—'no imposture, no waste, no proselytizing, no relief'—but insisted that charity organisation had a positive task to perform as well. Although it did not pretend to have a complete social programme, and, indeed, admitted that there were other and more powerful social forces in the world working for its reform, charity organisation still affirmed that charity, too, was a great social force which could and should co-operate with workers of every variety of social belief.[1]

Mary Richmond set to work to prove this faith. So zealously and effectively did she labour that it soon became obvious that in its assistant treasurer the Society possessed a potential leader. Early in 1891, when the general secretaryship became vacant, Miss Richmond, in spite of her youth, her sex, and her lack of the outward trappings of an academic, was elected to the position. This she filled for eight years, until in 1899 she was summoned to a wider stage by the Philadelphia Society for Organising Charity.

Since its inception in 1878, the Society had fallen into what Mary Richmond called 'a tangle of good intent'.[2] Following the pattern of the London C.O.S., the Philadelphia Society had

---

[1] 'What is Charity Organisation?' published in *Charities Review*, January 1900; reprinted in Joanna C. Colcord (ed.), *The Long View* (New York, 1930), pp. 131, 141.

[2] The title of a paper published in *Charities* in 1905; reprinted in *The Long View*, pp. 222–8, in which she described the confusion into which Pennsylvania's private charities had fallen.

decentralized its organisation to the point where it had become a loose collection of independent and autonomous 'ward associations'. These raised and disbursed relief within local limits with little, if any, control from the central office. At the same time, the people who organized the Society agitated so effectively against public and outdoor relief, that Philadelphia became the first large city in America to abolish the system. These two causes—decentralization with no uniform supervision, policy or standards and a failure to provide an adequate substitute for public outdoor relief—combined to corrode the position of leadership which the Society had enjoyed in its early days. By 1900 when Mary Richmond became its general secretary, the Society had become, as one of its members said, little more than 'a clutter of unwieldy mechanism' doling out from its local offices, 'ten-cent pieces in relief on rainy days, and maintaining two miserable lodging houses.'[1]

The new general secretary turned to the task of reorganizing the Society. Within a few months she had re-staffed the Central Office, introduced a new case record form, reorganized two district offices, established an embryonic training scheme, secured approval for a plan to build a model Wayfarers' Lodge, and introduced a system of letter appeals for possible new contributors. In addition, she also found time to lead an attack on corrupt city government, and to goad the Pennsylvania legislature into passing a number of reform bills dealing with wife desertion and non-support, child labour, housing, juvenile delinquency, and the care of the feeble-minded. She also organized the Pennsylvania State Conference of Social Work and the Philadelphia Social Workers' Club, and used her Society's facilities for training and supervising paid investigators for a group of day nurseries, a children's home, and the Philadelphia Hospital's Department of Mental Diseases.

It was in this world of sternly-won achievement that Mary Richmond learned to suspect the dichotomy between social action and casework and to endorse what she called 'the retail method of reform'[2] which stressed the necessity for both. 'The fruit will not be sound', she insisted, ' . . . unless it springs from the

[1] *The Long View*, p. 176.

[2] The title of a paper given before the Ethical Culture Society of Philadelphia, 17 April, 1905; printed in *The Long View*, pp. 214–21.

good ground of the individual case;'[1] while in later life, looking back over the period from 1905 to 1914, she confessed wistfully that it was 'uphill work to interest either the public or the social reformers in any reform that dealt with people one by one instead of in great masses'.[2]

The opportunity to explain her ideas to a wider audience came during the next stage of her career, when the newly formed Russell Sage Foundation in New York invited her in 1909 to be director of its Charity Organisation Department. One of the functions of the Department was 'to study, teach and publish in the charity organisation field, bounding that field broadly to include the better co-ordination of all social services'.[3] In pursuing this goal, Miss Richmond, among other activities, made a detailed study of the families of widows and their children, fashioned a conceptual framework for the craft of social work,[4] became embroiled in controversies over mothers' assistance and community chests, and acted as counsellor and teacher to the New York School of Philanthropy. But perhaps the educational enterprise nearest her heart was the Charity Organisation Institute which, from 1910 to 1922, she conducted for four weeks of each year so that practising caseworkers in the field of charity organisation could meet to discuss common problems. Working by the seminar and the committee method, the annual groups not only acquired fresh skills and refurbished old ones, but, in time, became a valuable sounding board for the various studies which the Department was assembling. Doubtless, too, these student caseworkers posed questions which their teachers had long since forgotten to ask. This can be an experience both stimulating and chastening and Miss Richmond was the first to admit it. 'The open door, the open mind', she said, 'the willingness to think things through all over again no matter how many times—these, I suppose, are the things that keep organisations as well as people young'.[5] If this be so, then

[1] 'Charitable Co-operation', *Proc. 28th N.C.C.C.* (Washington, 1901), p. 313; reprinted in *The Long View*, pp. 186–202.

[2] 'Possibility of the Art of Helping', *The Long View*, p. 587.

[3] From an unpublished report, quoted in *The Long View*, p. 629.

[4] *Study of Nine Hundred and Eighty Five Widows Known to Certain Charity Organisation Societies in 1910*, written in collaboration with Fred S. Hall (New York, 1913), and *Social Diagnosis* (New York, 1917).

[5] In a letter to a friend, quoted in *The Long View*, p. 277.

certainly neither the Foundation nor the director of its Charity Organisation Department could be accused of decrepitude.

It was during these years of intense activity in the field of charity organisation that Mary Richmond began that long, and for her often painful, process of conceptualization by which she was to teach her fellow caseworkers to see the treatment of individuals as a total process, the techniques of which could be ordered, described, analysed and transmitted from one generation of social workers to another. As her biographer has shown,[1] conceptualization was accomplished in groping, painful, piecemeal fashion. Beginning with a simple conception of the friendly visitor as 'a patient, persevering, faithful friend' who, through personal influence, would teach those less fortunate than herself 'habits of self control',[2] Mary Richmond applied herself to the task of finding out why, in spite of all efforts, 'restoration' of the individual did not always take place, what were the family, personal, neighbourhood, civic, private and public charitable forces 'with which the charity worker may co-operate', and how best these forces could be used to bring about an adjustment between the individual and his environment.[3] Inheriting the idea of a series of procedural steps undertaken by different people at different stages—investigation by a paid agent, case planning by a committee of volunteers, and 're-habilitation' by a friendly visitor—she began to study systematically the processes of casework help. Selecting and applying the concepts from some of the social sciences, she gradually hammered out her own ideas of social casework as a conceptual whole within the larger whole of social work. Within this conceptual whole, there were individual and component parts—a study of the facts of the situation, a diagnosis of the nature of the problem, and following in the direction pointed by this diagnosis, a plan and execution of treatment. These parts could be isolated, ordered, studied and taught at will.

The advent of *Social Diagnosis*, which expounded these ideas,

---

[1] Muriel W. Pumphrey, 'Mary Richmond's Process of Conceptualization', *Social Casework*, Vol. XXXVIII, No. 8 (October, 1957), pp. 399–406. See also Muriel W. Pumphrey, 'The First Step—Mary Richmond's Earliest Professional Reading, 1889–91', *Social Service Review*, Vol. XXXI, No. 2 (June, 1957), pp. 144–63.

[2] 'The Friendly Visitor. A speech delivered to the C.O.S. of Baltimore in 1890', *The Long View*, p. 40.

[3] 'Charitable Co-operation', *The Long View*, pp. 186–202.

has been likened to a child's experience of fumbling with a kaleidoscope, seeing a jumble of bright bits of glass, and then having someone turn them to the light so that suddenly the colourful but meaningless bits fall into patterns—discernible, orderly, describable and with a new exciting significance.[1] It was not that there was anything novel in Mary Richmond's analysis of study, diagnosis and treatment as the steps in the social casework process. Charity organizers had been hovering on the fringes of these concepts since the 1870's. Moreover, *Social Diagnosis* not only drew upon Mary Richmond's wide reading in the social sciences, so that it applied to social case-work concepts already familiar elsewhere, but it represented answers to questions which she had asked herself when she began charity organisation more than twenty years earlier. Therefore, far from presenting new ideas, the book bears the impress of an interpretation and a point of view which was prevalent before its publication in 1917. This explains why it was that just at the time when psychology and psychiatry were beginning to influence social work—and in fact, Mary Richmond herself was defining for her colleagues the psychological basis of social casework[2]—*Social Diagnosis* bore the impress of the preceding 'sociological' era, rather than of the 'psychological' era which was just beginning. Thus although Mary Richmond could plead for an understanding of what she called 'characterology', 'for which no satisfactory body of data yet exists',[3] she built her concept of social diagnosis on a foundation uncompromisingly sociological. There is in her work little indication that Freud, both through a personal visit to the country and through trans-lations of his writings which began to appear soon afterwards, was lending his eyes to social workers to interpret the meaning of behaviour, whether overt or inner, and the compulsive forces and inhibitions which directed it. This new knowledge, with its revolutionary implications, was not incorporated into the

[1] Helen Harris Perlman, *Social Casework. A Problem Solving Process* (Chicago, 1957), p. viii.

[2] E.g. 'The distinguishing marks of (our social agencies) were first, skill in discovering social relationships by which a given personality had been shaped; second, ability to get at the central core of difficulty in these relationships; and third, power to utilize the direct action of mind upon mind in their adjustment.' ('The Social Caseworker's Task', *Proc. 44th N.C.S.W.* (Pittsburgh, 1917), p. 114; *The Long View*, p. 399.)

[3] *Social Diagnosis*, pp. 55–56.

concept of social diagnosis. Nor was it intended to be, for Mary Richmond was more intent upon formulating the elements of social casework as it was being practised at the moment than of assimilating the knowledge and techniques of the new and sometimes suspect psychiatry. This was made clear in the preface of her book, when she defined the goal she had set herself. 'The elements of social diagnosis, if formulated,' she said, 'should constitute a part of the ground which all social case-workers could occupy in common, and . . . it should become possible in time to take for granted, in every social practitioner, a knowledge and mastery of those elements, and of the modifications in them which each decade of practice would surely bring'. The task of formulation, she continued, was made easier because casework had advanced to a point where it was becoming standardized. 'In essentials', she explained, 'the methods and aims of social casework were or should be the same in every type of service, whether the subject was a homeless paralytic, the neglected boy of drunken parents, or the widowed mother of small children. . . . The things that most needed to be said about casework were the things that were common to all'.[1] She then proceeded to describe in detail the processes which led up to social diagnosis and the shaping of a plan for social treatment. Treatment was described only very briefly. Originally planning to write a companion volume on it, she abandoned the idea, perhaps, as one of her colleagues has suggested, because she found the new psychoanalytic psychiatry disturbing if not alarming,[2] or perhaps because she had decided that this was an area which was not yet ready for generalization. But although the projected volume on treatment was still-born, she used the National Conference of Social Work as a sounding board for her ideas. Deploring the undue emphasis on the processes of investigation, which followed the publication of *Social Diagnosis*, she insisted that since there was no dividing line between investigation and treatment, a fusion of the two was needed so that 'more penetratingly helpful action' could ensue.[3]

[1] *Ibid.*, p. 5.

[2] Gordon Hamilton, 'A Theory of Personality: Freud's Contribution to Social Work', in Howard J. Parad (ed.), *Ego Psychology and Dynamic Casework* (New York, 1958), p. 12.

[3] 'Some Next Steps in Social Treatment', *Proc. 47th N.C.S.W.* (New Orleans, 1920), 254–8; reprinted in *The Long View*, pp. 484–91.

But although treatment was dealt with only in cursory fashion in *Social Diagnosis*, the nature and uses of social evidence[1] and the processes leading to social diagnosis[2] were described in the most minute detail. She discussed types of evidence, real, testimonial and circumstantial, rules of inference, and the collection of evidence from the client, from the family, and from outside sources. She included subsidiary sections on the 'main drift of family life', the father, the mother, the children, and other members of the family, and discussed principles governing the choice of outside sources of evidence such as doctors, teachers, employers, documents, neighbours, social agencies and letters of inquiry. This was followed by an analysis of the underlying philosophy of social work and a discussion of the reliability of questionnaires as a means of collecting information about groups with various disabilities. Nothing escaped her attention; and all the material so painstakingly amassed was used to illuminate the nature of the casework process.

This process, as analysed by Mary Richmond, fell into four stages—thorough investigation, accurate diagnosis, co-operation with all possible sources of assistance, and treatment. The first two stages constituted what she called 'social diagnosis'. This she defined as 'the attempt to arrive at as exact a definition as possible of the social situation and personality of a given client. The gathering of evidence, or investigation, begins the process, the critical examination and comparison of evidence follows, and last comes its interpretation and the definition of the social difficulty'.[3] Great importance was attached to this part of the process, and it was stressed again and again that for any given family (and the family for Mary Richmond was 'the cradle of immortal souls'),[4] there was only 'one best possible combination' which it was the social worker's duty to discover and to use.[5]

---

[1] Defined as 'any and all facts as to personal or family history which, taken together, indicate the nature of a given client's social difficulties and the means to their solution'. (*Social Diagnosis*, p. 43.)

[2] Defined as 'the attempt to make as exact a definition as possible of the situation and personality of a human being in some social need—of his situation and personality, that is, in relation to other human beings upon whom he in any way depends or who depend upon him, and in relation also to the social institutions of his community'. (*Ibid.*, p. 357.)

[3] *Ibid.*, p. 62.

[4] 'The Family and the Social Worker', *Proc. 35th N.C.C.C.* (Richmond, Va., 1908), 81; *The Long View*, p. 267.   [5] *The Long View*, p. 194.

After investigation and diagnosis came two further steps in the casework process, co-operation with all possible sources of assistance and treatment. Sources of assistance included not only the client's family, relatives, employers, teachers and neighbours, but were extended to include sources of financial aid and the philanthropic and social resources of the community as well. These it was the social worker's duty to organize in the interests of her client. Treatment was conceived largely in terms of this organisation of resources, although it was held to include the 'important inside truths of personality',[1] which involved a study of the family group and its inner resources. 'As society is now organized', said Mary Richmond, 'we can neither doctor people nor educate them, launch them into industry nor rescue them from long dependence, and do these things in a truly social way without taking their families into account. . . . Whatever eccentricities a family may develop, the trait of family solidarity, of hanging together through thick and thin, is an asset for the social worker, and one that he should use to the uttermost'.[2]

These, then, were the components of the process of case-work—investigation, diagnosis, co-operation with all possible sources of assistance, and treatment—and each was analysed in turn.

The point of view and method of diagnosis prevalent in 1917 and described and approved by Mary Richmond can be seen in the discussion of the Ames case.[3] This family, consisting of Thomas Ames, a tuberculous hatter of 38, with a wife of 28 and two daughters of 2 and 6, was reported as being in distress, to a charitable woman, Miss Delancey, when she happened to be visiting some of their neighbours. An interview conducted in the Ames home by one of the Society's caseworkers (who recorded that she had to see the husband, his wife and mother-in-law all together) revealed that Mr. Ames, employed at Caldwell's hat factory since his marriage, had been advised to apply for admission to the State sanitorium, but felt that he could not leave his family. The Church had helped, but was too poor to continue; the mother-in-law was not working 'for reasons unstated', and Mr. Ames had to overcome wifely

---

[1] *Social Diagnosis*, p. 126.
[2] *Ibid.*, pp. 134, 139.   [3] *Ibid.*, pp. 83–85, 91–93, 352–6, 361.

opposition in order to furnish addresses of his four brothers and sisters and his wife's two sisters, who might possibly help them. Outside visits were then made to the tuberculosis dispensary, Mrs. Ames' two sisters, her doctor, the school principal of the older child, one of Mr. Ames' brothers, and his two sisters. These were followed by an interview with Mrs. Ames alone, and then with her husband's employer, and the pastor of the church. The dispensary gave definite information about Ames' health, which was more serious than was supposed, and sanitorium treatment was found to be necessary. The interviews with relatives were limited to revealing a picture of the Ames family from the point of view of health, finance and character. Ames was described by his sisters-in-law as being industrious and kind to his family, Mrs. Ames by her doctor as 'always frail' and by her brother-in-law as 'too high-toned', while the older child was reported by the school principal to be quiet, well-trained, and diligent, but 'by no means bright'.[1] One relative offered an important clue to treatment by hinting that Ames was willing to go away, but that his wife was holding him back and urging him to find other work. This was followed up. Mrs. Ames was interviewed alone, was convinced by the caseworker that her husband's condition was graver than she realized, and was persuaded to let him go away. With the help of Ames' employer, who agreed to pay five dollars a week, and his pastor, who promised to supply whatever food was necessary, the waiting period was spanned until Ames could be admitted to the sanitorium. There he recovered under treatment and came back well enough to resume more healthful work under his old employers. But while her husband was receiving treatment, Mrs. Ames herself developed an incipient case of tuberculosis. This, however, was treated in time to prevent serious consequences, and the family, one supposes, eventually resumed their usual way of living.

Mary Richmond's comments on the case are interesting. While applauding the promptness with which the social diagnosis penetrated to the heart of the difficulty ('a personal as well as economic one') and rallied outside sources to meet it, she criticized weakness, 'which a competent supervisor would quickly discover', such as why a woman described as 'frail' was

[1] *Ibid.*, p. 353.

left with no medical diagnosis for four months, why the offer by Ames' brother to provide a home for Mrs Ames and her children was accepted without weighing more carefully the arguments for and against, and why an investigation was not made to discover whether the causal factors of Ames' disease lay in his family history, his home sanitation, or his occupation.[1] These seemed to her to be serious omissions in the social evidence which could result in an incomplete, unscientific and distorted diagnosis which might, in turn, lead to ill-conceived treatment. 'There would be few more dangerous things,' she warned, 'than a social diagnosis that was not subject to review in the light of other facts.'[2] But because her whole attention was centred on the problem rather than on the client, she showed little, if any, interest in the personalities concerned; no attention was paid to their relationships with one another, and always, it was assumed, the caseworker had the last word in deciding what was best for the client.

This is not to say that Mary Richmond was unaware of the importance of these factors. One of her most valuable contributions to social work was the concept that a knowledge of human behaviour was essential to understanding the individual, family life, and what she called 'the effect of mind upon mind'. The theory of 'the wider self', she claimed, lay at the base of social casework. 'The soul literally is, or is built up of, all its experience', she explained, 'and such part of this experience, or soul life, as is active at any given time or for any given purpose constitutes the self at that time and for that purpose.'[3] It was necessary, therefore, to study the differences between, and the relations of, individual men in the light of this concept of the wider self. Only in this way could a remedy be found for the ills which beset them.[4] In a later book, too, she applauded the fact that the theories, aims and practice of social casework seemed to 'have been converging of late years toward one central idea', the development of personality. 'Our physical heredity', she said, 'our innate qualities transmitted and unalterable are individual, but all that portion of our social heritage and our environment

[1] *Ibid.*, pp. 354–5.
[2] *Ibid.*, pp. 360–1.
[3] *Ibid.*, 368, quoting Helen Bosanquet, *The Standard of Life and Other Studies* (1898), p. 131.
[4] *Social Diagnosis*, pp. 369, 370.

which we have been able in day by day living to add to individuality and make a part of ourselves is personal; and the whole becomes our personality.'[1] Again, she recognized the interest and importance of studying interpersonal relationships. 'It occurs to me that a good deal could be dug out of fairly full biographies about the family relationships of the subjects',[2] she remarked on one occasion when discussing the psychological aspects of biography, while, commenting upon Abraham Flexner's characterization of social workers as 'middle men' unworthy to be called a profession,[3] she clearly recognized the importance of using relationships to effect an adjustment between men and their social environment. 'Many of our social agencies were something better than animated clearing houses', she remarked. '. . . . The distinguishing marks of their work were, first, skill in discovering the social relationships by which a given personality had been shaped; second, ability to get at the central core of difficulty in these relationships, and third, power to utilize the direct action of mind upon mind in their adjustment.'[4] Later, too, she insisted that by what she called 'direct and indirect insights, and direct and indirect action upon the minds of clients', the social relations of clients could be improved and their personalities developed.[5]

Again, although little is said in *Social Diagnosis* about the client-worker relationship—possibly because it was assumed that 'contact' was likely to be good and social diagnosis poor —it is obvious that Miss Richmond recognized the value of relationship as a medium through which aid to the client could be effected. 'Friendly visiting means intimate and continuous knowledge of and sympathy with a poor family's joys, sorrows, opinions, feelings and entire outlook upon life', she had written in 1899;[6] and in the years following, attention had become focused on the form taken by this knowledge and sympathy.

[1] *What is Social Case Work?* (New York, 1922), pp. 90, 92.

[2] From unpublished letters, quoted in *The Long View*, p. 428.

[3] E.g. 'Social work is . . . the mediator whose concern it is to summon the expert.' ('Is Social Work a Profession?', *Proc. 42nd N.C.C.C.* (Maryland, 1915), p. 588).

[4] 'The Social Caseworker's Task', *Proc. 44th N.C.S.W.* (Pittsburgh, 1917), 114; *The Long View*, p. 399.

[5] *What is Social Case Work?*, p. 255.

[6] *Friendly Visiting Among the Poor. A Handbook for Charity Workers* (1914), p. 180.

In 1905, James F. Jackson had outlined to the National Conference some aspects of 'expert personal service' and suggested 'a partial substitution of this for almsgiving',[1] while four years later, Mary Simkhovitch had added the idea that 'the investigated . . . becomes a co-operator in a common work and is filled with pride rather than animosity'.[2] With the publication of *Social Diagnosis*, casework not only emerged as a social technique, but the title of the book suggested a new kind of professional relationship between caseworker and client. This was rather misleading, because, critically examined, the relationship as envisaged by Miss Richmond was still on a friendly, naïve, unanalysed basis. 'To be really interested', she told the caseworker, 'to be able to convey this fact without protestations, to be sincere and direct and open-minded—these are the best keys to fruitful intercourse.'[3] In the first interview, she added, it was important, 'to establish, if possible, a sympathetic mutual understanding' and to use 'the tonic influence which an understanding spirit always exerts' to develop self-dependence in the client.[4]

In developing this self-dependence, not very much cognizance was taken of the wishes of the client. Although lip service was paid to the fact that 'the client's own hopes, plans and attitude toward life are more important than any single item of information',[5] there is a certain relentlessness about the 'slow, steady, gentle pressure' which the interviewer is called upon to exert in order to reach 'a certain goal' so clearly conceived by herself but hidden, apparently, until later, from her victim.[6] As Una M. Cormack has said, throughout the whole book, the interviewer, as it were, shoots a sitting bird, plucks him, trusses him, bastes him, and dishes him up finally settled 'in his right relation to society'.[7] But although there is this element of authoritarianism in the relationship between caseworker and client, it is obvious that Mary Richmond realized the therapeutic significance of the relationship, and directed attention to

---

[1] 'Considering Especially the New Emphasis in the Principles of Organised Charity', *Proc. 32nd N.C.C.C.* (Portland, 1905), p. 350.
[2] 'The Casework Plane', *Proc. 36th N.C.C.C.* (Buffalo, N.Y., 1909), p. 143.
[2] *Social Diagnosis*, p. 200.
[4] *Ibid.*, p. 114.   [5] *Ibid.*, p. 133.   [6] *Ibid*, p. 115.
[7] 'Developments in Case Work', in A. F. C. Bourdillon (ed), *Voluntary Social Services*, p. 104.

this no less than to the necessity to study the differences between and the relations of individual men.

Thus the casework of Mary Richmond was not narrowly social, as has sometimes been claimed, for she called attention not only to those 'insights' which yielded an understanding of the resources, dangers and influences of the social environment, but also to insights which promoted understanding of individuality and personal characteristics as well. 'If the development of personality is our task', she said, 'then the personality as it now is, together with the ways in which it came to what it now is, must be discovered.'[1] Likewise, although she described the caseworker as an artificer in social relations, and certainly laid stress upon the 'indirect action' of the social environment, she was also concerned with the ways in which personal relations with a client could be strengthened and used in the client's interests. Eagerness to be of service, frankness of intercourse, absence of officialism, the habit of keeping faith, a patience born of sympathy, of trained insight and of vision, and above all, the attempt to ensure the client's participation in the plans made for his welfare—these were the elements of what she called 'the direct action of mind upon mind',[2] and each could be used to attain the 'character-building' at which social casework aimed. 'The highest test of social casework is growth in personality', she wrote. 'Does the personality of its clients change, and change in the right direction? Is energy and initiative released, that is, in the direction of higher and better wants and saner social relations? Only an instinctive reverence for personality and a warm human interest in people as people can win for the social caseworker an affirmative answer to this question. But an affirmative answer means growth in personality for the caseworker himself. The service is reciprocal.'[3]

Here, then, are the three main concepts which Mary Richmond bequeathed to social casework—the concept of a systematic method by which a social diagnosis could be made to serve as a basis for treatment, the concept that a knowledge of human behaviour was necessary for a better understanding of the individual, his family life and the personal and social relationships by which he lived, and the concept of the process of social

[1] *What is Social Case Work?*, p. 103.
[2] *Ibid.*, pp. 108, 109.
[3] *Ibid.*, p. 260.

work as a democratic process in which the caseworker and client could co-operate to their mutual advantage. 'It is not enough for social workers to speak the language of democracy;' she said, 'they must have in their hearts its spiritual conviction of the infinite worth of our common humanity before they can be fit to do any form of social work whatsoever.'[1]

In spite of its contribution, however, *Social Diagnosis* was limited by the times in which it was written. In the first place, although there was more data available on 'characterology' than Mary Richmond believed,[2] it was still true that a more effective use of the scientific method which she propounded demanded a deeper knowledge of human behaviour than was available at the time she wrote. Until the psychologist and the psychiatrist provided this necessary knowledge, casework was forced to concern itself with the problem and the process rather than with the person. This was inevitable. Although there were some family agencies in the United States which used *Social Diagnosis* in as discriminating a fashion as its author could have wished, there were many more which, either through an excess of zeal or an inability to master the new concepts, were less successful in their attempts, so that an application of the Richmond procedures sometimes hampered rather than helped in the understanding of people and their problems. Many caseworkers in their social investigation paid meticulous attention to the gathering of case histories and the weighing of evidence, but showed little perception of what an inquisition did to the client, or any realization of how important it was for him actively to participate in, if not to determine, the decisions and plans made on his behalf. There was a tendency, too, to assume that the 'outsider's' version of the client's situation would be more objective, and hence more reliable, than the client's own, and there was little appreciation of that alchemy of the mind which enables a witness no less than a participant to invent or distort a piece of evidence or a situation without consciously realizing that he is doing so.

Again, the emphasis on method, especially when exaggerated as it often was by the disciples of *Social Diagnosis*, tended to

---

[1] *Ibid.*, p. 249.

[2] For further detail, see Virginia P. Robinson, *A Changing Psychology in Social Case Work* (Chapel Hill, 1939), Chapters II and IV.

concentrate attention on means rather than ends, so that many social workers were all but blinded to the fact that method was not the *raison d'être* of social casework, that it perforce must be guided by philosophy, and that the ultimate aim of the process, the reasons why it was undertaken, and its relationship to other activities would largely determine the methods to be employed.[1]

That her formulations were subject to misinterpretation and abuse was a matter of grave concern to Mary Richmond herself. Time and again, she deplored the fact that the procedure she had so carefully outlined was being misinterpreted or misapplied by her colleagues. 'I never intended they would do it all to one client!' she was reported to have cried despairingly at one convention,[2] and girded her literary loins to stimulate an interest in treatment[3] and to show the relationship casework bore to other forms of social work, such as group work, social reform and social research.[4] 'This topic of the interplay of different forms of social work deserves fuller treatment than I have been able to give it', she observed, 'but that all forms are inextricably woven in the great task of furthering social advance should be evident.'[5]

In spite of such efforts, however, jubilation at the success of *Social Diagnosis* was often diluted by an anxiety that a specific technique, which she saw as one component of a larger process, should be mistaken for the whole. 'I have spent twenty-five years of my life in an attempt to get social casework accepted as a valid process in social work', she exclaimed on one occasion. 'Now I shall spend the rest of my life trying to demonstrate to social caseworkers that there is more to social work than social casework'.[6]

But although she did spend the rest of her life demonstrating this truth, perceptive use of *Social Diagnosis* had to wait until

---

[1] Frank J. Bruno suggests that this concentration on method, which he sees as an effect of Abraham Flexner's paper to the National Conference of Charities and Correction in 1915 (see p. 112, n.3) was responsible for diverting attention from research, and comments 'It is tragic that an impetus in that direction was given social work at the very inception of its professional consciousness'. (*Trends in Social Work 1874–1956* (New York, 1957 ed.), p. 141.)

[2] Muriel W. Pumphrey, 'Mary Richmond's Process of Conceptualization', *op. cit.*, p. 401.

[3] E.g. 'Some Next Steps in Social Treatment', *The Long View*, pp. 484–91.

[4] *What is Social Case Work?*; see especially Chapter X.

[5] *Ibid.*, p. 242.   [6] Quoted by Frank J. Bruno, *op. cit.*, pp. 186–7,

the 'psychiatric' era, when the work of Freud and his colleagues threw a blaze of light upon the meaning of human behaviour, and social workers, becoming enmeshed in the new knowledge, began to refashion the theory and practice of casework in the light of those insights which psychiatry supplied. In preparing the ground for this new knowledge, *Social Diagnosis* played no small part. Although it bore the impress of an interpretation which was prevalent in the decade preceding its publication, it yet made a contribution, though indirect, to the new interpretation which was to come. In seeking to find a logical sequence in the elusive material of everyday human experience, Mary Richmond had begun the process of providing immediately usable tools for the standardization and refinement of procedures which hitherto had remained inchoate; while in stressing the importance of the detailed history as a preliminary to diagnosis and treatment, she had stimulated a deeper search for facts and for principles of interpretation other than the social facts and principles with which she herself was so much concerned. Perhaps, as Charlotte Towle suggests,[1] if social workers had been able to grasp and to use *Social Diagnosis* at Miss Richmond's level, the integration of psychiatry would have been gradual, and there would not have been the stage of disequilibrium which followed. This, however, was not to be, and after the First World War, the sociological basis of casework was rejected in favour of an over-emphasis upon the psychological. Although in this sense, *Social Diagnosis* may have failed, nevertheless, it still remains a landmark in the history of social work, for in its pages one can study the basis upon which social casework was operating until 1917 and, in addition, read the signs of what was to come.

[1] In a letter to the writer, dated 17 October 1958.

VI

◇◇◇◇◇◇◇◇◇◇◇◇◇◇◇◇◇◇◇◇◇◇◇◇◇◇◇◇◇◇◇◇◇◇◇◇

The Psychiatric
Deluge

◇◇◇◇◇◇◇◇◇◇◇◇◇◇◇◇◇◇◇◇◇◇◇◇◇◇◇◇◇◇◇◇◇◇◇◇

W<small>HEN</small>, in 1883, the Kensington Committee of the London
Charity Organisation Society was requested to investigate the
case of one 'R.M.' to decide whether he should be given a small
grant of money to begin life as a hawker of table brushes, the
Committee's recommendation was succinctly decisive, the
decision immediately applied, and the outcome economically
profitable to the applicant. 'We found his employers gave him
excellent characters', wrote the friendly visitor in her record of
the case. '. . . We reported to the gentleman interested that
we thought the man likely to do well and he sent us the money to
lay out a stock. From all we hear, the man is doing a good trade,
and making an independent living'.[1] In 1948, however, when
an unhappy client, Mr. Murray, sought the aid of the Family
Service Association of America to help him to solve a problem
of what his case record called 'unsatisfactory job adjustment',
the exploration of the problem was more prolonged, an entirely
different set of factors was considered relevant to the diagnosis,
the caseworker obviously conceived her role as something more
than dispenser of the loan requested, and the client's dividends
were psychological rather than economic. Mr. Murray, it is

---

[1] C.O.S., *Annual Reports of the Council of the District Committees 1883–1884*,
Report of the Kensington Committee, p. 53.

118

clear, was encouraged in interviews to talk about himself in relation to his parents, his friends, his job and his marriage; intelligence and aptitude tests were clapped upon him; he submitted to a Rorschach test, and was examined at intervals by a psychiatrist. From evidence so painstakingly amassed, the conclusion was reached that Mr. Murray was an emotional Peter Pan. His behaviour, according to this case record, was a reflection of his 'inner problems, tensions and fears'; he fell in 'the general classification of character disturbance'; and although 'chronologically adult', and with mature responsibilities of marriage, parenthood and economic support, he was 'emotionally still in need, like the child, of looking to adults for security, reassurance of his strength, and help in controlling his impulses'.[1] Helping him to overcome this handicap of emotional immaturity and to reach an understanding of himself as a first step towards adjustment was obviously considered to be more beneficial than giving him a 'sufficient financial backlog' to allow him to resign his present job and to seek another.

Comparing the two cases, it is obvious that the caseworker handling Mr. Murray's problem was dealing with different concepts, different values, and even different facts from those which troubled the mind of her occupational ancestor in the London suburb of Kensington in 1883. The relationship between worker and client was essentially different; the spotlight was focused on the person rather than the problem; a more thorough exploration of personal relationships in the home and the job was made, and treatment was conceived in terms of encouraging the client to know himself rather than of mending a hole in his pocket. So far had the caseworker of 1948 parted company with the friendly visitor of 1883.

In order to understand when, how, why, and with what result this change of emphasis occurred, one must turn to the years during and after the First World War. At that time the American social work scene—and a decade later, the English scene—were swept by a psychiatric deluge which, for the time being at least, deflected thinking about social work into entirely new channels. When it receded, it left rich alluvial soil in which new

[1] Cora Kasius (ed.), *A Comparison of Diagnostic and Functional Casework Concepts. Report of the Family Service Association of America Committee to Study Basic Concepts in Case Work Practice* (New York, 1950), p. 71. See full account of the case, *ibid.*, pp. 66–77.

concepts were to take root and flourish, and older ones were to be vitalized and shaped anew. From these developments, especially from the teaching of Freud and his disciples, there was to emerge not only a new way of thinking about people, but an entirely new way of helping them.

It was not that the early social workers in the United States were unaware of the importance of studying people as well as their environment. As early as 1880, when the Reverend Mr. McCulloch presented the first report of the Charity Organisation movement to the Conference of Charities and Correction, he stressed the fact that 'each individual is treated with respect, and with the desire to do that which shall permanently help him',[1] while five years later, he reiterated his claim that the ultimate object of the Charity Organisation movement was to reach the individual. 'While for purposes of investigation and control of causes it deals with classes', he said, 'its thought is to reach the individual man'.[2] In the following year, George B. Buzelle, discussing 'Individuality in the Work of Charity', put the matter even more plainly. 'Charitable work in the best sense', he said, 'must be done by the individual . . . for the individual . . . If the individual is lost, all is lost.'[3]

This principle of individualization, enunciated for the first time in 1886 and still the foundation of modern casework, took firmer shape as it became applied to the groups of people—such as deserted wives, widows with dependents, and delinquent, defective, crippled and deformed children—who now began to engage the attention of welfare workers in the United States. Although classification of these groups was very general and analysis superficial, now and again it was realized that before treatment could be given, a deeper knowledge of the individual was needed. Edward T. Devine, discussing the value and dangers of investigation, insisted that if help were to be given effectively, 'investigation cannot be too thorough or extensive or painstaking or the record too careful',[4] while another speaker

[1] Oscar McCulloch, 'Associated Charities', *Proc. 8th N.C.C.C.* (Cleveland, 1880), p. 132.

[2] 'The Personal Element in Charity', *Proc. 12th N.C.C.C.* (Washington, 1885), p. 341.

[3] 'Individuality in the Work of Charity', *Proc. 13th N.C.C.C.* (St. Paul, Minn., 1886), p. 187. See above, pp. 92–3.

[4] 'The Value and Dangers of Investigation', *Proc. 24th N.C.C.C.* (Toronto, 1897), p. 195.

in 1888, pleading for a more humane treatment of what he called 'moral imbeciles', stressed the need for a study of the mind along with the body and came to the conclusion that 'all the actions of man, physical, intellectual, and moral, are the inevitable consequences of preceding circumstances and conditions which absolutely control and dominate him'.[1] But although there were the few who recognized the need to know more about the individual, little was done to meet the need, both because social workers in the period up to 1910 were less preoccupied with the individual than with the environment and social action to correct abuses in it, and because psychology and sociology had not yet advanced to the stage where they could answer the questions asked. Therefore as late as 1900, at a time when in Europe Freud was already undergoing his painful self-analysis, William Smallwood could plead that 'the man should be studied psychologically', and yet show himself to be a child of his age in that he sentimentalized the study,[2] Edmond J. Butler could discuss the family with an understanding of the ties which bind it together but with little realization of the tensions which rend it apart,[3] and Mary E. Richmond could analyse the relation of community forces to the family and yet show little interest in the relationships which existed within it.[4]

In the decade from 1910, however, new influences from psychology and psychiatry began to make themselves felt. These were to result, in the United States, in a swing away from the socio-economic determinism of the previous era to the psychological determinism of the 1920's, and in England a decade later, were to temper the content and emphasis of social workers' thinking about family and individual problems. The child guidance movement in the United States had taught social workers to recognize the importance of the family in moulding

[1] P. Bryce, 'Moral and Criminal Responsibility', *Proc. 15th N.C.C.C.* (Buffalo, N.Y., 1888), pp. 88, 75, 85.

[2] E.g. 'Is there in him a latent moral force, a love of the beautiful, of music, of nature, of sunsets and skies? . . . Shall I have him in my home, suggest good books, · good plays to see, music to hear, and pictures to look upon? Shall I take him to walk with me in the country, where the language of the birds, fields, hills, and streams, may be revealed?' ('The Development of the Individual', *Proc. 27th N.C.C.C.* (Topeka, 1900), p. 270.)

[3] 'Needy Families in their Homes: Causes of Poverty', *Proc. 30th N.C.C.C.* (Atlanta, 1903), pp. 272–85.

[4] 'Charitable Co-operation', *Proc. 28th N.C.C.C.* (Washington, 1901), pp. 298–313; reprinted in *The Long View*, pp. 186–208. See above, pp. 105, 108.

the life of the individual, especially during the infant years, and even though there were times when this knowledge was not adequate to afford complete understanding of the child,[1] it did form a base from which later psychologists were to work. At the same time Krafft-Ebing, Forel, Havelock Ellis and others were beginning to explore the sexual factor in human behaviour, and social workers, influenced by this new knowledge, to achieve an understanding of the predominating importance of the emotional life in contrast to the intellectual aspects with which hitherto they had been so much concerned. This recognition of the ascendancy of the emotional was not altogether new. As early as the 1870's, the importance of emotional factors in the treatment of problems such as delinquency had been admitted, but although there were signs of what was to come, the National Conference had to wait until 1916 to hear a strong plea for the individual criminal to be studied 'medically, psychiatrically, psychologically and in every important known way',[2] and a further two years to hear a speaker stress how important emotional factors were in the treatment of the feeble-minded.[3]

Perhaps the main reason for this delay was that psychiatry, which, far more than psychology, was to influence social casework in the decade from 1910, had only recently graduated

[1] E.g. Charles Loring Brace's work in 'placing out' homeless and vagrant children, although based on the sound principle that a home is better for a child than an institution, shows a naïve, if not callous, understanding of children and their adjustment. Describing in 1876 his scheme to 'place' children in homes in the West 'where the assistance of children is needed', he said, 'The resident Western agent . . . procures the name of a few prominent citizens. . . . Public notice is given some weeks beforehand, that a company of orphans and homeless children from New York will come there on a given day. The little company of unfortunates . . . are billetted around among the families of the village . . . and then appear in the town hall or whatever place has been selected for the meeting. Here the agent . . . forms a committee of some of the leading men present. This committee decides upon the applications . . . each child is placed in a home. . . . The employers agree to send the children to school in the winter, and of course to treat them kindly.' (*Proceedings of the Conference of Charities*, 1876, p. 139). In 1899, the same naïveté was shown when C. R. Henderson commented, 'The homeless child is taken to a childless home, or to family care where love makes room for one more object of mercy and hope. . . . The old sad history is forgotten; with a new home begins new memories and a new career.' (*Proc. 26th N.C.C.C.* (Cincinnati, 1899), pp. 12–13.)

[2] E. E. Southard, 'Psychopathic Delinquents', *Proc. 43rd N.C.C.C.* (Indianapolis, 1916), p. 531.

[3] Jessie Taft, 'Supervision of the Feebleminded in the Community', *Proc. 45th N.C.S.W.* (Kansas City, 1918), pp. 543–50.

from its concern with the custodial care of the insane to an interest in causation and treatment. Mental disorder, of course, was no new phenomenon. It had plagued earlier societies, and the person so afflicted had been variously conceived as a madman, a fool, a sorcerer, or an offender against the gods. If he were possessed of evil spirits, they might be exorcized by incantations and ceremonials; if he were sick of soul, drugs and herbs might relieve his suffering; if he were being punished for his sins, prayer and sacrifice might propitiate the gods, but if these measures failed, then he might be physically scourged and tortured, and even burned, hanged or drowned as a witch. Thus was the study of insanity veiled from the understanding of men. The result was inevitable. By the nineteenth century there was still so little known about the origin of mental disease that society oscillated between punishment of the insane as criminals and indifference to them as enigmas, and while it was believed that mental disease, like physical disease, was organic in origin, treatment was conceived in terms of custody for the afflicted and restraint for the violent. As late as 1850, treatment of the insane was based on such ideas as those of Dr. Benjamin Rush of the University of Pennsylvania Medical School. He, while recognizing the power of kindness in dealing with the insane, found it too precarious for regular use, and recommended coercion to prevent destruction of furniture and clothing, and, if considered necessary, to punish the patient. As instruments of coercion, punishment and subjugation, he recommended use of the strait waistcoat, the restraint chair, the shower bath, chains and whips, and a 'gyrator' invented by himself to give the patient rotatory motion at a rate rapid enough to produce 'vertigo, nausea and a general perspiration'. He also remarked upon the advantages of solitude and darkness for the afflicted, and considered that the same means might be used for subduing mad men as had been found effectual for taming refractory horses. The horse was impounded, and then prevented from lying down or sleeping for two or three days and nights by thrusting sharp pointed nails in his body; the madman, considered Dr. Rush, could be kept awake and standing by less severe means for twenty-four hours.[1]

---

[1] *The Institutional Care of the Insane in the U.S. and Canada*, I, 234; quoted by Joseph L. Bodina, 'The Management of the Insane without Mechanical Restraints', *Proceedings of the Third Conference of Charities* (Saratoga, 1876), pp. 95–96.

These were measures invented by ignorant men fearful for their own safety, but even fearful men are chary of putting hand in pocket, and many were the complaints that the insane were a financial burden on the community, and that the increase of insanity was due to intemperance, prostitution and other vices widely practised but socially disapproved. 'I object to the magnificence of public buildings being erected in this state for these purposes', the Governor of New York wrathfully told the National Conference in 1876.[1] Twelve years later, an earnest doctor pleaded the cause for preventing insanity by what he called 'the timely control of the dissolute'. 'Intemperance, prostitution and associate vices', he warned, 'leave not a tissue of the body untouched by their depressing influence and disease-developing power, the direct and natural end of which is the insane asylum'.[2]

Throughout most of the nineteenth century, emphasis had been on the custodial care of the insane, and what study there was of mental disease concerned itself largely with description and classification. It was only when Freud began his studies of hysteria in the 1890's, thus inventing the science of psychoanalysis, that the causes of mental illness were studied, the role of psychogenic factors in mental disease was explored, and custody was supplemented and sometimes replaced by therapy. Freud's analysis of the unconscious gave an entirely new slant to the study of the human mind and personality, and even though controversy raged around his hypotheses[3] and many psychiatrists and neurologists refused to accept them, his teaching influenced dissenters as well as disciples and gave currency to a conception of personality which was to modify forever, if not eventually to replace, the old static view.

Thus by the first decade of the twentieth century, there were signs which presaged new developments in the study and treatment of mental disease. The old-time preoccupation with custody and classification gave way to a concern with causes and treatment; psychoanalysis was providing new insights into human behaviour, while psychology was tracing the growth of the child, stressing the importance of the family, and elaborating

[1] Samuel J. Tilden, 'Presidential Address', *ibid.*, p. 13.

[2] C. Irving Fisher, 'The Prevention of Insanity by the Timely Control of the Dissolute', *Proc. 15th N.C.C.C.* (Buffalo, N.Y., 1888), p. 92.

[3] For an account of the various schools of thought, see Ruth L. Munroe, *Schools of Psychoanalytic Thought* (1957).

mental testing techniques as a method of studying individual differences. The net result was an entirely new outlook upon mental health, and the launching of a mental hygiene movement which incorporated the principle that mental disease could be prevented if more was known about it, institutional care was improved, knowledge of causes, treatment and prevention disseminated, and ways and means found by which people could be helped to live more constructively and happily.

It was not long before this new point of view began to influence the content and emphasis of social casework. Prompted by the publication in 1908 of Clifford Beers' autobiographical *A Mind that Found Itself*, which popularized the cause of the mentally ill, and the formation in the following year of the National Mental Hygiene Committee, the National Conference of Charities and Correction began to show an increasing interest in the problem of mental disease. Previous speakers at the annual meeting had been interested in the custody of the feeble-minded and the insane. Now, however, attention came to be focused on treatment and prevention. 'When will our intellectual leaders begin to realize the agony to which we psychiatrists are put when we have to watch, too often helpless, the long illness and frequently the irresistible fading-out or perversion of human minds', asked Dr. Adolf Meyer despairingly in 1915;[1] while one of his colleagues, more hopeful than he, reported on the possibilities of research as applied to the prevention of feeble-mindedness, another, concluding that the disease was incurable, pleaded for 'some central government authority' to supervise, assist and control the feeble-minded not properly cared for by their friends, and yet a fourth proclaimed the prevention of mental defect to be 'the duty of the hour'.[2] At the National Conference in 1916 too, papers were presented on various aspects of feeble-mindedness and insanity. The question of 'borderlinity' was discussed; the need stressed for a 'Brain Institute' to carry out research into the nature, causes, results, prevention and treatment of mental disease, a study was made

---

[1] 'Where should we attack the Problem of the Prevention of Mental Defect and Mental Disease?' *Proc. 42nd N.C.C.C.* (Maryland, 1915), p. 306.

[2] H. H. Goddard, 'The Possibilities of Research as applied to the Prevention of Feeble-Mindedness', *ibid.*, pp. 307–12; Walter E. Fernald, 'What is Practical in the Way of Prevention of Mental Defect?', *ibid.*, pp. 289–97; Martin W. Burr, 'The Prevention of Medical Defect, the Duty of the Hour', *ibid.*, pp. 361–7.

of what was called 'psychopathic delinquents', and social workers were instructed in the medical facts which it was considered they should know.[1]

The following year saw the same unquenchable interest in the twin sciences of psychology and psychiatry. A Committee Organised for Mental Hygiene reported that failure to recognize 'underlying mental factors' in community problems resulted in conflicts in the individual, the home, the school, in social and industrial relationships, in the almshouse and in the court. A doctor carefully explained how the community should be organized for mental hygiene, while another discussed with worried relish some of the mental problems he had to deal with at Sing Sing. A social worker interpreted dependence in terms of psychology, and a psychiatrist emphasized the value of having 'accurate knowledge of the phases of mental life . . . synonymous with disability'. Mary E. Richmond spoke of 'the direct action of mind upon mind'. A realist sadly prophesied that the delinquent boy and girl of today would be the delinquent husband and wife of tomorrow, and social workers were again told how much medicine they should know, both for their own good and that of their clients.[2] Even more significantly, Dr. Macfie Campbell uttered the wise dictum that 'indigestion and headache may be mental disorders just as truly as are morbid phantasies and distorted attitudes',[3] and Dr. Healy applauded this interest in psychiatry, commenting that 'the one science that has most to contribute, now or ultimately, to social casework is unquestionably the science of the mind.'[4]

[1] Samuel C. Kohs, 'The Borderlines of Mental Deficiency', *Proc. 43rd N.C.C.C.* (Indianapolis, 1916), pp. 279–91; Owen Copp, 'Mental Disease and Mental Defect, a State and National Problem', *ibid.*, pp. 266–77; E. E. Southard, 'Psychopathic Delinquents', *ibid.*, pp. 529–38; Charles P. Emerson, 'Medical Facts that Social Workers should know', *ibid.*, pp. 495–501.

[2] Owen Copp, 'Report for the Committee Organized for Mental Hygiene', *Proc. 44th N.C.S.W.* (Pittsburgh, 1917), pp. 391–7; E. E. Southard, 'Zones of Community in Mental Hygiene', *ibid.*, pp. 405–13; Bernard Glueck, 'Some Mental Problems at Sing Sing', *ibid.*, pp. 420–1; Porter R. Lee, 'The Administrative Basis of Public Outdoor Relief', *ibid.*, pp. 146–54; William Healy, 'Bearings of Psychology on Social Casework', *ibid.*, pp. 104–12; Mary E. Richmond, 'The Social Caseworker's Task', *ibid.*, pp. 112–15; E. Bosworth McCready, 'Mental Problems in the Courts', *ibid.*, pp. 413–19; Richard C. Cabot, 'What Medical Diagnosis should the social caseworker know and apply?' *ibid.*, pp. 101–4.

[3] 'The Mental Health of the Community and the Work of the Psychiatric Dispensary', *ibid.*, p. 437.

[4] 'Bearings of Psychology on Social Casework', *op. cit.*, p. 105.

This 'psychological' stream, which in 1917 ran alongside the faster flowing 'sociological' river represented by Mary E. Richmond's *Social Diagnosis*, was considerably strengthened when the entry of the United States into the First World War brought new social problems to plague the mind and sharpen the wits of those who guarded America's welfare. 'We would show ourselves unfit to enjoy the blessings of democracy', one speaker told the National Conference in 1917, 'if, while sending our soldiers to the front . . . we permitted their families at home to fight want, disease and moral dangers alone'.[1] Another warned her audience of the difficulties attendant upon adjusting returned soldiers to civilian life, while the following year, an enthusiastic description of the work of the Division of Neuro-Psychiatry in the army ended with a plea that the knowledge so gained would be carried over into civilian life after the war. A further speaker, by experience wise, recommended the speedy organisation on a national scale of medical and social care of war neuroses, while yet another advocated continuing into the years of peace 'this great new regimentation of the free which the American nation is achieving'.[2]

It was obvious that the appearance of these new clients on the scene raised challenging problems for the social worker. How to assist the family of a sailor overseas, to care for a soldier broken by the boredom of barracks or the barbarity of combat, how to fill for a convalescent long hours of nothingness, or to help a serviceman become a civilian? In 1918, cases such as these posed new problems of approach, of contact and of training. These, when met, evoked a new kind of service. In 1918 a Red Cross worker drew the attention of the National Conference to this growth of what she called 'casework above the poverty line'. It depended for its existence on the satisfaction of the client, she said, and since the average family had overcome whatever dislike it may have had for 'investigation', the number of cases had increased to the extent that the busy worker might

[1] Eugene T. Lies, 'Red Cross Work among Families of Soldiers and Sailors', *ibid.*, p. 142.

[2] Helen Y. Reid, *ibid.*, pp. 126–39; Richard H. Hutchings, 'The Work of the Division of Neuro-psychiatry in the Army', *Proc. 45th N.C.S.W.* (Kansas City, 1918), p. 521; Mary C. Jarrett, 'War Neuroses after the War: Extra-Institutional Preparation', *ibid.*, pp. 558–63; Robert A. Woods, 'The Regimentation of the Free', *ibid.*, p. 10.

be tempted to go ahead with her investigation 'without the close co-operation that ought to be present'.[1] It was obvious, too, that since much of this casework was not only above the poverty line, but dealt with maladies hitherto outside the case-worker's ken, it was necessary to link hands with the psychiatrist and to become versed in his interpretation of human nature. By 1919, this need for new knowledge had been clearly realized and generously met. The programme of the National Conference of that year displayed the verbal fruit of this intellectual mating of psychiatrist and social worker. Delegates crowded into halls to listen to discussions on what the psychiatric worker's task was and how she should be prepared for it, how frequently the mentally disabled soldier presented a difficult problem, whether the study of mental life was fundamental to any activity 'having for its object the better adjustment of the individual', and how, since all family situations could be analysed in terms of the dominant figure, the individual, rather than the family, should be the unit of casework.[2] 'This psychiatric eruption', as Dr. Cabot said, 'is the best thing that has happened in the history of social work during the last thirty years.'[3]

The following year, although the eruption had almost spent itself, the main theme of the previous conference was reiterated. Once again, the psychological nature of the caseworker's task was emphasized. The individual, as Dr. Macfie Campbell said, had 'a most complicated pattern of reactions' which a physician must take into account when treating him for a disease. 'Headache may be a reaction to eye strain', he explained, 'but it may be a reaction to a mother-in-law . . . Indigestion may be more

[1] Agnes Murray, 'Casework above the Poverty Line', *ibid.*, pp. 340–3.
[2] Jessie Taft, 'Qualification of the Psychiatric Social Worker', *Proc. 46th N.C.S.W.* (Atlantic City, 1919), pp. 593–9; Bernard Glueck, 'Special Preparation of the Psychiatric Social Worker', *ibid.*, pp. 599–606; Douglas Singer, 'The Function of the Social Worker in Relation to the State Hospital Physician', *ibid.*, pp. 632–7; V. May Macdonald, 'Function of Psychiatric Social Work in Relation to the Community', *ibid.*, pp. 637–43; Edith R. Spaulding, 'The Training School of Psychiatric Social Work at Smith College', *ibid.*, pp. 606–10; Arthur F. Sullivan, 'Some Special Medical Problems in the After Care of Disabled Soldiers', *ibid.*, pp. 351–7; Mary C. Jarrett, 'The Psychiatric Thread running through all Social Casework', *ibid.*, pp. 587–93; F. E. Southard, 'The Individual versus the Family as the Unit of Interest in Social Work', *ibid.*, pp. 582–7.
[3] In informal discussion, *ibid.*, p. 593.

closely related to a troubled conscience than to poor cooking; palpitation is not always an indication of organic heart disease, it may be the expression of the romance of life gone astray.' This, he hastened to add, was not the whole story. Environment, too, was important, for individual shortcomings could spring from a social source. 'Let us keep in mind', he said, 'that delinquency may be delinquency not of the individual, but of the society.'[1]

This, however, was an environmentalist voice crying in a wilderness of individualism. So intent were Dr. Campbell's colleagues upon the psychology of the individual and how best it could be studied, that their thoughts strayed to the social context only insofar as it impinged upon the individual. Thus Dr. Salmon, outlining the tasks of mental hygiene organisations emphasized the fact that attention must be directed 'first, last and all the time' to the individual,[2] but how the individual was affected by the structure and functioning of the social order was never considered, nor were the ways in which his mental processes were influenced by the prejudices and predilections of society. A similar disregard for social factors was shown by his successors to the rostrum, for one speaker, with a womanly yet myopic eye on what was profitable and what was not, applauded the fact that all points from which industry was studied—economics, medicine, engineering, labour and capital—were coming to a focus upon the 'basic fact that production rests upon mind', while a sister in economy estimated the cost to industry of the psychopathic employee and urged society to correct that unprofitable state of mind which led it to treat all mental abnormalities as mysterious and dangerous.[3]

This, then, was the beginning of the psychiatric deluge. It was not at first particularly Freudian. In fact, as Virginia Robinson pointed out,[4] there was an indiscriminate interest in any new psychological theory, but gradually, and especially in the decade from 1930, terms such as 'ego', 'super-ego', 'libido' and 'ambivalence' began to invade the caseworker's vocabulary;

---

[1] 'Minimum of Medical Insights required by Social Service Workers with Delinquents', *Proc. 47th N.C.S.W.* (New Orleans, 1920), pp. 66, 69.

[2] 'Some of the Tasks of Organised Work in Mental Hygiene', *ibid.*, p. 65.

[3] Mary C. Jarrett, 'The Mental Hygiene of Industry', *ibid.*, p. 341; Margaret J. Powers, 'The Industrial Cost of the Psychopathic Employee', *ibid.*, pp. 342–6.

[4] *A Changing Psychology in Social Case Work* (Chapel Hill, 1939), p. 83.

the concept of 'relationship', as developed in psychoanalytic literature, became part of casework's stock-in-trade; clients were encouraged to relate the story of their lives on the basis of Freudian 'free association'; 'dynamic passivity' was accepted as a guiding principle for caseworkers; and 'therapy' based on relationship became a significant part of the 'helping process'. The era of frenzied Freudianism had begun. By 1940, according to one American writer, any deviation from Freudian psychology in the theory of social work 'was looked upon by some with the same horror as a true Stalinist appraising a Trotskyite'.[1] The reasons were the same in both cases; both had become a religion with a theology, an organisation, and an inquisition to discover and to punish heresy.

Why, one might ask, this surrender to Freud?[2]

The most obvious reason was that the new psychology, fed by contributions from psychiatry and psychoanalysis—whether of Freud, Adler, Jung or Rank—could help to explain facets of human behaviour hitherto ignored as irrelevant or dismissed as irrational. Whereas in pre-Freudian days, attention had been focused on the problem—whether it was one of desertion, alcoholism, dependency or delinquency—now the person became the centre of the case. What assumed significance were his emotional attitudes as they mirrored the repressions, conflicts and struggles within his unconscious life. Often these attitudes were expressions of deep-seated conflicts within his personality, and help was needed to bring them to the surface and to face them, to accept them, to live with them or to change them. This, it was thought, was the caseworker's task. At first her role was conceived in negative terms, but as it was realized that the emotional rehabilitation of the client demanded that the worker be something more than sounding board or safety valve, she began to play a more positive part, and, armed with the new knowledge and sharper interviewing skills, she sought

[1] Arthur P. Miles, *American Social Work Theory* (New York, 1954), p. 9.

[2] The two main 'schools' of casework theory are the *diagnostic*, which derives its philosophy and methods from the theory of personality created by Freud, and the *functional*, based upon the theory of 'will therapy' developed by Otto Rank, at first a disciple, then a dissenter, of Freud. For an account of the differences between these two approaches, see Cora Kasius (ed.), *op. cit.*, especially pp. 7–13, and Grace Marcus, 'Family Casework in 1948', *Journal of Social Casework* (now called *Social Casework*), Vol. XXIX, No. 7 (July 1948), pp. 261–70.

to help the client to become master of his emotional fate. In accordance with this new emphasis, a different kind of case history was evolved. Instead of the older type of social history which furnished relentlessly utilitarian details about parents, children, wages, delinquencies, sicknesses, operations, schooling, and jobs there now appeared a case history recording the client's introspection and the attempt of the worker, often in alliance with the psychiatrist, to edit and interpret the client's subconscious. 'Mr. Martin's fear about his arm . . . was deeper than reality justified', ran the record of a sufferer from an accident, 'It was as if his virility is threatened'.[1]

Sometimes, of course, the caseworker was carried away by her self-imposed mission to explore the subconscious. Often she had drunk so deeply of Freudian draughts that she claimed to know more about the client than he knew himself; or else she insisted upon taking the hard way out, refused to accept at face value the emergencies which propelled many people to seek the aid of an agency, and sought to penetrate below what she called 'the presenting problem' to the 'something deeper' that was assumed to lie beneath. Sometimes, too, her description of 'the relationship' between worker and client was couched in terms so grandiloquent that relationship loomed larger than the main task of mobilizing forms of assistance for the client, while often her attempts to describe her activities led her into making formulae so comprehensive and claims so ambitious, that she drew down upon her head the scorn of the humbler and the wrath of the outraged.[2]

In spite of abuses, however, the new psychology had much to offer. Beginning as a study of the mind diseased, it had early turned its attention to the psychopathology of everyday life, where its exploration of human behaviour and relationships yielded new knowledge and insight which the social worker was quick to seize. A deeper understanding of the forces which control human behaviour, a concern with the motives which prompted a person to seek help, an emphasis upon his past experiences and the seemingly non-essential areas of his life, an appreciation of the factors which might conceivably lie

[1] 'The Martin Case: from a Family Service Agency', quoted by Gordon Hamilton, *Theory and Practice of Social Case Work* (New York, 1940 ed.), p. 350.

[2] E.g. see Barbara Wootton, *Social Science and Social Pathology* (1959), Chapter IX.

beneath the immediate problem—these were some of the concepts which psychoanalysis bequeathed. And as they were read, learned and inwardly digested, not only did the emphasis of the social worker's philosophy and practice change, but, in accordance with the new preoccupation with the psychological rather than the economic, she began to see herself in a new light. No longer was she a dispenser of charity, interested primarily in the poverty of the poor; no longer did she divide those who sought her help into the deserving and the undeserving. Now, shorn of her old-time censoriousness, armed with a vocabulary richly strewn with medical terms, and convinced, apparently, that the poor were no longer with us, she saw herself as a species of social physician, concerned with problems of psychological maladjustment rather than material need, and versed in the arts of treating such symptoms of a sick society as broken homes and juvenile delinquents.[1]

This change in emphasis from the economic to the psychological meant that once more the individual became the centre of the stage. Whereas in the period from 1900 to the First World War, the caseworker, faced with the problem of man's adjustment to his social environment, had been concerned primarily with the environment and the possible ways in which social action could repair individual failure, now in the post-war years, it was assumed that if adjustment was not achieved the individual was to blame. Moreover, it was believed that individual therapy was the process by which a better world could be achieved. 'Important as are good wages', said Gordon Hamilton in 1928, '. . . . they are not guarantees of what the social worker is inclined to call adjustment. . . . The unit, personality, as men

---

[1] This is not to say that no material relief was given. On the contrary, the 'psychological' trend was paralleled by a trend towards much relief giving. As Joanna C. Colcord pointed out in 1923, families formerly considered 'unsuitable for relief because of moral judgments (e.g. cases involving desertion, venereal disease, or families of criminals) were now frequently granted relief on a budgetary basis which seemed to indicate that caseworkers had lost their fear of relief as a danger to strength of character, 'feeling with good reason that casework has adequate methods to avoid this danger', ('Relief', *The Family*, 4 (March 1923), pp. 13–17). Similarly, it should not be inferred that the psychoanalytic approach in casework eliminated the sociological point of view of *Social Diagnosis*, as an analysis of the Milford Conference Report of 1929 will show. This Report, bent on defining social casework and relating the various specialized fields to the whole, was sociological rather than psychological in its approach, and probably had a more immediate effect on casework than the new psychology.

come to understand more the means of releasing it, has the power, in a true sense, to socialize the world'.[1] 'The true springs of action are in the internal nature of man', echoed another, 'hence the uselessness of programs, particularly those dependent upon state action or force.'[2]

This emphasis upon the individual and the consequent refusal to face harsh social and economic facts not only reflected the social worker's new preoccupation with psychiatry and psychoanalysis. It reflected also the conservative social and economic climate of the post-war years. During the preceding Progressive era, Oliver Wendell Holmes might challenge the view that *laisser-faire* principles were embodied in the constitution and Woodrow Wilson advocate 'the new freedom' to ensure that the individual gets 'fair play', but during the glittering twenties, the Progressive plea to adjust industrialism to democracy was temporarily forgotten. In its place came that kind of liberalism which valued private enterprise and wanted to keep state control at bay. Perhaps the reason was that by the time the soldiers returned from France a different way of life had already begun, a way of life which embraced such distractions as jazz, the radio, crossword puzzles, bathing beauty contests, speak-easies, racketeers, the cinema and the confession magazine. Perhaps the reason was that in the complacent years of 'normalcy' there seemed justification for Hoover's claim that, given a chance and the help of God, 'poverty will be banished from this nation'.[3] Or perhaps the reason was that the Republican Party was so successful in using the government as an instrument to promote private profit, that many came to believe the Coolidge dictum that 'the business of America is business', and fell down to worship at the shrine of private industry. 'The man who builds a factory builds a temple', intoned the president, 'the man who works there worships there, and to each is due not scorn and blame but reverence and praise.'[4]

[1] Quoted by Jacob Fisher, 'Social Work and Liberalism', *Social Work Today*, Vol. I, No. 2 (May–June 1934), p. 11.

[2] Miriam van Waters, 'Presidential Address: Philosophical Trends in Modern Social Work', *Proc. 57th N.C.S.W.* (Boston, 1930), p. 19; reprinted in Fern Lowry, *Readings in Social Case Work, 1920–1938* (New York, 1939), pp. 38–53.

[3] Speech of 11 August 1928, in Avery Craven et al, *A Documentary History of the American People* (New York, 1951), p. 693.

[4] Quoted by C. A. and M. R. Beard, *Rise of American Civilization* (New York, 1930 ed.), II, 700.

This belief in the sanctity of private industry—and its corollary that government should be the high priest to guard the sacred flame—coincided with the views of the self-conscious, organised business man of the period in whom a sense of power was combined with an acute political awareness. 'As a nation we are occupying Alpian heights of economic prosperity hitherto unexplored', the President of the National Association of Manufacturers told a meeting of his confrères in 1926. 'Yet it must be admitted that . . . even as death loves a shining mark, so conspicuous success attracts the lustful attention of political expediency. Hence the more successful and prosperous our industry is, the greater its peril and the larger our collective responsibilities.'[1]

Why American industry was so conspicuously successful, the president was only too willing to explain. 'Our system . . . is the best so far that has been evolved from the wisdom of all the ages',[2] he claimed, and considered that there was evidence on all sides to prove it. Any poverty which existed, he said, was the result of 'voluntary unemployment, thriftlessness, sin in various forms, disease and other misfortunes'. Basically, unemployment was not an economic but a moral problem, and to lift the individual's economic responsibility by legislation was to promote 'the very habits of thriftlessness in his life' which produced his dependency upon such a process. Therefore, to seek to abolish unemployment or poverty was 'neither a legitimate nor proper function of government'; such incentives to indolence as old age pensions were to be strongly deplored;[3] the working-classes were to be protected against 'excessive leisure';[4] and

[1] John E. Edgerton, 'Presidential Address', *Proceedings of the Thirty-First Annual Convention of the National Association of Manufacturers of U.S.A.* (New York, 1926), pp. 67, 68–69.

[2] 'Presidential Address', *Proceedings of the Thirtieth Annual Convention of the National Association of Manufacturers of U.S.A.* (New York, 1925), p. 12.

[3] 'Presidential Address', *Proceedings of the Thirty-Fifth Annual Meeting of the National Association of Manufacturers of U.S.A.* (New York, 1930), pp. 14, 15, 13, 53.

[4] E.g. 'The working masses of our country . . . have, for the most part, been so busy at their jobs that they have not had time to saturate themselves with false theories of economics, social reform, and of life. They have been protected in their natural growth by the absence of excessive leisure and have been fortunate not only in their American made opportunities to work, but in the necessities which have compelled its reasonable indulgence.' (*Proceedings of the Thirty-First Annual Convention of the National Association of Manufacturers of U.S.A.* (New York, 1926.) p. 5.)

the National Association of Manufacturers was to continue to co-operate with the government 'in the wise performance of its just and proper functions'.[1] If these simple rules were followed, the president thought, all would be well. Not even a depression could disturb his cheerful faith. 1929 was, no doubt, a great trial, but greater faith in the system was warranted by its mere survival. 'Certainly, nothing has happened to weaken the confidence of understanding minds in . . . our American economic system and its adaptability', said he. '. . . . on the contrary, while depression has brought into clearer view some egregious abuses of both our economic and political mechanisms, it has at the same time demonstrated their sufficiency of strength for as severe a test as has yet been known.'[2]

This conservative social climate was conducive to refocusing attention on the individual, not only in the economic sphere, but in the sphere of social work as well. The conviction, deeply rooted in the soil of American individualism, that moral inadequacy lay at the root of most problems of poverty and dependency was now reinforced by an over-emphasis upon psychological inadequacy, and little, if any, attention was paid to the social realities which the individual had to face in a highly industrialized and fiercely competitive society. It is no wonder, then, that although there were enthusiasts in the psychiatric cause who believed that with the coming of psychoanalysis, social casework was for the first time placed on a scientific foundation, there were others who gave horrid warning of the dangers of neglecting economic and cultural factors, and who pleaded somewhat wistfully that sociological research on subjects such as personality and group behaviour could be adapted for use in social work. Nor was it surprising that although Jane Addams could advocate a policy of political action[3] and Karl de Schweinitz see social work as 'the interpreter of the longings of people for a more wholesome order',[4] the majority of their

---

[1] *Proceedings of the Thirty-Fifth Annual Meeting of the National Association of Manufacturers of U.S.A.* (New York, 1930), p. 19.

[2] *Ibid.*, p. 12.

[3] E.g. 'When the ideas and measures which we have long been advocating become part of a political campaign, which is after all but an intensified method of propaganda, would we not be victims of a curious self-consciousness if we failed to follow them there?' ('Pragmatism in Politics', *The Survey*, XXIX (1912), 12.)

[4] 'Social Work as it contributes to the Strengthening of Family Life', *Proc. 50th N.C.S.W.* (Washington, 1923), p. 299.

colleagues should agree that social work should proceed on a non-partisan basis, that social workers should be 'adjustors' and 'ameliorators' rather than innovators and reformers,[1] and that a cool reception be given to the challenging call to social workers to build up 'a political class party of the producers' committed to public control of natural resources, public utilities, money and credit.[2] These were demands too radical to be accepted by the intensely individualist social workers of the 1920's, and it was not until the following decade, when the psychiatric deluge had given way to an economic deluge, and attention was swept from the super-ego to the trade cycle, that the tide of individualism was turned back.

If, in the United States, there was a psychiatric deluge in the 1920's, in England during the same period there was nothing more than a trickle which, even though it was to grow in the following decades, never reached the majestic swell of its American counterpart. True, there was some interest in the individual personality and the forces which shape and control it. From its earliest days casework had been conceived, in Loch's words, as 'a social regenerator'[3] and a 'healing art',[4] while the friendly visitor was regarded as 'a good physician',[5] who, if she was to fulfil her aim of restoring a fellow in distress to healthy self-dependence, should have a knowledge of his personality and the way it could be modified. 'The possibility of helping depends on knowing alike the strength and the weakness of those in distress', Loch had said, 'the man as he might be, as

---

[1] E.g. Miriam van Waters said, 'We do not plan and build communities, rather we are adjustors, maybe the ameliorators, or we just dodge the traffic'. ('The New Morality and the Social Worker', *Proc. 56th N.C.S.W.* (San Francisco, 1929), p. 70.)

[2] Roger N. Baldwin, 'The Challenge to Social Work of the Changing Control in Industry', *Proc. 51st N.C.S.W.* (Toronto, 1924), p. 378.

[3] 'Charity is a social regenerator; she has to support new desires; to revive old instincts; to keep alive family affections . . . to preserve the humane in man. . . . We have to use charity to create the *power* of self help.' ('The Future of Charity', *C.O. Reporter*, Vol. XIII, No. 551 (27 September 1884), pp. 320, 321.) See above, pp. 50–1.

[4] 'Charity organisation is not mere investigation and detection; it is a diagnosis and the art of healing.' (C.O.S., *Eleventh Annual Report*, April 13, 1880, p. 16).

[5] 'Go, learn all about him, and treat him like a man. . . . Strengthen him where he is weak, aid him when he is tempted . . . and if you have moral power over him . . . make him from a beggar, a man, and make yourself from a charitable spendthrift a good physician.' (*Diary of Charles Stewart Loch, 1876–1892* (unpublished), entry for 28 May 1877.)

well as the man as he has become.'[1] But although the English social worker early realized this need to know more about the individual, little was done to meet the need, and attention was focused on environment to the exclusion of the individual. When, in 1903, the training scheme, established by the C.O.S., in 1896, blossomed into the School of Sociology and Social Economics, the whole emphasis of its teaching was sociological. E. J. Urwick, lecturer and tutor to the sixteen students enrolled, certainly paid lip service to the importance of psychology as one of the departments of 'a new knowledge',[2] but the administration of the School and the programmes drawn up for the edification of the social worker seemed to belie his words. The work of the School was divided into three departments, Sociology, Social Theory, and a specialized department in poor law administration, while the lectures given, both by Urwick and by distinguished visitors to the School, were dissertations on sociological subjects, such as good citizenship, social improvement and methods of thrift, rather than intimate studies of the psyche of the citizen, the improved or the thrifty.[3]

The same sociological emphasis can be seen in the training schemes developed outside the C.O.S. and London, such as the Women's University Settlement at Southwark, the School of Social Science in Manchester, the later schemes in Birmingham, Bristol, Leeds, Liverpool, Edinburgh and Glasgow, and the many unorganised specialized schemes which sprang up outside the academic pale.[4] For little of the new psychological and psychiatric knowledge which so bedazzled the American social

---

[1] 'The Development of Charity Organisation', C.O. Review, (N.S.), Vol. XV, No. 86 (February 1904), p. 73.

[2] The four divisions of this 'new knowledge' which might furnish 'the scientific basis for the social education we need' were 'the natural history of society', 'social philosophy', 'social economics' and a knowledge of the mental processes on which development depends or 'individual and social psychology'. (E. J. Urwick, 'Social Education of Yesterday and Today', C.O. Review (N.S.), Vol. XIV, No. 83 (November 1903), pp. 254–64.)

[3] A great deal of information is given by C. S. Loch in a paper entitled 'The School of Sociology', included in C.O.S. Pamphlets—C. S. Loch (in possession of the Family Welfare Association), in which he includes material from the annual reports of the School for 1904–5 and 1905–6. See also Marjorie J. Smith, Professional Education for Social Work in Britain (1952), App. III, which gives extracts from the 'Confidential Report of the Social Education Committee of the C.O.S., submitted June 8, 1903'.

[4] For further detail, see E. Macadam, The Equipment of the Social Worker (1925).

worker found its way across the Atlantic. As late as 1917, when Cyril Burt was invited to tell the C.O.S. whether social workers could improve their efforts by a study of psychology, his answer was decidedly ambiguous. 'Psychology is as yet in its infancy', he said. '. . . . It has not yet reached the mature stage of an applied science'; therefore, it could form for the social worker nothing more than 'an entertaining and even a suggestive hobby'. That it was 'obligatory and essential, or even in any direct way helpful and important to his work, no one could conceivably maintain'. On the other hand, he added, since the decisions of a case committee of a C.O.S. depended chiefly upon the circumstances and character of the applicant, psychology could help. 'With the circumstances of the case', he said, '. . . . psychology cannot directly be concerned. But where character or personality is in question, there psychology, were it in any way a complete or well-established discipline, should be the master science.'[1]

In spite of this lukewarm attitude, there were signs in the 1920's that more attention was being paid, even if a little grudgingly, to the new science. Cyril Burt himself, exploring the psychology of juvenile crime, taught his confrères that a crime is not 'a detached or separable fact', but a 'mental symptom with a mental origin'.[2] A mysterious correspondent called 'X' informed the *Charity Organisation Review* that he was convinced there was a psychological factor in public assistance.[3] A secretary to the Glasgow C.O.S. warned his audience that they must be psychologists first and economists second,[4] and in 1929, owing to the good offices of the Commonwealth Fund of America, the London Child Guidance Clinic and Training Centre was set up at Islington to train psychiatrists, psychologists and social workers and to conduct research on delinquent, dull, backward and disturbed children. At the same time the London School of Economics invented a Mental Health Course which, using the London Child Guidance Clinic as the

[1] 'Individual Psychology and Social Work', *C.O. Review* (N.S.), Vol. XLIII, No. 253 (January 1918), pp. 4–6.   [2] *The Young Delinquent* (1925 edn.), p. 4.
[3] 'Public Assistance: The Psychological Factor', *C.O. Review* (N.S.), Vol. XLIII, No. 253 (January 1918), pp. 19–29.
[4] 'We must set to work in the belief that the most significant things we shall discover will not be the economic facts but the indications of states of mind.' (L. V. Shairp, 'An American View of Casework', *C.O. Review* (N.S.), Vol. XLV, No. 265 (January, 1919), p. 10.)

centre for its practical work, became the first recognized training course for psychiatric social workers,[1] while a comparative
study of eighty case records, made in 1904 and 1934, showed a
significant change in content which indicated the influence of
the new developments. For whereas the earlier comments were
more concerned with material conditions or with certain kinds
of behaviour, such as 'cleanliness', 'honesty' or 'sobriety', the
later records dealt in far more detail with different aspects of
personality and the nature of family relationships.[2] These, however, were but straws in a wind which was to blow more freely
in the following decade. In the 1920's, although there were
some social workers who applauded the verdict that 'the provision of surgical appliances or artificial teeth . . . often leads to
the discovery and treatment of more serious needs',[3] and that
'serious needs' were often of a psychological nature, there
were many more who accepted at face value the emergency
which drove a person to seek help from an agency and did not
seek to probe for the 'something deeper' which might conceivably lie beneath the surface. This may have been the social
worker's line of least resistance. As a member of the C.O.S.
confessed, 'It is far easier to understand the benefit of a splint
to a crippled child or a stay at a sanitorium to a consumptive
than to grasp such elusive conceptions as personality and family
life';[4] but in most cases it was due to the fact that the British
social worker, although influenced by the arrival from America
by these psychological methods and ideas, did not accept them
and apply them with the same wholehearted enthusiasm as did
her sisters across the sea.

Why, then, this resistance to Freud? Perhaps the main
reason was that the English social soil, fertilized as it was by
the practice of Shaftesbury no less than the precepts of Owen,
was not as receptive to individualist seeds as that of the New
World. This had bred an approach to the problem of poverty
which differed from its American counterpart in several respects. In the United States, the munificence of Nature had lent

[1] For further detail, see Margaret Ashdown and S. Clement Brown, *Social
Service and Mental Health* (1953).

[2] S. Clement Brown, 'The Methods of Social Caseworkers', in F. C. Bartlett,
M. Ginsberg et al. (eds.), *The Study of Society* (1939 edn.), pp. 384–7.

[3] C.O.S., *Fifty-Sixth Annual Report*, April 27, 1925, p. 9.

[4] C.O.S., *Fifty-Seventh Annual Report*, May, 17 1926, p. 10.

substance to the legend that the road from log cabin to the White House was open to all, and consequently it was believed that poverty was the fault of the individual and that where it existed, it should be treated from the standpoint of individual circumstance. In England, on the other hand, nature had been less kind, and the problem of poverty had proved so obtrusive that public responsibility for the care of the poor had been early acknowledged. Usually this responsibility had been interpreted in niggardly terms, but by the beginning of the twentieth century the principle of 'less eligibility', incorporated into the Act of 1834, had been undermined on all sides. New forces in the electorate, unleashed in 1867 and 1884, had demanded reforms which could not be denied. The reforms, when achieved, indicated a new concept of government which ran counter to the idea that rule should be in the interest of the wealthy. Likewise investigations of poverty made by Charles Booth in London and Seebohm Rowntree in York suggested a new attitude to poverty and a more effective mode of handling it, while the coming of the Fabian Society, vociferous in its criticism of the existing order and insistent in its demand for change, emphasized the concept of a society whose structure could be manipulated by its members in the interests of all. Sooner or later the forces represented by this new concept of government, this new electorate, this new attitude to poverty and this concept of a malleable social order had to come to grips with the forces standing behind the principles of 1834. The conflict came at the beginning of the twentieth century and was staged with outward calm in sedate surroundings. The ring was a Royal Commission appointed in 1905 to enquire into and make recommendations about the working of the poor law and the relief of distress. It sat for four years and after a hundred and fifty-nine hearings in which four hundred and fifty-two witnesses answered more than a hundred thousand questions, it declared itself unable to agree and issued two reports to prove it. In one corner of the ring sat the Poor Law Division of the Local Government Board supported by the C.O.S.; in the other, the four recalcitrants led by that determined Socialist, Beatrice Webb.[1] The issue at

[1] For two different versions of the Poor Law Commission of 1905–9, see Una Cormack, *The Welfare State* (Loch Memorial Lecture, 1953, printed by the F.W.A.), and Beatrice Webb, *Our Partnership* (ed. Barbara Drake and Margaret I. Cole, 1948), Chapter VII.

stake was whether the Poor Law should be 'broken up' and its place taken by departments dealing with different aspects of the problem of destitution; and the result was the beginning in England of a debate on social welfare which was to last for forty years.

The differences between the Majority and the Minority Reports were not so profound as their makers believed, for while the more conservative were undoubtedly forced by the Minority along paths more radical than they were wont to tread, the Minority, in turn, were tamed by royal commissionership into reaching agreement where once there was none. In the early days of the Commission, the official attitude towards relief had been clearly revealed in the examination of James Stewart Davy, principal officer of the Poor Law Division. The destitute man, he admitted, had a right to relief, but it was not a complete right 'for the necessary sanctions are lacking'. Since he could not sue for his rights, it was the duty of the State to see that he got them. Davy admitted the moral liability to relieve, but he maintained a rigid attitude on the principle of deterrence. The lot of the pauper was still to be less eligible than that of the independent labourer, he said, and defined less eligibility as consisting of 'loss of personal reputation . . . the loss of personal freedom, which is secured by detention in a workhouse, and . . . the loss of political freedom by suffering disfranchisement'. 'In all large urban communities', Davy summed up, 'You must have test houses where you can have task work for the able-bodied loafer'. The work given should be both irksome and unskilled, for, as he added darkly, 'It is the compulsory labour, the discipline and the classification which are the real objects of the pauper's dislikes.'[1] This attitude, however, was to soften considerably during the course of the Commission, so that by 1909, the Majority could report that since the name Poor Law had gathered about it 'associations of harshness, and . . . hopelessness', it hoped to show the way to 'a system of help which will be better expressed by the title of public assistance than by that of Poor Law.'[2] Although this did not go as far

---

[1] *Report of the Royal Commission on the Poor Laws and the Relief of Distress.* Cmd. 4499, 1909. App. Vol. I: Minutes of Evidence: See answers to questions 2027, 2229, 2230, 2375, 2366, 2318, 2033, and 2036.

[2] *Ibid.*, Part IX, para. 3, p. 596.

as the Minority Report, which advocated the complete break-up of the Poor Law and the substitution of a State system of insurance, health service and labour exchanges,[1] the use of phrases, such as 'a system of help' and 'public assistance', did indicate a definite departure from the principles of 1834. Whereas the Royal Commission of that year had blamed the individual for his poverty, the Commission of 1909 drew attention to 'modifications and developments in our industrial system which cannot be ignored'.[2] Whereas in 1834 the government's policy was one of deterrence rather than prevention, in 1909 recommendations were made for a national system of employment exchanges, the extension of technical education, the tightening up of child labour laws, and even the institution of public works.[3] There was a significant change, too, in the attitude to the workhouse. Accepted without question in 1834, in 1909, it had been abandoned, by implication, as a 'test' of pauperism. Here was the essential difference between 1834 and 1909. Pauperism was to be treated, not tested, and the concept of 'less eligibility' was to give way to the concept of social provision against poverty. On this, both Reports were agreed, but whereas the Minority Report wished to replace the old Poor Law with specialized services to meet specialized needs, the Majority Report, under the influence of the C.O.S., put its faith in a combination of public assistance and private charity.

This, then, was the first concerted attack upon the Poor Law, and although forty years were to elapse before it was wiped off the Statute Books, a beginning had been made.

The attack, however, was not confined to the theorist. Men of action, too, came to join the fray. In 1906 when, after more than a decade on the back benches, the Liberals came to power, they began to pour into legal mould the philosophy of Lloyd George, then President of the Board of Trade, who saw occurring in England changes which he believed amounted to social revolution. 'I believe there is a new order coming from the people of

[1] *Separate Report by the Rev. P. H. R. Wakefield, Mr. Francis Chandler, Mr. George Lansbury and Mrs. Sidney Webb:* See 'Summary and Conclusions of Recommendations of Part I and Part II', pp. 1218–38.

[2] *Majority Report,* para. 304, p. 359.

[3] *Ibid.,* Part IX ('Review of Existing Conditions and Proposed Changes'), pp. 596–645; 'List of Principal Recommendations Contained in Report', pp. 647–70.

this country'. he said. 'It is a quiet but certain revolution, as revolutions come in a constitutional country, without over-throwing order, without doing an injustice to anybody, but redressing those injustices from which people suffer'.[1] Whether these changes constituted revolution is debatable, but certainly they came without overthrowing order; they did no obvious injustice to anybody, except perhaps to the working man,[2] and they did redress certain injustices from which people suffered. Between 1906 and 1912, school-children gained the social right of free meals and medical inspection without fear of their parents' losing the vote; an old age pension of five shillings a week was granted to the needy and deserving of seventy and over; while by the National Insurance Act of 1911, a man could claim a small health insurance benefit for himself and, if he were in certain industries, an even smaller insurance payment if he became unemployed. At the same time, a Coal Mines Regula-tion Act gave miners a nominal eight-hour day; labour exchanges were created to speed up the movement of labour; local authori-ties were given power to build houses and plan towns; and members of parliament were, for the first time, paid a salary.

These Acts charted a new course for government activity, and several were designed gradually to overthrow the Poor Law, but because at the time there were no alternative ideas to work with, nor were there new insights into the social phenomena of human need and human behaviour, many of the ideas and as-sumptions of the old Poor Law remained to be transferred, often unwittingly, to the new social services. If, for example, poverty was often the outward and visible sign of an inward and spiritual disgrace, then the poor needed to be punished or rewarded. The Old Age Pensions Act of 1908 sought to apply this principle by separating the worthy poor from the unworthy and with-holding pensions from those deemed lazy or improvident. Again, since it was assumed that each man was an island, need was con-ceived in terms of the individual rather than the family or the work group. Accordingly, in 1911, National Health Insurance

---

[1] Speech at Bangor, 19 January 1906, in *Slings and Arrows—Sayings chosen from Speeches of the Rt. Hon. David Lloyd George* (1929), p. 5.

[2] E.g. By the 'People's Budget of 1909', the working man probably contributed more through indirect taxes on beer and tobacco than the amount paid from revenue to benefit him in social services. See Bernard Mallet, *British Budgets* 1887–1888 *to 1912–1913* (1913), pp. 298–313.

provided cash benefits during a period of sickness which were the same for a single man as for a man with a family, and thirty-seven years had to elapse before the State grudgingly recognized the fact that sick workers usually had wives and children to support. Thus many of the social services which were born in this period embodied the moral assumptions of the nineteenth century, with the result that tensions were created then which still remain today.[1]

In spite of this, however, the years from 1906 to 1912 saw the foundation laid for the present Welfare State. Certainly work on the superstructure was interrupted by the First World War, but it was resumed immediately afterwards, and the country's lawmakers continued to break off further fragments of need from the Poor Law or from the unco-ordinated activities of voluntary organizations, and to build new services around them. In 1920, pensions were granted for the blind, while in the following year, unemployment insurance was extended to most manual workers, cash benefits for the unemployed were raised, and the period during which benefits were paid was extended. Thus, somewhat timidly, did England's government seek to deal with the poverty and unemployment which beset the country after the First World War. In the following decade, when the cold wind of depression forced the problems once more to the front, the need for more drastic measures was realized, but although an Unemployment Assistance Board was created in 1934, it was only in the 'forties that an attempt was made to set up a unified and comprehensive programme of social services to combat, in Lord Beveridge's phrase, the 'Five Giants' of Want, Disease, Ignorance, Squalor and Idleness which lay across the path of social progress.

This system of social security was Britain's way of handling the problem of poverty. By government policy and a network of welfare services, she hoped to provide employment for those who were unemployed, to insure her citizens against the major hazards of life, and eventually to give them 'a national minimum' of health, wealth and well-being. These were not favours to be dispensed by the bountiful, nor were they privileges to

---

[1] On this antithesis between social purpose and administrative policy, see Richard M. Titmuss, 'Social Administration in a Changing Society', in *Essays on 'The Welfare State'* (1958), pp. 13–33.

be won by the sycophant. They were social rights to be secured to the citizen, and since to accept assistance no longer meant loss of personal liberty or disfranchisement, social rights were not alternative to political and civil rights as they once had been. Instead, political, civil and social rights were now embodied in the law of the land, institutions were being fashioned through which they could be realized and guaranteed, and the rights of citizenship were established in their modern form.

Since the English social context differed so much from that of the United States, it is not surprising to find divergencies developing between the two countries in the theory and practice of their social work. The main difference stemmed from the fact that whereas the American social worker surrendered whole-heartedly to Freud, her English counterpart was much more reserved in her embrace. She did not reject psychiatric advances entirely. Even such a sober document as a report of the Unemployment Assistance Board showed traces of a flirtation with the new knowledge,[1] while the English caseworker often spoke words reminiscent of those used by her sisters in psycho-analysis. But despite a certain similarity in speech, there were differences in the basic assumptions made by the English and American social worker, especially the caseworker employed in the administration of public social services. England was building up a system of National Assistance which aimed, eventually, at complete coverage, a uniform standard, and a single efficient administration. In the United States, on the other hand, even as late as the 'fifties, public assistance was not only fragmentary in coverage and diverse in procedure and standards, but there was a tug-of-war between the pressures of public opinion for and those against a liberal system of assistance. Again, there was a fundamental difference between the two countries in the ultimate objectives of their programmes, and this affected the approach of the worker to the applicant for assistance. In Great Britain, the programme was primarily to maintain income; the officer was concerned mainly with determining whether or not the applicant was in need of assistance,

[1] E.g. Stating that the consequences of long unemployment for an applicant are not merely economic but psychological as well, the Report concluded that 'the problems of need in a household are not simple; often they cannot be fully met by a grant of money'. (*First Report of the Unemployment Assistance Board for period ended Dec. 31, 1935*, Cmd. 5177, pp. 16–17.)

and if so, how much; and it was assumed that people, individually or in groups, were capable of solving their own problems. 'The people receiving assistance from the Board are . . . in the main competent to manage their affairs and differ from other people only in point of income', proclaimed the National Assistance Board in 1949. '. . . The primary business of the Board is to ensure that people applying to them have a sufficient income, and have it in the majority of cases with as little trouble and inconvenience to themselves as is possible'.[1] In the United States, programmes of public assistance aimed not only to assess the person's need and eligibility, but also to reveal the causes which led him into need. It was assumed, further, that people have problems which are not solved by bread alone, and hence an attempt was made to establish a relationship which would help the client to use money payments as a means of rehabilitation rather than as an end in itself. Thus whereas in England the provision of relief was regarded as a service, in the United States, on the other hand, it was often seen merely as a tool in the process by which the individual was to be rehabilitated.

This difference in approach between the American and English caseworker reflects the response of social work to the social environment of the New World and that of the Old. Because during the 1920's the political and social climate of the United States was conducive to the growth of a rampant individualism, the ground was prepared for the acceptance of psychiatric and psychoanalytic theories which focused attention on the individual to the exclusion of the social matrix in which he lived. Moreover, since it was a decade during which the dollar seemed to glint with even more than usual brilliance, it was considered desirable to rationalize the fact that there were many who did not share the good things which belong to prosperity. In the low-vaulted past the individual was poor through personal inadequacy. Now in the Freudian present he could be poor because of his early childhood.[2] This not only justified the

---

[1] *National Assistance Board, Report for 1949*, pp. 16–18; quoted by Barbara Wootton, *op. cit.*, pp. 294–5.

[2] E.g. 'Even today there are some social workers who are unable or unwilling to see poverty except as a purely economic event, without acknowledging the possible existence of childhood dependency wishes which, if they do not actually cause, may certainly prolong dependency.' (Gordon Hamilton, *Theory and Practice of Social Case Work* (New York, 1940 edn.), p. 346.)

exclusion of the unsuccessful, but it distracted the social worker's attention from possible alternative explanations for poverty, such as low wages, lack of protective labour laws and an inequitable social system. In England, on the other hand, it was the low wages and labour laws which were the focus of attention, and since the beginning of the century, if not before, the scaffolding of the present Welfare State had been erected to safeguard England's citizens against the most acute forms of social distress. In this setting, so different from that of the United States, the task of the social worker was not so much to explore the psyche of the individual, as to 'individualize' social services and institutions in order to direct clients' attention to the forms of practical assistance relevant to their problems. Thus the English social worker was less susceptible to the new psychology than her American counterpart, and although in the 'thirties the influence of psychoanalysis was more strongly felt in England than in the preceding decade, the Welfare State, by then, was so firmly entrenched that it formed a bulwark against which the waves of individualism beat in vain.

PART THREE

From Lady Bountiful to Social Welfare

VII

◇◇

The State as Social Worker

◇◇

In October, 1928, Herbert Hoover, closing his campaign for the presidency of the United States, congratulated his countrymen on being born into a land from which poverty had been banished. 'Our American experiment in human welfare has yielded a degree of well-being unparalleled in all the world', he said. 'It has come nearer to the abolition of poverty, to the abolition of fear of want, than humanity has ever reached before.' This, he claimed, was due not only to the wealth of the country's resources and industry, but also to the blessing of having lived for a hundred and fifty years under 'our form of government and our social system'.[1] In 1931, however, before a Committee of the United States Senate, evidence was given that in Philadelphia a family of ten had just moved into a three-roomed apartment which was already occupied by a family of five. 'However shocking that may be to the members of this Committee it is almost an everyday occurrence in our midst', said the witness. 'Neighbors do take people in. They sleep on chairs. They sleep on the floor. There are conditions in Philadelphia that beggar description. There is scarcely a day that calls do not come to all our offices to find somehow a bed or a

---

[1] Speech of 22 October 1928, New York City, in H. S. Commager (ed.), *Documents of American History* (New York, 1958 edn.), II, 405.

chair. The demand for boxes on which people can sit or stretch themselves is hardly to be believed.'[1] Two years later, Grace Abbott, Chief of the United States Children's Bureau, reported to the Committee that a new army of transients was moving across the country, riding the freight trains, hitch-hiking, and travelling by car. It was impossible to secure the exact numbers, she said, but evidence was abundant that it was 'a very large problem'. The railroads were overwhelmed by it. Along the right of way of the Southern Pacific, small towns in Texas, New Mexico, and Arizona reported as many as two hundred a day coming into the towns, while the railroad men in Kansas City estimated that every day approximately 1,500 men and boys went through that city riding the freights.[2]

This is what the great depression meant to the United States in terms of human beings. What it meant in terms of declining national production, factory employment, manufacture and foreign trade can be shown through statistics. Totals and averages are always cold and often misleading. Nevertheless they indicate what was happening. In 1929 the national income was 81 billion dollars; in 1932 it had dropped to 40 billion. The national income paid out in the form of wages, salaries, dividends and interest dropped from 78½ billion dollars in 1929 to 49 in 1932. All sectors of the economy told the same story. The level of economic activity reached its peak about 1929, and thereafter till 1932 it fell at an unprecedented rate. The hopes of the post-war decade had received a shattering blow. No more could promises be made of a car in every garage and a chicken in every pot; no longer could a senator from Louisiana envisage every man as a king with a home, a motor-car, an electric refrigerator and a college education. Even the *Ladies' Home Journal* carefully forgot one of its articles entitled 'Everybody ought to be Rich', which invited its readers to retire with an income of four hundred dollars a month after twenty years of saving and investing in common stocks.

Various reasons were given for the depression into which

---

[1] *Unemployment Relief: Hearings before a Sub-Committee of the Committee on Manufactures, U.S. Senate, Dec. 28–30, 1931, Jan. 4–9, 1932* (Washington, 1932), p. 75.

[2] *Hearings before a Sub-Committee of the Committee on Manufactures U.S. Senate, Jan. 13–25, 1933* (Washington, 1933), pp. 23–35; printed in Grace Abbott, *From Relief to Social Security* (Chicago, 1941), pp. 49–68.

the country was plunged from 1930 to 1932. Some explained it as a lack of adjustment between costs and prices, others in terms of the disappearance of the frontier. Some saw it as an aftermath of war, others as the inevitable result of over-investment, under-consumption or excessive speculation. Only one thing seemed certain. The United States was producing more than it could consume, and this was caused, partly at least, by a maldistribution of wealth. Too large a proportion of the National Income was going into the pockets of a small percentage of the population, who promptly turned it back into savings or investment, and not enough of the income found its way to the worker, the farmer and the white-collar class upon whose continued purchasing power the whole business system seemed to rest. This conclusion was borne out by a study undertaken by the Brookings Institution which sought to analyse the relation of the distribution of national wealth and income to economic progress. According to this, twelve million families, or 42 per cent of the total, received the same proportion of the National Income (13 per cent) as 36,000 families or 0·1 per cent of the total. In other words, at the top of the scale one family in a thousand received as much as 420 at the bottom. Furthermore, the authors went on to claim that, at 1929 prices, a family income of 2,000 dollars 'may perhaps be regarded as sufficient to supply only basic necessities', and that in 1929, a boom year, 16 million families, or practically 60 per cent of the total number, were below this standard.[1] This marked inequality of wealth, combined with the fact that power was being concentrated into the hands of two hundred giant corporations—one of which, the Telephone and Telegraph Company, controlled more wealth than was contained within the borders of twenty-one of the States in the country[2]—seemed to indicate a national economy which was fundamentally unhealthy.

Government action to repair the breaches in prosperity was not forthcoming. President Hoover, while not entirely repudiating the obligation of the government to act, still held so firmly to the myth that prosperity was just around the corner, that

[1] M. Leven, H. G. Moulton and C. Warburton, *America's Capacity to Consume* (Washington, 1934), pp. 54, 55, 56.
[2] A. A. Berle and G. C. Means, *The Modern Corporation and Private Property* (New York, 1935 edn.), p. 19.

153

every proposal for the direct relief of the poor was rejected. Looking after the destitute was considered to be the exclusive concern of private charity and local governments. As late as December, 1930, therefore, he could approve congressional appropriation of 45 million dollars to feed the livestock of Arkansas farmers, and yet oppose an additional 25 million dollars to feed the farmers. Red Cross, he thought, could take care of them.[1]

In face of the magnitude of the problems created by the depression, the methods to handle them were quite inadequate. In many respects the American public relief system—with the exception of mothers' aid, workmen's compensation, and, in a few states, old age and blind pensions—was a copy of the system established in Elizabethan England and transplanted to America in the early seventeenth century. This English heritage made poverty a disgrace, branded the poor man as shiftless, and attached to relief an indelible stigma. This attitude of scorn and superiority had been embodied in the laws and institutions of the country designed to deal with the problem of poverty. The almshouse was still the chief means of caring for the poor; in fact, up to 1929, the laws of ten states did not mention outdoor relief as a possible alternative. In some states care of the poor was let out to the lowest bidder; destitute children were indentured or apprenticed to those who could support them; an applicant for relief was required to take the 'pauper's oath' by which he swore he was absolutely destitute; relatives who had 'sufficient ability' could be called upon to support poor persons, and if they refused, could be prosecuted; and as late as 1934 the constitutions of fourteen states deprived the recipients of relief of the right to vote and to hold office. Poor relief, for the most part, was locally financed, often administered as a part-time or extra duty, was confined to persons who had 'settlement' in the local unit, and was made disagreeable in the hope that the recipient would be driven into self-support. This doctrine of 'less eligibility', more than any other single factor, accounts for the low level of standards of relief in the three hundred years from the founding of the first colony to the passing of the Social Security Act in 1935.

[1] Harold L. Wilensky and Charles N. Lebeaux, *Industrial Society and Social Welfare* (New York, 1958), p. 42.

Because this system of poor relief was recognized as degrading, efforts were made to secure alternative provision for those regarded as destitute through no fault of their own. Victims of disasters, such as floods, crop failures and earthquakes, or veterans of war, who were regarded as employees of government engaged in work of a peculiarily hazardous or 'seasonal' kind, were given temporary assistance out of State treasuries, while in a few states the 'unsettled poor', who belonged to no town or place, were given pensions for a certain period. Early in the nineteenth century, too, state governments began to assume responsibility for the institutional care of certain categories of paupers whom the local governments found too costly to support. The almshouse had been a dumping ground for dependants of any age, of either sex and with every kind of disability. Within its walls there lived the insane, the sick, the deaf, the dumb, the crippled, the infirm, the young and the old, but so unsatisfactory were conditions and so inadequate the treatment, that certain categories of persons with special handicaps were drawn off from local communities and placed in state institutions. First the insane, then the defectives who were teachable, then the deaf and dumb were separated, while later special State provision was made for juvenile delinquents, for the feeble-minded and the crippled. Virginia established a state hospital for the insane in 1769; Kentucky founded the Lexington Asylum for the Insane in 1822, and another institution for the deaf and dumb in the same year; New York opened state institutions for delinquent boys in 1826, for the crippled in 1863 and for the blind in 1865, while in 1894, Ohio established the first State Institution for Epileptics. Dependent children, as distinct from other categories, were not classified as needing special state institutions until comparatively late. Although private institutions, both secular and religious, were early established to receive children from almshouses, it was not until the mid-nineteenth century that the states assumed responsibility for child care or contributed any considerable funds for that purpose.

At the beginning of the twentieth century, a further step was taken when several states began to enact legislation to grant assistance in their own homes to persons considered especially needy or 'deserving'. This state assistance took the form of aid to the blind, widowed mothers' pensions, and, during the 'twenties, old age pensions; but although they represented the most important participation of state governments in the direct care of groups of people outside of institutions, these laws were only permissive, state appropriations to supplement local funds were extremely niggardly, and, despite a crop of newly created State Boards of Charities, administration was usually left in local hands with little or no state supervision. Thus although these provisions softened the stigma attached to public relief and provided aid on less humiliating terms than previously, it was only in a few counties that they were put into effect in a manner or to an extent which met the problem of economic insufficiency.[1] Nor did the federal government assume responsibility for administering financial first-aid to people in need. Although Section 8 of the Constitution of the United States gave to Congress power to levy taxes, duties, imports and excises in order to provide for 'the common defence and general welfare of the United States', President Pierce's veto of Dorothea Dix's bill to secure federal help for the insane guided federal relief policy for more than three-quarters of a century and was not reversed until the Federal Emergency Relief Act became law in 1933. By that time the federal government had developed some welfare activities, such as the correction and confinement of federal offenders, the care of disabled soldiers and sailors, and above all, the Children's Bureau of the Department of Labor, which was established in 1912 to study all phases of child health and child welfare. Despite these beginnings, however, the federal government still denied any responsibility for the relief of persons in need. The principles embodied in the English Poor Law of 1601 and the interpretation which President Pierce had given in 1854 to the 'welfare clause' in the federal constitution were still effective in 1929. Poor relief, it was considered, should be local, private, deterrent and minimal.

[1] E.g. In 1934, the year before the Social Security Act was passed, of the 24 states which then had laws providing aid to the blind, only 11 spent any state funds; the total amount spent by counties in the 24 States was 3,480,000 dollars, only about 100,000 dollars more than the amount spent for the blind by the 11 state governments. Likewise of the 28 states with laws for old-age assistance in 1934, state funds were spent in 16; mothers' aid laws were limited in Alabama, not operative at all in New Mexico, Arkansas and Mississippi, and non-existent in Georgia and South Carolina. In the remaining 42 States, probably less than half the counties were actually administering benefits. (Josephine Brown, *Public Relief 1929–1939* (New York, 1940), p. 27.)

This was not surprising. The social philosophy underlying the principles of 1601 and 1854 had been reinforced by a fear of public poor relief as a source of political power and patronage no less than by a dislike of the harsh methods so often used to administer it. Canon Barnett's plea to abolish all outdoor relief fell on deaf ears in England, but in the United States it was put into practice. In 1879, Brooklyn and Philadelphia abruptly stopped all financial aid without, it was claimed, any ill effects,[1] and for many years there was more vociferous support for private charity than for public relief. Even within the growing profession of social work, there were few who regarded public relief with anything but distrust. Certainly a lone voice in 1891 could cry that all relief should be dispensed 'by public authorities only',[2] but the great preponderance of opinion was in favour of private charity, which was considered to be more personal, less damaging to self respect, more easily controlled, not so liable to political corruption, and less likely to be regarded as a right.[3] Even the attempts to improve the administration of such public poor relief as existed were hampered by the same scepticism and distrust. This was shown very clearly in the attitude of social workers to the growing child welfare movement. Child welfare had been the subject of the first White House Conference on Dependent Children summoned by President Theodore Roosevelt in 1909. This conference had accepted as a basis of public policy the principle that poverty alone should not be cause to separate mother and child, and, as a corollary to this, that if assistance had to be given, it was better to give it in the home than in an institution. This provoked a storm of dissent in the ranks of social workers, many of whom,

---

[1] E.g. 'The stoppage of public outdoor relief, wonderful as it seems, appears to have thrown absolutely no additional burden upon the only general relief-giving society in Brooklyn, the Society for Improving the Condition of the Poor. . . . Of Philadelphia, as of Brooklyn, it may be said that the public outdoor relief has been found to be unnecessary. . . . No reason occurs to the writer why a similar experience would not follow the abolition of outdoor relief in any city or town sufficiently large to enable private benevolence to organize and act in concert . . . and that outdoor relief, in the United States as elsewhere, tends inevitably and surely to increase pauperism.' (Seth Low, 'Outdoor Relief in the United States', *Proc. 8th N.C.C.C.* (Boston, 1881), pp. 149, 150, 153.)

[2] I. F. Wright, 'Arguments in Favour of Public Outdoor Relief', *Proc. 18th N.C.C.C.* (Indianapolis, 1891), pp. 28–30.

[3] See 'Arguments against Public Outdoor Relief', by Charles R. Henderson and others, *ibid.*, pp. 34–49.

although approving the principle, opposed public assistance to mothers as a class on the grounds that it would do more harm than good. It could undermine the family by lessening the relatives' sense of responsibility; public officials could not provide supervision as efficient as that of private children's and family agencies, and the administration of such public relief, it was considered, could well induce political chicanery. Mary E. Richmond, advocate-in-chief for the private agency and individualized casework, argued that 'family problems and child-helping problems' should be undertaken by the agency best able to secure good results, but that no responsibility should be given to a government body until it could guarantee an administration with standards of social casework equal to that provided by private charity organization societies. There was evidence, she said, that during the last decade many private social agencies engaged in family work had made great advances in child welfare, but she added darkly, 'We have no evidence from the public agencies charged with the same duty.' No plumb line had been dropped into their daily activities.[1]

This view, however, was not to go unchallenged. Amos Butler, secretary of the Indiana State Board of Charities, pointed out to his colleagues how much greater was the demand for official relief, 'though that is not what it is called', and that 'while we are all proud of what private relief has accomplished, it as yet does not seem able to do all that is required'.[2] The director of the Department of Social Welfare in Denver went further. She not only stated her belief in the responsibility of government to help persons in need, but described the progress which her public agency had made in applying techniques of social casework as practised under private auspices. 'I believe that the principle of poor relief by public authority is absolutely right', she said.

> . . . the poor and suffering are so, not only by their own fault or peculiar misfortune, but also by the fault of us all . . . It is only just that organised society as a whole should struggle with the responsibility and pay the cost . . . It would seem necessary, then,

---

[1] '"Pensions" and the Social Worker', in *The Survey*, 15 February 1913, reprinted in *The Long View*, p.348. See also *ibid.*, pp. 346–9, 350–64.

[2] 'Official Outdoor Relief and the State', *Proc. 42nd N.C.C.C.* (Maryland, 1915), p. 439.

to find some division of the field that is clear and convincing. In the past, this division has come upon the quality of the work done and the element of personal service which was given by the private and not ordinarily by the public administration. But if that difference is to be removed, as I think it must be, and soon will be, what useful divisions remain?[1]

This question pinpointed the change which was taking place in the attitude towards public and private relief. From now on, especially in cities and rural counties which boasted 'socialized' departments of public welfare, social workers no longer debated whether or not the needy had a right to public relief, but how much public relief there should be and where the line of demarcation should be drawn between the work of public and private agencies. Public relief, it was clear, had come to stay. Roscoe Pound, Dean of the Harvard Law School, saw the State as 'a great public service institution . . . bound from the nature of its undertaking to furnish a reasonable service to all alike',[2] while an enthusiastic Commissioner of Public Welfare in Raleigh, North Carolina, convinced 'that public welfare is a democratic concept', exhorted her fellow commissioners to see their jobs 'in all their bigness and beauty'.[3] Likewise somewhat anxious attempts were made to measure the increased demand for trained social workers,[4] and the astonishing, and to some, intimidating, fact was revealed that in the field of family social work, the government was so firmly ensconced that its efforts made those of private societies 'seem dwarfed by comparison'.[5]

It cannot be said that the controversy about the respective

---

[1] Gertrude Vaile, 'Principles and Methods of Outdoor Relief', *ibid.*, pp. 479, 483.

[2] 'Society and the Individual', *Proc. 46th N.C.S.W.* (Atlantic City, 1919), p. 106.

[3] Mrs. Clarence A. Johnson, 'The Work of a Commissioner of Public Welfare', *Proc. 49th N.C.S.W.* (Providence, Rhode Island, 1922), pp. 437, 442.

[4] Ralph G. Hurlin, 'Measuring the Demand for Social Workers', *Proc. 53rd N.C.S.W.* (Cleveland, 1926), pp. 587–95. He placed the number of positions calling for trained social workers at 25,000, more than half of which were in the larger cities, and deplored the fact that the 'social work force' was 'unstable' and salaries so unfavourable (*ibid.*, pp. 594–5).

[5] A. W. McMillen, 'Some Statistical Comparisons of Public and Private Family Social Work', *Proc. 56th N.C.S.W.* (San Francisco, 1929), pp. 514–22. McMillen's figures showed that in 1928, 71·6 per cent. of all relief in 21 cities came from public funds, and that in Detroit and Grand Rapids, the figures were as high as 98·2 per cent. and 91·8 per cent. respectively. New Orleans, on the other hand, had a figure of 0 per cent. (Chart II, *ibid.*, p. 517).

merits of private charity and public relief had been settled in favour of the latter, or even that there was a more willing acceptance of the fact that, necessity being the mother of intervention, circumstance had forced the state to invade fields hitherto occupied by private philanthropy. Homer Folks might plead that relief be made 'respectable'[1] and Harry L. Lurie see public relief as a collective responsibility for the inadequacies of a faulty economic system,[2] but there were many still fearful that a socialist lurked behind every relief roll,[3] or who believed that public relief when given was 'more stingy',[4] and that in any circumstances, private charity was much better than public relief could ever be.[5] Even as late as 1929 it was still generally believed that public relief was a favour granted to the mendicant poor, that an application for public aid was one of the greatest humiliations a person could endure, that relief (preferably in the form of commodities and always lower in amount than wages for real work) should be granted only to those who had legal claim of settlement, and that workers engaged in labour disputes should not be eligible for relief at all. In other words, the United States came into the depression with a public assistance programme still grounded in the law and social philosophy of the Elizabethan code of 1601. In this she was several generations behind the countries of Western Europe. England, though not fully prepared for the deluge of destitution which descended on the world in 1929, was yet in a better position to deal with it than was the United States. Workmen's compensation had been adopted in 1897, and non-contributory old age pensions and compulsory contributory sickness and unemployment insurance had been placed on the statute books several years before the war. By amendment of the National Insurance Act,

[1] 'Making Relief Respectable', *The Annals of the American Academy of Political and Social Science*, 176 (November 1934), pp. 151–61.
[2] 'The Drift to Public Relief', *Proc. 58th N.C.S.W.* (Minneapolis, 1931), p. 214.
[3] E.g. 'There is great danger of going too far in giving power to the state. Socialism can arise from the acts of those who would push centralization into the domain of individual rights, as much as from the blatant demagogues decried by all reasonable men.' (Rev. D. J. M. Mahon, 'Private Institutions and Public Supervision', *Proc. 29th N.C.C.C.* (Detroit, 1902), p. 139.)
[4] E.g. Frederic Almy, 'Adequate Relief', *Proc. 38th N.C.C.C.* (Boston, 1911), p. 291.
[5] E.g. 'The chief objection to this public outdoor aid is, in brief, to many of us, the sincere belief that organized charity is far better.' (Jeffrey R. Brackett, 'The Treatment of Needy Families in their Homes', *Proc. 30th N.C.C.C.* (Atlanta, 1903), p. 302.)

widows' and orphans' insurance and limited old age annuities were provided in 1925; grants-in-aid from the national exchequer covered part of the costs of poor relief, public health, housing and education; and during the depression years, the old boards of guardians were quietly discarded and the general local authorities made responsible for 'public assistance'. In 1934, too, the Unemployment Assistance Board was established and the central government took over the care of the unemployed. These measures constituted England's first wall of defence against the tide of depression, and although fissures were to appear and cracks to widen, the foundations of the Welfare State, which had been laid in the previous three decades, stood firm to receive additional building in the '40's.

In the United States, on the other hand, the tools of social reform had been laid aside in 1917. Consequently, the country in 1930 was so unprepared to feed the hungry, that in the large eastern cities, selling apples could be earnestly considered as a way of saving the destitute, and the employment committees, which President Hoover had organised on a local state and national basis to create jobs, could sit in the midst of swirling unemployment, dedicated to the idea of prevention but with no programme to carry it out. Expansion of private relief was attempted, too, and amounts far in excess of anything previously spent for home relief were raised by voluntary gifts, but these, although of temporary value, were usually too localized, often too desultory and always inadequate to meet the problem. Other means had to be found, and found they were.

Franklin D. Roosevelt, as governor of the state of New York, was the first chief executive to ask a state legislature for funds to help local governmental authorities to meet the needs of the unemployed. In doing so, he placed unemployment in the same category of non-culpable misfortune as old age, widowhood and industrial accidents. 'One of the duties of the State is that of caring for those of its citizens who find themselves the victims of . . . adverse circumstances', he said in a message to the state legislature on 28 August, 1931.

> . . . While it is true that we have hitherto principally considered those who through accident or old age were permanently incapacitated, the same responsibility of the State undoubtedly applies when widespread economic conditions render large numbers of men and

women incapable of supporting either themselves or their families because of circumstances beyond their control . . . To these unfortunate citizens aid must be extended by government—not as a matter of charity but as a matter of social duty.[1]

'Social duty' was interpreted in practical terms to mean the setting up of a Temporary Emergency Relief Administration to dispense state aid to local governments unable to provide adequately for their unemployed. Although this widening of the governmental unit responsible for the relief of distress did not alter drastically the nature of the relief personnel, their attitudes to poverty, and the services given, it did establish principles, policies and procedures which were later carried over into the federal programme when Governor Roosevelt became President of the United States. The purpose for which emergency relief funds could be spent, a definition of eligibility consistent with the law's intent, the principle that there must be no discrimination on the grounds of religion, race, creed or colour, the policy of work relief for the able-bodied, the inception of projects to meet the needs of professional and other 'white collar' unemployed, the beginning of educational projects and other special programmes—these were some of the issues debated on the smaller stage of the New York state before they were transferred to the wider one of Washington. Some of these issues were to have a direct bearing upon social work. An official report of the Temporary Emergency Relief Administration, issued in January 1932, stressed the need for trained social workers to administer relief. 'The Administration has come to appreciate how important training and experience are in the field of social work', it said.

> Those in distress are naturally sensitive and the approach by untrained or unsympathetic workers, or the promiscuous mingling with long lines of applicants . . . tends to aggravate that distress. The Administration desires . . . to express the hope that most, if not all of the communities with which it has been in contact . . . will wish in the future to include among their executives trained personnel to handle social problems.[2]

[1] Message to the legislature, 28 August 1931, in Samuel I. Rosenman (ed.), *The Public Papers and Addresses of Franklin D. Roosevelt* (New York, 1938–40), I, 458–9.

[2] *Social Service Personnel in Local Public Relief Administration: Research Bulletin, TERA Division of Research and Statistics (February, 1935)*, p. 30; quoted by Josephine Brown, *op. cit.*, pp. 93–94.

Here was official recognition of the contribution which the caseworker could make in the field of public assistance. It was recognition long overdue. So long as public welfare had concerned itself in the local community with pauper relief, and in the state government with institutional care and management, there was little occasion to use, let alone to recognize, the services of casework. For while private agencies selected their clients and public institutions had to take the rest, little attention was given to the individual needs of persons asking for public relief. It was assumed that they were poor through their own perversity, that they were beyond the redemption of private charity, and that public relief was merely the means of keeping them alive. But when, in the 'thirties, the public agency was created to administer a service on a scale far beyond the means of the private agency, then public assistance, too, became a means of restoring economic and spiritual self-dependence, and people asked how this could be done on a mass basis without impairing the quality of the service to the individuals who received it. As early as 1903, Jeffrey R. Brackett had asked why the work of officers of public aid should be limited to giving or refusing material help.[1] It remained for later social workers, faced with the problem of helping to administer the Social Security Act of 1935, to stress the importance of casework in public assistance and, even when dealing with larger numbers of clients than ever before, to cherish the principle of individualization on which good casework was based.

This, however, was in the future. Public assistance in 1932 was still on a state and local basis; the very name of New York's Relief Administration indicated official expectation that it was merely a temporary and emergency measure; and although, by the end of the year, twenty-four states had followed New York's example and set up relief agencies of their own, it was only when the electors of November, 1932, rejected Hoover, the Republicans and 'rugged individualism' in favour of Roosevelt, the Democrats and 'a new deal', that it was officially recognized that state attempts to handle depression, unemployment and economic apathy had proved inadequate. It was obvious that action was now necessary on a national scale, and that Washington itself must step in to put the 'new deal' into practice. 'The

[1] 'The Treatment of Needy Families in their Homes', *loc. cit.*, p. 302.

only thing we have to fear is fear itself', President Roosevelt had told his audience in his inaugural address. 'Our distress comes from no failure of substance. We are stricken by no plague of locusts. . . . Our greatest primary task is to put people to work. . . . I am prepared under my constitutional duty to recommend the measures that a stricken Nation in the midst of a stricken world may require.'[1]

Putting people to work was a gargantuan task. Unemployment had reached its peak; fifteen million people were out of work; in some states 40 per cent of the total population were receiving relief; thousands of families were losing their homes and their farms; and security—whether it meant assurance of a job, a home, shares of stock, deposits in banks, or a life insurance policy—seemed an illusion.

President Roosevelt's way of tackling the problem was to pass the Federal Emergency Relief Act of 12 May, 1933. This Act, coming as it did after three years of pressure upon Congress for federal aid, represented a radical change in federal relief policy. It meant that unemployment was recognized as a problem national in scope, and that concerted action had been taken to meet it by the only agency large enough, rich enough and powerful enough to deal with the situation. The administration of the new law was assigned to the Federal Emergency Relief Administration (FERA); Harry L. Hopkins, a trained social worker and an ex-director of the New York Temporary Relief Administration, was appointed Federal Administrator; and FERA began to administer grants to the states for unemployment relief, to supervise and control programmes of state relief, to collect relief statistics to provide information necessary to administer federal funds, and to rehabilitate the farmer. From the beginning, it was clear that FERA intended to use federal funds to help the unemployed who were victims of the depression through no fault of their own. 'I am not going to hide behind the cloak of the intent of Congress as to what federal funds can be used for', the Federal Administrator told a conference of social workers in 1933. 'It is my belief that the people who fought for this bill . . . were trying to get it for relief for the unemployed, and not for a number of other perfectly fine

[1] First Inaugural Address, 4 March 1933, in *Public Papers and Addresses*, II, 11, 13, 15.

and worthy social objectives.'[1] Although the terms of the act allowed a liberal interpretation of eligibility, and almost any type of need suffered by a person could be considered 'the hardship and suffering caused by unemployment', nevertheless an attempt was made to distinguish between 'employables' and 'unemployables'. Help for the employables meant work—public works, if no private employment was available, and work relief, until public works could be developed or private industry revived. The 'dole' or direct relief for the able-bodied unemployed was considered to be palliative, if not pernicious, and was to be discarded as quickly as possible. 'To dole out relief in this way is to administer a narcotic, a subtle destroyer of the human spirit', President Roosevelt was later to explain, 'It is inimical to the dictates of sound policy. It is in violation of the traditions of America. Work must be found for able-bodied but destitute workers.'[2]

When the federal government treated unemployment as a social problem, it changed radically the social setting within which social work operated. The army of unemployed had to be dealt with en masse. Social work, with its traditional interest in the incompetent, the indigent and the disabled, was dominated by a philosophy of casework which interpreted all problems and remedies in terms of individual needs and characteristics. Certainly there had been some who looked beyond the case history to the social order. Even in the 1920's, when interest was focused with Freudian intensity on the psyche of the individual, Karl de Schweinitz had seen social work as 'the interpreter of the longings of people for a more wholesome social order',[3] while a labour counsellor, conceiving social work as 'community moral building', warned its exponents not to become 'mere apologists for the present social order'.[4] But it was not until the depression had forced men to recast their notions about the relation of government to economic life that social workers began, once again, to see themselves as something

[1] Harry L. Hopkins, 'The Developing National Program of Relief', *Proc. 60th N.C.S.W.* (Detroit, 1933), p. 66.
[2] Message to Congress, 4 January 1935, in *Public Papers and Addresses*, IV, 19–20.
[3] See above, p. 135.
[4] Arthur J. Todd, 'The Responsibility of Social Workers as Interpreters of Industrial Problems', *Proc. 47th N.C.S.W.* (New Orleans, 1920), pp. 271, 273.

more than custodians of the individual and to ask themselves—as they did in Washington in 1934 at a conference on 'Governmental Objectives for Social Work'[1]—how to use the unprecedented opportunity which existed to convert emergency relief into a permanent public programme for the welfare of all people.

It was not only that the 'social service divisions', which FERA created to give interviews, establish eligibility and dispense aid, now began to bring social workers and the methods they used into practically every county and township in the country. It was not only that, strengthened by a new sense of power, born of society's recognition of their worth, more social workers began to agree with those who preached the necessity for having a planned economy as a national objective for social work.[2] In less dramatic ways, too, the changes were rung. For the federal government, in establishing the principle that provision of public benefits for persons in need was the responsibility of government and not of private citizens, however organized or however charitably disposed, had revolutionized the system of public relief. In doing this, the government had changed the social context in which social work operated. The result was that the philosophy, attitudes and methods of social work were influenced by these changes no less than they themselves influenced the administration of emergency relief and, later, public assistance and social insurance. The traditional attitudes and methods of social casework, as we have seen, had already undergone drastic changes following the First World War. Partly because a new clientele had emerged, composed of the families of itinerant servicemen, and partly as a result of the application of new concepts derived from psychology and

[1] This conference, attended by 200 representatives from 44 chapters of the American Association of Social Workers, is reported in detail in *The Compass*, Vol. XV, No. 6 (March 1934), and criticized in even more detail in *The Compass*, Vol. XV, No. 7 (April 1934), and Vol. XV, No. 9 (June 1934).

[2] E.g. At a conference called by the American Association of Social Workers on 22 April 1933, Mary van Kleeck gave an address entitled 'A Planned Economy as a National Objective for Social Work', in which she stated that: 'The issue is whether capitalism as we know it now, which after all is only a hundred and fifty years old, must claim our permanent allegiance or whether we are ready with entirely open minds to consider the fundamental questions of economic organisation which the present crisis of unemployment presents to us. We have to decide whether the attainment of our social objectives requires a different form of economic organisation at the base.' (*The Compass*, Vol. XIV, No. 8 (May 1933), p. 23.)

psychiatry, there had come, in the late 'twenties a new democratic approach to the people who sought the caseworker's aid.
The depression, and the subsequent frenzied attempts of public
and private agencies to administer relief to the constantly
increasing army of unemployed, gave ample opportunity to test
in practice the validity of the new principles. It was obviously
absurd to suggest that the average applicant for relief was a
self-made pauper. Likewise the social worker, who sat at an
application desk in an unemployment relief office, realized as
never before that the casework relationship was a reciprocal
one in which she had to 'accept' herself and her client equally.
Too many of the applicants were people like herself with much
the same or sometimes better cultural background, education,
and previous earning capacity. She knew that, but for the grace
of a relief programme which put a premium on her work, she
would be on the applicant's side of the desk. She knew, too, that
although many of the people who sought her aid must have
other problems in their lives, they came to the office for relief,
and not usually for help or advice in other spheres. The social
worker, unless requested to do so, did not consider it her duty,
nor had she the time, to try to uncover and to treat these other
problems which might exist, but on which the applicant was not
seeking advice.[1]

This democratic philosophy of social casework developed just
in time to serve as a rationalization for the administration of
unemployment relief by governmental agencies. It dovetailed
into the tenets of the federal government which in 1933 maintained that local, state and federal governments had a direct
responsibility for the welfare of its citizens. If, as President
Roosevelt had said, each man has a 'right to life' and this meant
that 'he has also the right to make a comfortable living',[2] then
each person in need had a right to share in the provision made

[1] E.g. 'If the unemployed request advice and assistance with these other problems, the relief administration may furnish social treatment as an additional public
welfare function, but only when there are workers available who are well equipped
to give it.' ('Social Work in the Administration of Unemployment Relief',
Federal Emergency Relief Administration, 5314, *April 30, 1935*, cited by Josephine
Brown, *op. cit.*, p. 229.) Later, however, there was some controversy as to whether
relief was an end in itself, or a tool in the rehabilitation process. See above, pp.
145–6.
[2] In an address delivered before the Commonwealth Club at San Francisco,
23 September 1932, in *Public Papers and Addresses*, I, 754.

by the government to meet the ravages of depression. Because he had this right, an applicant for public relief incurred no stigma, asked no favour, and was expected to express no gratitude. He, as well as his application, was treated with respect; his eligiblity was determined impersonally in the light of legal requirements, available funds, and the claims of others equally in need of assistance; it was specifically stated that there should be no discrimination because of race, religion, non-citizenship, political affiliation, or membership of any special or selected group; and relief, sufficient 'to prevent physical suffering and to maintain minimum living standards', was to be given in cash in order that the recipient might be free to spend it as he had spent his wages when he was employed.[1]

These changes in the philosophy of public relief did not gain universal acceptance, even among social workers administering the policy. Many of the latter, borrowed or released from private social agencies, had brought with them the philosophy, attitudes and methods of the agencies and schools where they had been trained. Therefore, the social service divisions of FERA, far from being specialized, uniform and esoteric, represented all kinds of philosophy and practice. Every stage of development was represented from the most primitive of poor relief customs to a well-integrated philosophy and technique of modern public welfare. In spite of these differences, however, the administration of public relief under the Federal Emergency Relief Administration marked a turning point in the philosophy and practice of social work as applied to relief. Not only was the responsibility of government established once and for all, but public relief was recognized as an indisputable right of people in need, and their worth and dignity as human beings was respected. Moreover, since the administration of public relief was a new form of social work often at variance with the assumptions and methods of the older family casework, it meant that ideas inherited from the past had to be re-examined and, if necessary, recast to fit the new conditions or else discarded as an atavism.

Relief alone, however, and especially relief on an emergency basis, was not enough to assuage the economic insecurity growing out of the Great Depression. Even when relief was placed

---

[1] *Rules and Regulations No. 3. FERA Monthly Report, May 22, through June, 30* 1933, quoted by Josephine Brown, *op. cit.*, pp. 231, 230, 244.

on a permanent basis, and the Public Works Administration, created under the National Industrial Recovery Act, set the 'employable unemployed' to work on projects safely outside the purview of private enterprise, it was obvious that something more than relief was needed. Some countries, such as Germany and Italy, faced with mass unemployment, had resorted to Fascist dictatorship, but this was not acceptable to Americans. For many of them still believed that the State should stand above the contests in the market place, and, if forced by circumstance to intervene, should do so in the way most likely to leave the strongest contestant in command and the market-place intact. Other countries, such as England, had embarked upon programmes of public assistance and social insurance as a shelter against economic and political storms, but although some of the American states had adopted old-age assistance laws and workmen's compensation, it took the force of the great depression for the United States government to consider more positive ways of aiding and abetting the economic recovery of the farmer, the industrialist, the businessman and the worker. From these attempts, there was to emerge a series of acts culminating in the Social Security Act of 1935 which was to lay the foundations of the American system of social security.

Some of these acts were purely negative in character. The Agricultural Adjustment Act, for example, was designed to solve the dilemma of the American farmer who, even though confronted with European markets closed to him through satiation or protection, still continued to produce as much as before. The Act provided a negative solution to this problem of 'farm surpluses', for, faced with the paradox of plenty in the midst of poverty, the Act abolished the plenty. Its solution to the problem of too much farm produce at too low prices was to cut down production and so raise prices, to pay the farmer to reduce acreage, and, in the cause of induced scarcity, to control both production and prices. This was the gist of the Act, and, judged in the short run and by its own norms, the policy paid off. The annual cash income of the farmer doubled between 1932 and 1937, and even when Nature lent aid to the A.A.A. policy of crop reduction and unleashed drought and dust to lay waste thousands of square miles and to set the inhabitants adrift upon a desperate migration such as Steinbeck portrays in *The Grapes of Wrath*, certain farmers at the top of the agricultural pyramid were better off than they were before the New Deal. That their tenants and farm labourers did not share in the newly-made prosperity must have seemed to them as immaterial as the fact that the programme of aid to the farmer had been carried out largely at the expense of the consumer.

Likewise, even though the National Industrial Recovery Act was more positive in its approach than its fellow act dealing with agriculture, it was still far from being a long-range programme to plan production according to the needs of the nation. Such a programme would have involved far-reaching changes in the economic system which President Roosevelt and his government did not for one moment contemplate. Moreover, because the Act aimed to appease the industrialist, who advocated government aid to business as a means of recovery, and the worker, who advocated government aid for labour, it tended to be a compromise which worked in some ways and not in others. There was no doubt that the Act with its codes of fair competition, its limitations on child labour, its efforts to assure the workers minimum wages, maximum hours and the right to collective bargaining, did enjoy a large measure of success, and, with the other acts of the New Deal, helped to inject a feeling of hope into both big business and labour; but performance still fell short of promise. In spite of the Public Works Administration, it could not make business thrive, even though it helped to put it back on its feet. It did not solve the problem of unemployment, even though it created employment for more people; and although it raised the wages of the lowest-paid, and, moreover, by legalizing the workers' right to organize and bargain collectively, helped to build up a labour organisation, it did not fulfil its promise of giving all the workers a living wage. In fact, looking at these measures to promote agricultural and industrial recovery, rather than at the more imaginative programmes of power production and housing, one might be tempted to agree with Professor Beard's verdict of the New Deal as 'a tempest in a teapot' which would subside when wheat sold again at a dollar a bushel and the U.S. Steel Corporation resumed payment of dividends.[1]

Seen against this background of classic conservatism, the Social Security Act of 14 August, 1935, was a landmark in the

[1] Charles A. and Mary R. Beard, *America in Mid Passage* (1939), p. 248.

history of the social services, for it proclaimed the federal government's assumption of responsibility, to at least a part of the population, for public assistance in the form of social insurance and other forms of service, both remedial and preventive. But it fell short of its title of 'Social Security', for it contained merely two proposals for social insurance, three proposals for general assistance, provisions for maternal and child welfare services, aid to the blind and to dependent and crippled children, and a plan to strengthen public health work. It was hesitantly framed and, in some parts, it proved unworkable. Although it made some provision for old age security and unemployment compensation, it left millions of needy people unprotected. But most serious of all, the Act, supposedly designed to meet the challenge of insecurity, fell short of its aim, for it omitted provision for the unemployed able-bodied worker and for the care of the chronically sick. As Frank Bruno pointed out, the Social Security Act could only be called a measure to furnish such means of security as did not arouse serious opposition.[1]

This Act inevitably proved disappointing to many social workers. The New Deal, in a sense, meant that for the first time in American history, a political party had made a policy of social welfare its concern on a grand scale. For some social workers, this meant that the responsibility for social policy was no longer theirs, and that now they could return to their work with the individual and family on problems of emotional adjustment and development. Other workers, however, interpreted the searing experience of the 'thirties as proof that economic forces were at the root of the problems with which social work dealt, and that the social worker could best make her contribution by allying herself with those groups in society working towards economic, political and social change. 'Social workers . . . should interest themselves in measures for social reform and economic protection . . . because they appear to be consistent with the objectives of a planned society', announced a conference committee in 1933,[2] while in the same year the National Conference of Social Work heard a speaker declare

[1] *Trends in Social Work, 1874–1956* (New York, 1957 edn.), p. 309.
[2] Statement by the Committee on Federal Action on Unemployment, at a conference on 'National Objectives for Social Work', called by the American Association of Social Workers on 22 April 1933, reported in *The Compass*, Vol. XIV, No. 8 (May 1933), p. 11.

that it was the duty of social work to cast aside its former role of 'ferry-boat between the shores of poverty and wealth' and to ally itself with an organised body of people 'which is striving definitely, consciously and militantly to bring about a new and radically different social order'.[1] The following year, William Hodson, Commissioner of Public Welfare in New York, warned the social worker that so long as she remained a beneficiary of the existing order, she would be expected to support the fundamental principles upon which that order was based.[2] Mary van Kleeck, Director of Industrial Studies at the Russell Sage Foundation, insisted that labour and social work now had 'common goals'.[3] Later, Katharine Lenroot, describing the great task of the twentieth century as the reconciliation of individual freedom and social security, announced that social work in general, in common with other professions, was now facing the need for thinking and planning in terms of 'profound and permanent changes in our economic and social structure'.[4]

For this group of militant social workers—as well as for the less implacable group, who now began to draw a distinction between what could be done on the job and what could be done by the social worker as a citizen and a member of a professional association—the New Deal in general, and the Social Security Act in particular, represented merely the first step in that process of change through which economic security was to be accomplished for all people.

Seen even in this limited light, the Social Security Act had serious short-comings. Edith Abbott pointed out to her colleagues in 1936 that there was no civil service method of selection of personnel to implement the Act, and, moreover, no provision for general relief, or, as she called it, 'the home assistance bureau'.[5] Another critic, sterner than she, deplored the fact that not only were there large numbers of people exempt

[1] Karl Borders, 'Social Workers and the New Social Order', *Proc. 60th N.C.S.W.* (Detroit, 1933), p. 594.

[2] 'The Social Worker in the New Deal', *Proc. 61st N.C.S.W.* (Kansas City, 1934), p. 12.

[3] 'The Common Goals of Labour and Social Work', *ibid.*, pp. 284–303.

[4] 'Social Work and the Social Order', *Proc. 62nd N.C.S.W.* (Montreal, 1935), pp. 26, 29; reprinted in Fern Lowry (ed.), *Readings in Social Casework, 1920–1938* (New York, 1939), pp. 54–63.

[5] 'Public Welfare and Politics', *Proc. 63rd N.C.S.W.* (Atlantic City, 1936), pp. 27–45.

from the operation of the Act, but that since old age security and unemployment compensation were to be financed by a tax on the employers, the cost could easily be passed on to the consumer in the form of a disguised sales tax. The result would be that 'the poor pay for the poor' and, in the case of old age benefits, the young would carry the cost of the aged.[1] Similarly, in 1937, Edith Abbott returned to the fray to plead that the 'means test' for old age pensions be abolished and to insist that contributory pension systems were 'un-American',[2] while in 1940, she laid her cards on the Fabian Socialist table and came out squarely for nationalizing the care of the unemployed. The cost, she said, should be borne by taxation and should provide for the maintenance, retraining and placement of workers.[3]

The main cause of dissatisfaction with the Social Security Act, however, was that, in the field of social insurance, it fell far short of the ideas which social workers had been nurturing in public address and private conclave. As far back as 1902, the National Conference on Charities and Correction had appointed a Commission, under the chairmanship of Charles R. Henderson of the University of Chicago, to consider 'plans of so-called insurance for wage-earners in case of accident, sickness, invalidism and old age'.[4] Although two members of the commission issued unfavourable reports on how social insurance worked in Europe and was likely to work in the United States,[5] and the chairman himself endorsed only half-heartedly the principle of social insurance,[6] interest in the scheme still persisted. In 1911,

[1] Solomon Lowenstein, 'What Price National Security?', *ibid.*, pp. 68, 69.

[2] 'Presidential Address: Public Assistance—Whither Bound?', *Proc. 64th N.C.S.W.* (Indianapolis, 1937), p. 19.

[3] 'Relief, the No Man's Land and how to reclaim it', *Proc. 76th N.C.S.W.* (Grand Rapids, 1940), pp. 187–98.

[4] *Proc. 29th N.C.C.C.* (Detroit, 1902), Minutes and Discussion, p. 377.

[5] E.g. 'We need at least ten years' more evidence.' (John Graham Brooks, 'Report on German Workingmen's Insurance', *Proc. 32nd N.C.C.C.* (Portland, 1905), p. 454.) Likewise Frederick L. Hoffman, in a report on the German system of government insurance, criticized the cost of the scheme which, he claimed, was 'a tremendous handicap to the extension of German trade to other countries and especially the United States', and concluded that 'the evidence is not conclusive to prove that as the result of the system of workingmen's insurance the mortality of workingmen and hygienic conditions of employment have materially improved', (*ibid.*, pp. 447, 448).

[6] 'Your committee has the conviction that the time is ripe for an enlargement of the scope and an improvement in the method of industrial insurance . . . and therefore urge the continuance by the Conference of study and discussion which

173

Louis D. Brandeis, later to be associate justice of the United States Supreme Court, voiced the first unqualified support for working men's insurance as 'the road to social efficiency'. 'Men are not free while financially dependent upon the will of others', he said. 'Financial dependence is consistent with freedom only where claim to support rests upon right and not upon favour.'[1] In 1917 the cause was again publicly espoused. Royal Meeker, the U.S. Commissioner of Labor Statistics, confessed that his sole interest in social insurance was 'to put the cookies on the lower shelf' and to provide adequate protection to all members of society who need protection.[2] A covey of supporters began devising a scheme of health insurance as a means to that end.[3] This enthusiasm for social insurance, however, bore no lasting fruit. Twenty-four years after Mr. Justice Brandeis's call for a system of social insurance to cover all the foreseeable contingencies which menace the wage earner, the Social Security Act covered only two categories of need, old age and unemployment, while even today, there is still no federal provision to protect the unemployed worker caught in the maelstrom of depression, nor, it would seem, any conviction that such protection should exist.

In spite of its shortcoming, however, the Social Security Act reversed the policy pursued for a century and a half by the federal government of leaving the care of the indigent to the states. And when Judge Cardozo, on behalf of the Federal Supreme Court, declared in 1937 that the tax imposed by the Act on employers was valid and that the federal government's right to establish old age insurance was constitutional,[4] he

may tend to promote and direct this movement which is so deeply interesting to all nations of the civilised world.' (Charles R. Henderson, 'Workingmen's Insurance and Old Age Pensions', *Proc. 23rd N.C.C.C.* (Philadelphia, 1906), p. 456.)

[1] 'Workingmen's Insurance—The Road to Social Efficiency', *Proc. 38th N.C.C.C.* (Boston, 1911), p. 157.

[2] 'Social Insurance in the U.S.', *Proc. 44th N.C.S.W.* (Pittsburgh, 1917), p. 530.

[3] John B. Andrews, 'Progress toward Health Insurance', *ibid.*, pp. 535–42; A. E. Forrest, 'Compulsory Social Health Insurance', *ibid.*, pp. 542–50; Eugene T. Lies, 'Sickness, Dependency and Health Insurance', *ibid.*, pp. 550–3; Ernst Freund, 'Constitutional and Legal Aspects of Health Insurance', *ibid.*, pp. 553–8; Joseph P. Chamberlain, 'The Constitutionality of Health Insurance and the Relation of the Social Worker thereto', *ibid.*, pp. 558–67.

[4] See 'Steward Machine and Co. v. Davis', printed in H. S. Commager (ed.), *op. cit.*, II, 514–19, and 'Helvering *et al. v.* Davis', *ibid.*, pp. 519–21.

closed the long controversy over whether or not the federal government could legally enter the field of the social services. 'When money is spent to promote the general welfare, the concept of welfare or the opposite is shaped by Congress, not the states,' he said. 'Only a power that is national can serve the interests of all.'[1]

From this moment when the Social Security Act was assured of its constitutionality, the United States had the opportunity to develop a national policy in public welfare. The opportunity was taken; public assistance, which already showed an enormous increase from 1929, increased again in the period from 1936 to 1948 by more than 260 per cent. The nation, for the first time in its history, had become public welfare-minded, and, from now on, relief became a major item in federal financing and federal planning. In practical terms this meant the spread of public welfare units into every locality of the United States. It meant, too, the establishment of a national pattern in the grant of public assistance which, based on the concepts of eligibility, confidentiality, unrestricted money payments, and the right of appeal, not only confirmed the applicant's legal right to public assistance, but protected his worth and dignity as a human being. And when, by the amendments of 1939, the merit system was incorporated into the Act, there was established, too, a competency in personnel which, at best, embraced not only a knowledge of the arts of social work, but also a broader knowledge of public affairs, the acquisition of skill in public relations, and an understanding of the basic principles of democracy.

These developments of the 1930's, whereby social work became an accepted function of government, meant that social workers have had to recast many of their ideas in order to meet and solve a host of new and challenging problems. For example, they have had to face the problem of how to forge links between the two fields of private and public welfare. This has proved difficult to do, for whereas the former field has remained local, is concerned primarily with the problems of individuals and families, and uses a casework which has remained individualized and therapeutic, the field of public welfare has become a state and federal domain in which the problem of maintaining the economic and social security of the American people has

[1] *Ibid.*, pp. 521, 520.

demanded a revision of the traditional methods of casework and a sharpening of the newer skills of social group work and community organisation. Again, social work has had to face the issue of whether or not it shall take an active part in politics, and, if so, in which fields and by what means. During the presidential campaign of 1928, William Hodson, director of the Welfare Council of New York City, was hotly criticized because he headed a national committee organized to canvass votes. He defended his action before the National Conference of 1929 by stating that since the social worker is accepted by the community as one skilled in adjusting human relationships, he or she would be looked to for leadership in the wider problems of governmental policy and administration.[1] In saying this, he raised a host of queries hinging upon the extent of responsibility implicit in the word, 'social'. How 'social' should social work be? How much of the social worker's attention should be devoted to the welfare of society and how much to the welfare of the individual? What form, if any, should leadership take? These are questions which are still being debated three decades later, and to which no final answer has yet been found.

Thus the economic deluge of the 1930's not only brought a new deal for social work, in the sense that for the first time it became a recognized and respected function of government, but it brought, too, a series of problems arising out of its new position which was to occupy the attention of social workers for the next two decades. In meeting the challenge of these new demands, social work, in subtle ways, changed its form. As early as 1929, Porter R. Lee had pointed out to his colleagues that social work had added to its original character as a cause, that of being 'a function of well organized community life'. Contrasting the 'shibboleth' and 'flaming spirit' of the cause with 'the program and the manual . . . fidelity, standards, and method' of the function, he had said, 'I am inclined to think that in the capacity of the social worker . . . to administer a routine functional responsibility in the spirit of the servant in a cause lies the explanation of the great service of social work'.[2] These

---

[1] 'The Social Worker and Politics', *Proc. 56th N.C.S.W.* (San Francisco, 1929), pp. 103–12.
[2] 'Social Work: Cause and Function', *ibid.*, p. 20; reprinted in Fern Lowry, *op. cit.*, pp. 22–37.

words were to be proved correct in the following decade. For especially after 1935, when social workers entered the established structure of government to carry on the activities entailed in the new programmes, social work was operating both as a cause and a function on a scale never before envisaged.

VIII

<hr>

The Simple Dues of
Fellowship

<hr>

W<small>HEN</small>, in 1831, Alexis de Tocqueville left his native Paris to spend eighteen months in the United States, his patrician, prejudiced, yet penetrating eye roved beyond the prison system which he had come to investigate to the whole panorama of American political and social life. 'I wished to show what a democratic people really was in our day', he wrote to a friend when, two years later, the first volume of his *Democracy in America* leapt into print. '. . . I wished to diminish the ardor of the republican party and . . . to abate the claims of the aristocrats'.[1] In this dual role of narrator and iconoclast, de Tocqueville explored political and economic institutions in America, seeking to discover the permanent factors affecting the working of democracy. While doing so, he drew attention to what he called 'the immense assemblage of associations'. 'Americans of all ages, all conditions and all dispositions constantly form associations', he wrote.

> They have not only commercial and manufacturing companies, in which all take part, but associations of a thousand other kinds, religious, moral, serious, futile, general or restricted, enormous or

[1] M. C. M. Simpson (ed.), *Memoirs, Letters and Remains of Alexis de Tocqueville* (1861), I, 397, quoted by Phillips Bradley in his Introduction to de Tocqueville's *Democracy in America* (New York, 1948), I, xx–xxi.

diminutive. The Americans make associations to give entertainments, to found seminaries, to build inns, to construct churches, to diffuse books, to send missionaries to the antipodes; in this manner they found hospitals, prisons and schools. If it is proposed to inculcate some truth or to foster some feelings by the encouragement of a great example, they form a society.[1]

This he found in contrast to the English community where—because it was aristocratic and 'in aristocratic societies men do not need to combine in order to act'—the principle of association was by no means so constantly or adroitly used. 'The English often perform great things singly', he explained, 'whereas the Americans form associations for the smallest undertakings'.[2] De Tocqueville noticed, too, that the Americans, individualist empiricists though they were, seemed much more addicted to the use of general ideas than did their forbears across the sea, and concluded that this, too, was the result of living in a more egalitarian society.[3]

These conclusions drawn more than a hundred years ago seem to be borne out in the field of social work. During the 1940's and '50's, the American social worker had been so busily developing the art of using groups to achieve her ends, that she has raised social group work and community organisation, if not to professional status, then at least to the position of respected members of social work's trinity. In England, on the other hand, 'community organisation' is a term used much less frequently, and although 'social group work' is well ensconced in the social worker's vocabulary, there is still some scepticism about its function and status. Sir Philip Morris, Vice-Chancellor of the Bristol University, has said he finds it difficult to believe that group work has so specialized a technique as to amount to

[1] Phillips Bradley (ed.), *Democracy in America*, II, 106.

[2] *Ibid.*, p. 107.

[3] 'The Americans are much more addicted to the use of general ideas than the English and entertain a much greater relish for them. . . . When the conditions of men are very unequal and the inequalities are permanent . . . each class assumes the aspect of a distinct race. . . . Those who live in this aristocratic state of society never, therefore, conceive very general ideas respecting themselves; and that is enough to imbue them with a habitual distrust of such ideas . . . . He, on the contrary who inhabits a democratic country sees around him on every hand men differing but little from one another. . . . All the truths that are applicable to himself appear to him equally and similarly applicable to each of . . . his fellow men. Having contracted the habit of generalizing his ideas . . . he transfers the same habit to all his pursuits.' (*Ibid.*, pp. 14–15.)

'a mystique', for 'is it not just using one of the ordinary facets of society deliberately for a given end?'[1] Another sceptic has questioned group work's existence as 'a legitimate form of professional activity'. 'Is it justifiable', he asks, 'to grant it that status of a branch of social work, or is it more accurate to regard it as an artificial response to particular situations?'[2]

Community organization and social group work, then, are two corners of the field of social work which have been tilled more sedulously in America than they have been in England. Perhaps the explanation for this is to be found in what de Tocqueville called the 'greater relish' which the more egalitarian Americans entertained for forming associations and for finding general principles underlying the myriad manifestation. If this is so, then historical circumstance, as well as native predilection, must explain why it is that the Americans have been so much more willing than the English consciously to use and to analyse what Elizabeth Barrett Browning once called 'the simple dues of fellowship and social comfort'.

It is not that the English have been reluctant to form groups. The nineteenth century, as we have already seen, abounded in societies, clubs, associations and settlements which, unknown to themselves, were to become the source of our modern group work and community organization. In the twentieth century, too, new groups were devised to meet the new needs of industrial city and countryside. Women's Institutes, for example, first established at Llanfair in 1915 as 'the centre of good' in the neighbourhood, fulfilled so well the needs of countrywomen for recreation, discussion and the acquisition of skills in rural and domestic matters, that they have persisted in spite of dramatic changes in village life wrought by improved transport, the growth of local industry, the disappearance of the traditional

---

[1] Quoted in the *Report of the Conference of the Association of Social Workers (of Great Britain) on 'The Social Worker and the Group Approach'*, May 28–29, 1954, p. 28.

[2] John Spencer, 'Historical Development (of Social Group Work)' in Peter Kuenstler (ed.), *Social Group Work in Great Britain* (1955), p. 47, Cf. the comment in the recent Younghusband Report: 'Of these (casework, group work and community organisation) only the first is at present systematically taught and practised in this country.' (*Report of the Working Party on Social Workers in the Local Authority Health and Welfare Services* (1959), para. 15.) And again, 'So far, casework . . . is the only method which has begun to reach a satisfactory stage of development in this country.' (*Ibid.*, para. 629.)

leadership of squire and parson, and the growth of social services.[1]

Again, there was a keen realization of the inherent possibilities of group work (although it was not so called) during the economic deluge of the 1930's, when government efforts to cushion the worst effects of unemployment were paralleled, and in fact, dwarfed by the efforts of voluntary bodies. Unemployed clubs, youth organisations, community service clubs, and occupational centres sprang up by the score, both in the smaller towns and in the large cities. Primarily these sought to help the workless man to use his leisure more profitably and to restore to him that sense of purpose denied him in the enforced isolation of unemployment. This was difficult to do. Many of the unemployed felt lost, bitter, hopeless and apathetic. Others had settled down to living on the dole. The young men who had never known steady work and a regular wage did not fret at the lack of them. In 'the England of the dole', as J. B. Priestley said, they were 'the dingy butterflies of the backstreets'[2] with no sense of waste and tragedy in themselves. How to keep these men physically and psychologically fit for work and, if necessary, to retrain them for new jobs, was the problem which faced the government and voluntary organisations. The Ministry of Labour tried to solve it by operating training and instructional centres for men and domestic training centres for women. Voluntary organisations went a step further. As early as 1926, bodies, such as the Workers' Educational Association in Lincoln, established clubs and workshops for their unemployed members, while a group of Quakers founded at Maes-Yr-Haf in the Rhondda Valley an educational settlement which was to become what has been described as a 'spiritual power house for the valleys'.[3] But it was not till 1933 that the social service movement for the unemployed got under way. In that year, the National Council of Social Service held a public meeting at the Albert Hall at which the Prince of Wales spoke before he set off on a well-advertised inspection of England's 'distressed areas'. Later in the year, the government made the first

[1] For further detail of the Women's Institutes, see Inez Jenkin, *The History of the Women's Institute Movement of England and Wales* (Oxford, 1953).

[2] *English Journey* (1937 edn.), pp. 407, 306.

[3] *Men Without Work. A Report made to the Pilgrim Trust* (Cambridge, 1938), p. 304. See particularly Part V for a description of the social service movement.

experimental grant of £20,000 for social work to help the unemployed, and appointed the National Council of Social Service
to direct and supervise the project. Before long, clubs for the
unemployed were springing up all over the country. These
clubs not only provided recreation and better social amenities
for their members, but taught useful occupations, such as
tailoring and hair-cutting, encouraged, via subsidized tools,
seeds, fertilizers, and chicks, the raising of crops and poultry,
and, in the case of Tyneside clubs, acquired fishing boats and
tackle in order to bring home useful catches from the North Sea.
It could be argued that this was merely tinkering with externals,
and that, because they mitigated the first and most superficial
effects of unemployment, these clubs concealed, for the time
being at least, the necessity for more dramatic social change.
This is true, but limited as they were, the clubs were in keeping
with the conservatism of the times. In the 1930's, despite evidence to the contrary, there was still a widespread tendency to
identify economic misfortune with personal inadequacy, and to
assume that the poorest classes were cesspools of anti-social
habits. The social surveyors of Merseyside, for example,
blandly included among their 'subnormal types' the 'chronically unemployed', along with 'poverty stricken widows' and
'deserted wives',[1] and claimed that the majority of social
maladies, 'not merely poverty and overcrowding', were 'conspicuously centred in certain classes'.[2] In an environment as
conservative as this, the winged seeds of social revolution must,
perforce, lie cold and low. This is the background against which
England's unemployed clubs must be seen. If they appear as
pale solutions to a gargantuan problem, it must still be recognized that within the limitations imposed by the circumstance
of their birth, they did provide for the unemployed an interest,
a status, and a function which saved many from the worst
psychological effects of their enforced idleness.

[1] D. Caradog Jones (ed.), *The Social Survey of Merseyside* (1934), III, 445.
[2] 'Now the majority of our social maladies—not merely poverty and overcrowding—are conspicuously centred in certain classes, the members of which
are handicapped in one way or another from the very beginning or quite early in
life. . . . Some . . . are chronic sufferers from ill-health or unemployment, or they
are constantly coming to the Public Assistance Authority or some charitable agency
for relief. Many are not born with these defects or disabilities, but in some way or
other acquire them.' (*Ibid.*, p. 344.)

Again, when after the First World War, local authorities, subsidized and supervised by the Ministry of Health, began to build council estates on the outskirts of large towns, community centres and associations were formed to meet the social needs of the new inhabitants. Working class families, rudely thrust into neighbourhoods unprepared for their coming, found their new environment isolated, hostile, monotonous and bleak. The story has been well told in the case of Watling, Dagenham and Becontree,[1] and, although unrecorded in estates which lacked a scribe, was repeated in all. The sense of loneliness, the hostility of neighbouring areas, the lack of social amenities, the uncertain boundaries of local jurisdiction, and the sheer need for unity in the face of common obstacles, led to the growth of associations prepared to fight for what they wanted. In some cases, after the immediate needs of the early settlers had been met, the associations disintegrated, but more often they developed into community associations representing a variety of local groups and with a local habitation and a staff of their own. Especially was this so after 1929, when the National Council of Social Service formed a New Estates Community Committee, financed by the Carnegie United Kingdom Trust, to develop social work on the new estates and to devise the necessary central administration. And since the same kind of social problems existed, although not so acutely, in privately-built estates, in large blocks of flats, in homes for the aged, and, indeed, almost everywhere in the large towns, community associations quickly multiplied. By 1939 there were more than two hundred of them, while during the following years, when the world let slip the dogs of war, the necessities of defence forced the development of neighbourhood activities still further. Faced with this mounting evidence of success, the government and public began to acknowledge the possibilities inherent in community

[1] See Ruth Durant, *Watling: A Social Survey* (1939), E. Sewell Harris and P. N. Molloy, *Watling Community Association: The First Twenty-One Years* (1949), T. Young, *Dagenham and Becontree: A Report made for the Pilgrim Trust* (1934). See also Sir Ernest Barker, *Preface to New Housing Estates and their Social Problems* (1938), Harvey Sheppard, *The Response to a Community Centre* (1948), Henry A. Mess and Harold King, 'Community Centres and Community Associations', in Gertrude Williams (ed.), *Voluntary Social Services since 1918* (1947), Ernest Barker et al, *Community Centres* (1938), and, as a delightful study of what happens to family life when people move to a housing estate, Michael Young and Peter Willmott, *Family and Kinship in East London* (1957).

organization. The end of the Second World War saw much enthusiasm for Community Centres, and despite a shortage of material and manpower the work of exploration and experiment went on.

In other ways, too, the war stimulated the formation of groups. Some were permanent, official, tightly knit and purposive; others casual, spontaneous, discursive and neighbourly. Some sprang up to lend aid in an emergency; others were created to ease the burden of living for working wives or evacuated mothers. Some were designed to tide victims of war over a period of distress; others sprang up quite spontaneously to provide a feeling of warmth and security for those who found comfort in the presence of their fellows. For when he is faced with death, man finds moral aloneness even more intolerable than he does in peace, and it is only by relating himself to his fellows and to ideas, values and social patterns that give him a sense of 'belonging', that he can escape from his feeling of isolation and powerlessness. Thus in addition to the organized, directed groups, such as the children evacuated from crowded cities, the bombed-out families billeted or re-settled in new homes, the boys and girls in England's hastily created hostels, and the mothers clustered around forms of social care newly created for their needs, there was, as well, the mutual aid—it might perhaps be called the 'unconscious' group work—of the air-raid shelter, the bombed-out neighbourhood, the recreation centre and the hospital ward.[1]

In view of this number and variety of groups which England had fashioned to serve the needs of her people, it is surprising that so little attempt has been made to develop a theory of group work. Certainly Canon Barnett's accounts of his work at Toynbee Hall can be read as a treatise on the subject (although the author, no doubt, would be astonished to hear it), while the diary which Edward Denison kept as a 'settler' in London's East End contains suggestions not only of adult education, which is closely related to group work, but casework, community organisation and social action as well.[2] But apart from

[1] For further detail of the welfare services created or extended during World War II, see Richard M. Titmuss, *Problems of Social Policy* (1950).

[2] E.g. the entry for 7 August 1867: 'My opinion of the great sphere of usefulness to which I should find myself admitted by coming to live here is completely

such personal narratives as these, the English social worker, until quite recently, has been extremely reticent in writing of herself and her work. This may be due to several factors. It may be because the number of social workers in England is still so small, despite the vastly increased demand for their services, that the task of writing books must be bequeathed to a more leisurely future. It may be, as one of its members suggests,[1] that only in the post-war years has the English social worker been dragooned into the role of university teacher who, in the process of training recruits, writes books for her own and her students' edification. Or, it may be, in the case of the two newer comers to the field, that social group workers and community organizers in England are not unequivocally social workers, as they are in the United States. Consequently, the written exploration of their work has been carried on within the precints of education, sociology, or whatever happens to be the professional interest of the writer, rather than as part and parcel of the theory and practice of social work. Whatever the cause for her reticence, the English exponent of group work and community organisation, even more than the caseworker, has been content to leave most of the talking to her more loquacious cousin. The result, of course, is that English social work has been dominated by American practice and writing; and although, obviously, American precept has had to be adapted to English practice, and an attempt made to fashion new forms indigenous to England, so closely has the English worker kept

justified. All is yet in embryo—but it will grow. Just now I only teach in night school, and do what in me lies in looking after the sick, keeping an eye upon nuisances and the like, seeing that the local authorities keep up to their work. I go tomorrow before the Board at the workhouse, to compel the removal to the infirmary of a man who ought to have been there already. I shall drive the sanitary inspector to put the Act against overcrowding in force, with regard to some houses in which there have been as many as eight and ten bodies occupying one room. It is not surprising that the street in which this occurs has for months been full of small pox, scarlet fever, and typhus. . . . These are the sort of evils which, where there are no resident gentry, grow to a height almost incredible, and on which the remedial influence of the mere presence of a gentleman known to be on the alert is inestimable.' (Sir Baldwyn Leighton (ed.), *Letters and Other Writings of the Late Edward Denison* (1872), p. 37.)

[1] Foreword in Cherry Morris (ed.), *Social Case Work in Great Britain* (1950), p. 7. See also the Foreword in Peter Kuenstler (ed.) *op. cit.*, where the editor stresses the need for classification and for teaching material, and 'perhaps strongest of all, the need to establish Social Group Work as a practice and discipline in its own right', (*ibid.*, p. 7).

her own counsel that the process of adaptation and creation has been carried on in monastic silence.[1]

The American group worker and community organizer, on the other hand, have been much less inhibited in putting pen to paper. Although controversy still flourishes as to what exactly constitutes group work and community organisation and where the line should be drawn between them, there have been valiant attempts in recent years to analyse the processes and methods of each. This is not to say that either is of recent origin. Man has always lived, worked and played in groups, and whenever he has sought to mobilize the community's resources to meet his needs, he has called upon his fellows to help him. Social group work and community organisation, then, were practised long before they were defined, and an appreciation of their achievements and an intuitive understanding of their techniques preceded the systematic study of their processes and methods. Early in the century, Jane Addams showed that she clearly understood the techniques of both. In praising 'The Society for Superseding the Work of Climbing Boys' for its efforts to substitute a sweeping machine for a boy and to pass a bill to protect him, she gave a fascinating glimpse of an early chapter in community organisation,[2] while in describing how Hull House used the gang spirit in a group of young drug addicts to help them overcome their addiction, she indicated her faith in

[1] There are, of course, exceptions to this. Especially since the end of the Second World War, there has been a growing interest in the early history of social work and in what Elizabeth Macadam called 'the new philanthropy', or the 'unique partnership' between statutory and voluntary organisations in England. (*The New Philanthropy* (1934,) p. 18). See, for example, A. F. Young and E. T. Ashton, *British Social Work in the Nineteenth Century* (1956); Elizabeth Macadam, *The Social Servant in the Making* (1945); Peter Kuenstler (ed.), *Community Organisation in Great Britain* (1960); Josephine Klein, *The Study of Groups* (1956); A. F. C. Bourdillon (ed.); *Voluntary Social Services* (1945); Gertrude Williams (ed.), *op. cit.*; Mary Morris, *Voluntary Organisations and Social Progress* (1955); Madeline Roof, *Voluntary Societies and Social Policy* (1957). In spite of this, however, the fact remains that very little has been written in England about the theory and practice of social casework, group work and community organisation.

[2] E.g. 'We have here an epitome of the most advanced philanthropy, stimulation of inventions which shall relieve the poor from degrading drudgery, co-operation with commercial enterprises, and finally protective legislation. But these obscure people whose hearts were wrung over the conditions of chimney sweeps did even better than that. They were pioneers in the establishment of the modern principle of inspection. . . . May we not credit to their initiative this most valuable instrument of the modern state?' ('Presidential Address: Charity and Social Justice', *Proc. 37th N.C.C.C.* (St. Louis, 1910), pp. 3–4.)

what later came to be known as group work.[1] But although in the atomized industrial society of the twentieth century, men were devising social techniques to replace controls supplied in an earlier age by custom, little was done to analyse the process. Several decades had to pass before the group worker began to study systematically the art of developing personality through group activity, and the community organizer to study the ways in which the community's resources could be marshalled to achieve goals considered socially desirable.

In fashioning a theory, social group work was less of a laggard than community organisation. By the 1920's, although there was little attempt to define terminology, Mary E. Richmond was rejoicing at modern caseworkers' tendency to view their clients from the angle of 'what might be termed "small group psychology"',[2] 'the group approach' was being advocated as a means of dealing with immigrants,[3] principles of leadership and strategy in community organization were being thrashed out,[4] and an analysis begun of the processes that go into creating 'common interests' which bind groups together.[5] In 1923, too, the School of Applied Social Sciences at the Western Reserve University cleared a space in its curriculum for what it called 'Group Service Work', and social group work, with the brisk intemperance of youth, set out on its struggle to capture professional status. In the following decade, its practitioners began to develop a theory of their own. Until then, they had been combing through the literature of progressive education and social psychology, seeking to discover the characteristics of groups, the criteria by which they should be classified, the

[1] 'It is doubtful whether these boys could even have been pulled through unless they had been allowed to keep together through hospital and convalescing period, unless we had been able to utilize the gang spirit and to turn its collective force towards overcoming the desire for the drug.' (*The Spirit of Youth and the City Streets* (New York, 1909), p. 66.)
[2] 'Some Next Steps in Social Treatment', *Proc. 47th N.C.S.W.* (New Orleans, 1920), p. 256; reprinted in *The Long View*, p. 487.
[3] Thomas L. Cotton, 'The Group Approach', *Proc. 52nd N.C.S.W.* (Denver, 1925), pp. 360–66.
[4] Paul Franklin, 'Observable Results of the Organisation of the Local Community', *ibid.*, pp. 366–9; Robbins Gilman, 'The Development of Local Initiative', *ibid.*, pp. 385–90; Jane E. Robbins, 'Bureaucratic and Political Influences in Neighbourhood Civic Problems', *ibid*, pp. 391–5.
[5] Alfred D. Sheffield, 'The Organization of Group Thinking', *Proc. 56th N.C.S.W.* (Memphis, 1928), pp. 424–8.

importance for human growth of free activity within groups, and the settings in which group work could best be used. In 1930, group work went a step further. In that year a book appeared which was to hold as significant a place in the evolution of group work as Mary Richmond's *Social Diagnosis* does in the history of casework. This was *Social Process in Organized Groups*, in which the author, Grace L. Coyle, presented for the first time a complete theory of group work. In her analysis of the behaviour of groups, Miss Coyle was unashamedly eclectic. In discussing the way groups form, she adopted from sociology the concept of 'grouping process' developed by Professor Charles H. Cooley. Clubs, according to her, 'determine their interests . . . by moving from one to another in succession as circumstances present opportunities which appeal to them. Women's rural organisations, for example, rooted primarily in the need for social contact, take on from time to time a series of interests ranging from retail marketing direct to the consumer to the promotion of local libraries'.[1] Again, in order to explain how the structure of the group evolved, she adopted John Dewey's definition of structure as 'the agreed-upon instrument' through which the group puts its purpose into action, and which changes as the group creates, uses and modifies it for its own purpose. The functions of leadership, too, she interpreted in terms of Dewey's philosophy of pragmatism, acknowledging the necessity for investing certain individuals with authority, while recognizing the fact that the ultimate source of this authority would determine the direction of its 'flow'. 'Psychological reactions of a most complex sort', she said, 'are constantly remaking both leader and group. . . Out of that interaction group morale and decision are born and group functions performed.'[2]

This was considered socially beneficial as well as individually desirable. Like de Tocqueville before her, Miss Coyle saw her country's array of associations as part and parcel of the working of democracy. Moreover, unlike de Tocqueville, she had seen what happened to groups, such as trade unions and

[1] *Social Process in Organized Groups* (Topside, N.H., 1930), quoted by Arthur P. Miles, *American Social Work Theory* (New York, 1954), p. 161, from which the material in this paragraph has been derived.

[2] Grace L. Coyle, *op. cit.*, pp. 79, 105, 126, quoted by Arthur P. Miles, *op. cit.*, pp. 162, 163.

political parties, when the fabric of democracy was re-cut with Fascist knife. To her and her colleagues, groups were a primary medium in education for democracy which could flourish only within the protective framework of a democratic society. 'One of our purposes is to contribute to the creation of a socially awakened and socially intelligent body of citizens,' she wrote. '. . . . Such a result can only be attained by an educational method that starts within the actual experience of the group and encourages the growth of a sense of social responsibility to the larger whole'.[1] It was in this role of an 'experience in collective living' that group work, by careful selection of programme and direct education on social questions, could make a contribution to cultural and social change. Only in this way, she believed, could the group worker become 'an adequate group worker', or, for that matter, 'an adequate citizen of a new age'.[2]

What Miss Coyle began, others continued, and the 'thirties and 'forties saw a further search for principles to guide leader and led through the intricacies of the group. In these attempts to explore the alchemy of her art, the American group worker had a rich storehouse of theory and practice on which to draw. Not only were there the traditional sources of group work, such as the Settlement and the Y.M.C.A., but there was also the vast assembly of clubs, groups, leagues, and societies which had been summoned into life by the vicissitudes and aspirations of the twentieth century. When, in 1948, a survey was made of group work during the preceding decade, the surveyors not only pursued their hare through fields as diverse as camping, education, Red Cross, child welfare, low-rent housing, management, public administration and fighter squadrons, but, in no

---

[1] Grace L. Coyle, 'Education for Social Action', in Joshua Lieberman (ed.), *New Trends in Group Work* (New York, 1939), pp. 1–2. See also Coyle, *Group Experience and Democratic Values* (New York, 1947); Eduard Lindeman, 'Group Work and Education for Democracy', *Proc. 66th N.C.S.W.* (Buffalo, N.Y., 1939), pp. 342–7; and Clara A. Kaiser, 'Social Group Work Practice and Social Responsibility', *Proc. 79th N.C.S.W.* (Chicago, 1952), pp. 161–7.

[2] 'Group Work and Social Change', *Proc. 62nd N.C.S.W.* (Montreal, 1935), pp. 393–405. It should be noticed that, since this was written, group work has tended to place more emphasis on problems of individual adjustment than on helping people to become involved in social change. The importance of the social goal, however, is still recognized. See, for example, Alan F. Klein, *Society—Democracy—and the Group* (New York, 1953), especially chapters I, II and X, and Bernard M. Shiffman, 'Effecting Change through Social Group Work', *Proc. 85th N.C.S. Welfare* (Chicago, 1958), pp. 190–202.

way spent by their efforts, they forecast that in the next ten years, group workers would take their techniques into 'many places in community planning and living that have never used them before'.[1] How to find, in this array of groups, principles and precepts common to all, was the task which faced the hardy few who undertook the search for a conceptual framework.

In addition to practice tried and proved, the group worker had a fund of relevant theory on which to draw. Group dynamics, as conceived by Kurt Lewin, first at the Massachusetts Institute of Technology and later at the University of Michigan, was busily studying the forces underlying the behaviour of groups.[2] Group therapy, under the guidance of S. R. Slavson, was proving that the techniques of group work could be successfully applied to children suffering from severe personality disorders. In achievements within the protective shell of the group, he taught, a child could discover some recompense for failure to secure the love and appreciation he needs in his own home.[3] By the 1940's, too, psychoanalytic concepts had invaded the group worker's domain,[4] while the anthropologist, stock-piling his knowledge of societies of men, had made it easier for the group worker to understand how and why people think, act and live their lives. 'Much of what the group worker knows of human personality and its development has come from the research of the psychologist', complained one advocate of 'the culture concept'. This was inadequate. Man the world over has 'certain needs and drives that he must fulfil and satisfy'. Since the way he meets these needs and fulfils these drives is determined

[1] Charles E. Hendry (ed.), *A Decade of Group Work* (New York, 1948), pp. 181–2.

[2] For a succinct account of the work of the Research Center for Group Dynamics at the University of Michigan and its relation to the practice of social work, see two monographs issued by the American Association of Group Workers in 1950, 'Current Developments in Group Dynamics' by Leon Festinger, and 'The Relation of the Research Center for Group Dynamics to the Practice of Social Work' by Grace L. Coyle.

[3] See S. R. Slavson, *An Introduction to Group Therapy* (New York, 1943), which records an experiment of the Jewish Board of Guardians of New York to develop, under the guidance of Slavson, a 'group therapy' for selected cases of problem children.

[4] E.g. See Gertrude Wilson and Gladys Ryland, *Social Group Work Practice* (New York, 1949), especially Chapter II, entitled 'Understanding the Dynamics of Group Life', which is riddled with Freudian concepts such as 'suppression', 'repression', 'sublimation', 'symbolization', 'displacement', 'projection', 'identification', etc. (*ibid.*, p. 46).

by the cultural training he has received from his society, the group worker must know and understand the cultural milieu within which the members of her group are born and reared.[1]

Thus did the social sciences underpin the practice of this new-comer to the fold. From this storehouse of theory and practice, the social group worker, if she so desired, could select concepts and principles to light up the intricacies of personal relationships within groups of people. By the end of the 'forties, although there was still no unanimity of definition as to what constituted social group work—and, indeed, there were some who con-sidered it no more than the extension of the techniques of case-work to the group—there was sufficient agreement among the ranks for the braver members to state what they considered to be the essential elements of their craft. Social group work, they agreed, was a 'helping' process, carried on with voluntary groups, and directed by a leader who consciously used the group as a means to promote individual growth and social development.[2] In this way, it was hoped, not only would the citizen's voice be made more compelling, but participation within the group would bestow upon men that sense of 'be-longing', so essential to happiness, which had been lost in the chilly atomization of modern industrial society.

By the 1940's, too, social workers were beginning to look more intently at the process, structure, principles and tech-niques of community organisation. This, like social group work, was practised long before it was defined. Its main roots, as we have seen, are to be found within the Charity Organisation Society in England, where a divergence between those who were convinced that social ills were caused by individual wrong-doing, and those, equally convinced, that the social system was

[1] Alan F. Klein, *op. cit.*, pp. 76–78.

[2] E.g. Harleigh B. Trecker, in his *Social Group Work. Principles and Practice* (New York, 1948), described social group work as 'a process and method through which individuals in groups in social agency settings are helped by a worker to relate themselves to other people and to experience growth opportunities in accordance with their needs and capacities. In social group work, the group itself is utilized by the individual with the help of the worker, as a primary means of personality growth, change and development. The worker is interested in helping to bring about individual growth and social development for the group as a whole as a result of guided group interaction.' (*Ibid.*, pp. 8–9.) Later definitions of social group work theory echo and extend Trecker's refrain. See, for example, Gertrude Wilson, 'Social Group Work Theory and Practice', *Proc. 83rd N.C.S.W.* (St. Louis, Mo., 1956), pp. 143–59.

191

at fault, led to a dual approach to the problems which social work tried to solve. On the one hand C.O.S. visitors continued to give individualized service to those who sought their aid, granting help to tide them over difficulties, and working on their strengths to make them self-supporting members of society. At the same time, they began to advocate changes within the existing framework of society, which would produce less devastating effects upon the individual. For it was becoming increasingly obvious that if the social worker was to help her clients to live happier and more effective lives, she must not only take cognizance of the forces at work in society, but also mobilize the community's resources to meet human needs. This was the conviction which prompted the C.O.S. in London to support Octavia Hill's campaign for better housing, to undertake work for the blind, the sick and the mentally defective, and to establish new community services such as a tuberculosis dispensary and a hospital social service. This was the conviction, too, which later prompted the New York C.O.S. to found a national journal, to establish the first school of social work in the United States, and to help to conceive, plan and carry through the Pittsburgh Survey of 1907 which was to become the inspiration and the model for all later surveys.

From the soil of the charity organisation movement, too, there grew the social service exchange and the council of social agencies, which, with the community chest and the public welfare agency, today constitute in the United States the most significant instruments for community organisation. The first exchange was founded in Boston in 1876 by Joseph Tuckerman, 'minister at large' for the American Unitarian Society, who conceived the idea of a bureau of registration for common use by overseers of the poor and the benevolent societies, so 'that there shall be a discrimination in the distribution of alms by our charitable societies'.[1] Later, as a further attempt to avoid confusion and duplication of service, Milwaukee and Pittsburgh established councils of social agencies. That was in 1909, but by the time the First World War had been fought and won, not only had councils developed in various cities, but community chests for affiliated members had also come into existence in

---

[1] Joseph Tuckerman, *On the Elevation of the Poor. A Selection from His Reports as Minister at Large in Boston* (Boston, 1874), p. 90.

order to raise funds and to co-ordinate the health, welfare and recreational resources of the community.

Federated fund-raising, like so many other developments in social welfare, was first tried in England. In Liverpool, in 1873, a group of interested people developed a plan whereby charitable contributions could be made annually to one office. Subscribers could designate the various agencies to which they wished their money sent, and, in addition, the central committee was given an 'undesignated discriminatory fund'. Fourteen years later, the idea was transferred to the United States. Two Protestant ministers, a Jewish rabbi and a Catholic priest organized a federated drive through an agency known as the Associated Charities in Denver, while in 1896, a federation of Jewish agencies made a joint appeal to Cincinnati. Jewish agencies in Chicago followed suit, and in 1904, similar organisations were established in Philadelphia, Detroit and Cleveland. These were the first successful federated fund-raising agencies in America. Coming as they did in response to a demand for more business-like methods in the raising of money and its distribution to welfare agencies, the community chests settled down side by side with the councils of social agencies, which had been formed for much the same purpose, and together, chest and council set out to teach what Shakespeare called 'the act of order' to the charitably disposed of America's citizens.[1]

With the entry of the United States into the First World War in 1917, 'war chests' sprang up overnight, for thousands of people, who had never known what it was to give to a charitable agency, gave generously to drives on behalf of war charities at home and abroad. After the war was over, and particularly during the 1920's, war chests were converted into community chests, and as a council was often set up, too, or an existing council brought into close relationship with the chest, chest and council began to be regarded as inseparable allies in the campaign for joint financing, community planning, and co-ordination.

This impetus bore the community chests, and in most instances, the councils of social agencies with them, through the

[1] For further detail of the early history of the chest movement, see William J. Norton, *The Co-operative Movement in Social Work* (New York, 1927) and *Yesterday and Today with Community Chests* (New York: Community Chests and Councils, 1937).

depression of the 1930's. Although it soon became obvious that the needs of the depression would have to be met primarily from governmental funds, rather than from voluntary subscriptions, the chests continued to grow in number. By 1945, there were more than seven hundred of them in the United States, so generously supported by the public that, overshooting their target for the year, they could raise among them no less than 221,272,950 dollars.[1] For, despite criticisms made of the chest on the grounds that it would strip private agencies of their autonomy and would place the fate of social work in the horny hands of financial interests too much concerned with costs, the advantages have so far outweighed the disadvantages that the chest has remained the most important device for financing private social work. Moreover, since it combines the urge to organize with the managerial talent of the business man and the professional skill of the social worker, the community chest has been hailed—admittedly by the Americans themselves—as one of the unique and significant developments in American social work.[2]

Even more important than these voluntary bodies, such as the council and the chest, were the public welfare agencies which sprang up in the 'thirties in response to the demand that the federal government pilot the country through the high seas of depression. Vast new responsibilities were assumed by the government for developing programmes of social welfare, for setting standards, for marshalling support, and for all that these objectives implied in the way of collecting facts, educating the public, and co-ordinating the efforts of governmental and private agencies. Often there was formidable opposition to the

[1] Owen R. Davison, 'Community Chests', in *Social Work Year Book, 1954* (New York, 1954), Table 1, p. 116. Frank Bruno has suggested that these outbursts of generous gifts, through the war chests and through the American National Red Cross, are to be explained partly by the dramatic appeal of the incalculable sufferings of war, and partly by the Hollis Amendment to the Income Tax Law, which permitted the deduction for taxing purposes of 15 per cent. of one's otherwise taxable income. With surtaxes rising to 60 per cent. of income in the highest brackets during the First World War, and 90 per cent. during the Second, gifts might represent very little actual money to the giver. (*Trends in Social Work, 1874–1956* (New York, 1957 edn.), pp. 202–3.)

[2] E.g. by Arthur P. Miles, *op. cit.*, p. 193. There have been attempts, too, to 'sell' the idea of the community chest to Great Britain. See, for example, J. P. Brander, *The Community Chest and Chest Council System* (1941). So far, however, these attempts have not met with any great success.

federal government's usurping powers which had once belonged to the state or local authority. Often, too, there were no precedents to follow, and too little thought was given to asking who made the decisions about people in need, how, when, and where such decisions were reached, and why they were important to others than the applicants themselves.[1] But in spite of obstacles to be overcome, the federal government moved steadily into a position of leadership from which it could direct the mobilization of the community's resources to meet human needs. In spite of mistakes and omissions, the Social Security Act of 1935, as Arthur Dunham has pointed out, contained features which were significant from the standpoint of community organisation. It created a new federal agency, later called the Social Security Administration, which was entrusted with the task of devising programmes and standards. It established the 'state plan' as the basic administrative device by which a state would secure approval of its programme and the granting of federal aid. It laid down the principle of state leadership in planning and in carrying out programmes of public welfare. It incorporated certain concepts such as confidentiality, the explicit statement of requirements for eligibility, payment in money, and the right to a fair hearing; and it extended child welfare services to children in rural areas, emphasized the preventive as well as the rehabilitative aspects of casework, and envisaged 'developing state services for the encouragement and assistance of adequate methods of community child welfare organisation'.[2] The acorn planted by the Social Security Act was to grow in the following years into a cabinet department. Four years after the passage of the Act, the Social Security Board was transferred to the newly created Federal Security Agency; in 1946, the Agency was strengthened and partially reorganized, and in 1953, it was succeeded by a Department of Health, Education and Welfare. Thus a hundred

---

[1] This is a state of affairs which still exists. See Alan Keith-Lucas, *Decisions about People in Need. A Study of Administrative Responsiveness in Public Assistance* (Chapel Hill, 1957), in which the author bemoans the fact that so little attention has been paid, either by political theorists or those concerned with the implications for society of public administration, to the question of the basis of decisions made by public welfare agencies.

[2] Arthur Dunham, *Community Welfare Organization: Principles and Practice* (New York, 1958), p. 79.

years after President Pierce rejected Dorothea Dix's plea to make provision for the insane, the federal government in the United States established a cabinet department which was to be responsible for the health, education and social welfare of a large number of the country's citizens.

Since then, sometimes swiftly, sometimes haltingly, the work has gone on of building up a vast, sprawling, and complex network of services, in order to protect the American people against the four major human problems of dependency, ill-health, an unsatisfied need for recreation, and that composite of behavioural disorders which has come to be described as 'maladjustment'.[1] As a protection against dependency, community organisation aims to improve, simplify and consolidate services, such as public assistance and social insurance, and to provide help in cases of economic insufficiency. As a protection against ill-health, it seeks to extend public and private health services provided by hospitals, clinics, dispensaries and visiting nurses. To meet the recreational needs of an industrial, urban population, which has exchanged wandering through the woods for a seat in the local cinema, community organisation aims to provide public playgrounds, parks and auditoria, to organize sports, arts, and informal education, and to cultivate Boy Scouts, Girl Guides, and other youth groups; while to protect potential victims against emotional and mental disturbances, child neglect, juvenile delinquency and other outward and visible signs of 'maladjustment', community organisation aims to extend facilities for probation, correctional and parole services, diagnostic and treatment clinic, institutions for mentally disturbed patients, and casework services for families, children and adults.[2]

These four problems are not divisible. Some families have more than one kind of problem, and the solution often involves a number of skills and a variety of programmes. The result is that quite often a disproportionate amount of time and money is spent on a relatively small proportion of 'multiple-problem families' in the community. Bradley Buell found that in St. Paul, Minnesota, a group of 6,600 families, constituting about

[1] This classification is suggested by Bradley Buell and Associates, *Community Planning for Human Services* (New York, 1952), pp. 11–12.

[2] For more detail, see Bradley Buell, *op. cit.*, especially pp. 61–67, 125–35, 237–46, 356–61, 379–86.

6 per cent of the city's total, were absorbing more than half the services of the community's agencies dealing with dependency, health, and adjustment.[1] This underlines the need for a closer co-operation between the agencies which the community creates to provide the necessary services. In this way, the gaps in service may be closed, treatment by a coterie of specialists co-ordinated, duplication eliminated, and the client escape that segregation and stigmatization which too often accompany specialization. It underlines, too, the necessity to overhaul our ideas of how much the community can afford to give to social welfare. Giving is related to getting, and although it is now recognized that the low standard of relief in early colonial days in America was caused primarily by a deficiency in resources, rather than a lack of humanity in administrators,[2] there is still a deep-seated reluctance, in this more affluent society, to recast ideas and attitudes forged in a world in which poverty was man's normal lot and any other state was unimaginable. Wealth, as Galbraith has so trenchantly reminded us, is a relentless enemy of understanding, and an affluent society which conducts its affairs in accordance with rules formulated in a past and poorer age not only forgoes many opportunities which it could well use, but, in misunderstanding itself, it will, in time of difficulty, prescribe for itself the wrong remedy.[3]

Some of the same timidity of spirit has seeped into the analyses which community organizers have made of their craft. In the first place, even though community organisation has long been practised, there has been a reluctance to develop a theory to fit the facts. As early as 1901, Mary E. Richmond was teaching her 'charity workers' the way in which 'neighbourhood', 'civic' and 'public relief' forces could be used to help families in distress.[4] Later there were attempts to explore the possibilities of 'neighbourhood improvement',[5] and to explain how the

---

[1] *Ibid.*, p. 9. See also *ibid.*, pp. 412–13.

[2] See on this, Robert W. Kelso, *The History of Public Poor Relief in Massachusetts, 1620–1920* (New York, 1922) and Margaret Creech, *Three Centuries of Poor Law Administration* (Chicago, 1936).

[3] See the brilliant exposition of this theme in John Kenneth Galbraith, *The Affluent Society* (1958).

[4] 'Charitable Co-operation', *Proc. 28th N.C.C.C.* (Washington, 1901), pp. 298–313; reprinted in *The Long View*, pp. 186–202.

[5] Jane Addams, 'Neighborhood Improvement', *Proc. 31st N.C.C.C.* (Portland, Maine, 1904), pp. 456–8.

community should be organized for mental hygiene[1] and why war chests were such an unqualified financial success.[2] But it was not till 1939 when a study group, appointed by the National Conference of Social Work, presented a report on the concept of community organisation,[3] that a systematic attempt was made to explore the nature and characteristics of this newest comer to the field of social work. The following year a second group, encouraged apparently by the 'considerable agreement' of the first, met to explore the concept further and to decide, rather sadly, that in 1940 the study of community organization stood approximately where the study of casework stood in 1923 and that of group work in 1935.[4] There were at least four different concepts of community organisation, the group found, each expressing a partial truth about the process. Sometimes community organisation had been seen as 'group development', the essence of which was to assist a group of people to recognize their common needs and to help them meet those needs. At other times it had been seen as an educational process aiming to form satisfactory inter-group relationships, which could be used to move closer to such social goals as adequate child care for the community, proper sanitation, housing or recreation. A third concept identified community organization with integration of groups within the community in the interests of efficiency and unity of action; while a fourth described community organisation as the art of adjusting resources of social welfare to meet changing human needs. These four concepts of community organisation—group development, intergroup relationships, integration of groups, and adjustment of resources —were neither identical nor incompatible. Each was part of the whole, for each person undertaking the task of definition had done so in the light of prior interest or experience, tending to emphasize that aspect of the whole which he deemed most important. Beyond this, the group decided, it was unnecessary

[1] E. E. Southard, 'Zones of Community Effort in Mental Hygiene', *Proc. 44th N.C.S.W.* (Pittsburgh, 1917), pp. 405–13.

[2] Sherman C. Kingsley, 'Conserving War-time Spirit and Organization for Peace-time Needs', *Proc. 46th N.C.S.W.* (Atlantic City, 1919), pp. 697–702.

[3] Robert P. Lane, 'The Field of Community Organization', *Proc. 66th N.C.S.W.* (Buffalo, N.Y., 1939), pp. 495–511.

[4] Robert P. Lane, 'Report of Groups Studying the Community Organization Process', *Proc. 67th N.C.S.W.* (Grand Rapids, Michigan, 1940), p. 459.

to go, for it was better at the present stage to recognize the fact that these four concepts existed, rather than to try to find 'an artificial formulation of agreement for honest differences of opinion'. Similarly, although the group was at one on the type of training necessary and on the value of keeping records, it could not agree on the question of whether community organisation was a process, a field, or both, what its relation was to other processes of social work, and whether there were general principles underlying its theory and practice.[1]

Before these questions could be settled, however, America had entered the Second World War, and community organisation, impatiently laying aside its theories, prepared to face the problem of marshalling the community's resources to meet the myriad needs of war. There were large-scale movements in population as young men left their homes for military service, and men and women, and sometimes whole families, moved to industrial cities to work in factories. Special services were needed to help individuals and families take arms against this sea of troubles. Day care for children of working mothers, recreation for service-men on furlough and for war workers in cities, emergency housing projects, counselling services for teen-agers, programmes of training and re-training—these and other demands of the war brought thousands of citizens within the orbit of the Red Cross, the United Service Organisations, civilian defence councils, the social service exchange, and numerous other projects. The pressure of war brought many individuals into communal activities, too, and led many organisations for the first time to work together for the common good. This had a potent effect, not only upon the individual citizen, but upon community organisation for education, health, welfare and recreation. Health and welfare planning, it was said, was becoming more of a citizen's movement and less a mere federation of operating agencies.[2] The philosophy underlying social work, it was claimed, was 'definitely and wholly a democratic philosophy'. Community organisation could be considered a part of this if it focused on the guidance of the process by which people find 'satisfying and fruitful social relationships', if a

[1] *Ibid.*, pp. 465–73.
[2] Lyman S. Ford, 'The Effect of World War II on Community Organization for Health and Welfare', *Proc. 71st N.C.S.W.* (Cleveland Ohio, 1944), p. 396.

democratic philosophy permeated this process, and if the worker established a 'helping' and not a 'controlling' relationship with individuals and groups.[1] This marked the beginning of a more intensive self study, for, as the bonds of war were loosened, community organizers began to assess their efforts, seeking to discover the general principles implicit in the practice of their craft and to decide which were common to all three methods of social work and which characteristic of community organisation alone. By the 1950's some measure of agreement had been reached. The common elements, it was suggested, included a disciplined use of self in working with people, an emphasis on the principle of self-determination, the use of social diagnosis based on an analysis of facts, the formulation of a plan, and continuous evaluation of the results.[2] Beyond that point, however, community organisation assumed characteristics peculiar to itself. Whereas social casework was preoccupied with the needs of the individual, and group work with the activities of the group, this newest member of the trinity was concerned mainly with the structure of the community. It aimed to bring about a more effective adjustment between the needs of social welfare and the resources of the community,[3] and although,

[1] Kenneth L. M. Pray, 'When is Community Organisation Social Work Practice?', *Proc. 74th N.C.S.W.* (San Francisco, 1947), pp. 201, 204.

[2] See, for example, Violet M. Sieder, 'What is Community Organisation Practice in Social Work?', *Proc. 83rd N.C.S.W.* (St. Louis, Mo., 1951), p. 166, and Genevieve W. Carter, 'Social Work Community Organisation Methods and Processes', in Walter A. Friedlander, *Concepts and Methods of Social Work* (Englewood Cliffs, N.J., 1958), p. 222, footnote 6.

[3] Cf. Arthur Dunham's definition of Community Organisation as 'the process of bringing about and maintaining adjustment between social welfare needs and social welfare resources in a geographical area or a special field of service' (*op. cit.*, p. 23). On the other hand, Wilber I. Newstetter and his associates at the University of Pittsburgh have emphasized 'social intergroup work' as being the aspect of Community Organisation which is 'probably unique in social work practice' ('The Social Intergroup Work Process', *Proc. 74th N.C.S.W.* (San Francisco, 1947), pp. 205-17); Murray G. Ross defines community organisation as a process by which the community identifies its needs or objectives, establishes priorities among them, finds the resources for dealing with them, takes action in respect to them, 'and in so doing extends and develops co-operative and collaborative attitudes and practices in the community' (*Community Organisation: Theory and Principles* (New York, 1955), p. 39); and Violet M. Sieder makes the best of five approaches. She has described the five stages in the evolution of community organisation objectives: (1) as the effort, through such agencies as the social service exchange, to prevent 'client abuse of services' offered by independent voluntary agencies; (2) as an attempt to achieve integration of services particularly through community chests and community welfare councils; (3) as an

obviously, it was interested in the individual, and often enlisted the group as a means of reaching its goal, its main emphasis was on social needs and how the resources of the community might be marshalled to meet them.

How far did this marshalling of the community's resources involve the social worker in reform, or 'Social Action' as it was called? From the beginning of the century there had been a growing recognition that many of the problems with which social work dealt were essentially social in origin, and hence must be attacked from the standpoint of society as well as that of the individual. 'The dominant note of modern philanthropy is one which . . . relate(s) the work of charitable relief . . . to the all-absorbing social problem', Edward T. Devine had declared in 1906,[1] while Jane Addams had eloquently recounted the hopes with which social workers took part in the struggle for legislation to prohibit child labour, to limit hours of work for women, and to prevent industrial accidents and disease.[2] Again, in 1909, the National Conference of Social Work had set up a committee, which later presented a platform of 'Social Standards for Industry', which included recommendations for a living wage, an eight hour day, housing, compensation and insurance. These constituted 'the basement floor of our industrial organisation', the chairman declared, and it was the duty of social workers to use their influence 'in every place and through every agency' to see that these standards were maintained.[3] In 1917, too, a permanent Committee on Industrial Economic Problems was created which became 'Division V' of the National Conference. This presented a programme of papers until 1934 when the Conference again reorganized itself, and set up four sections on social casework, group work,

---

attempt to relate the resources of agencies, both public and voluntary, to the needs of the people; (4) as a method not only for meeting but for preventing social problems; (5) as a direct service to communities through which individuals and groups are helped to meet their own needs—and concludes that these approaches are 'not mutually exclusive'; rather, they are all 'still necessary and in effect in most community planning organisations' (*op. cit.*, pp. 161–3).

[1] 'The Dominant Note of the Modern Philanthropy', *Proc. 32rd N.C.C.C.* (Philadelphia, 1906), p. 2.

[2] *The Second Twenty Years at Hull House* (New York, 1930).

[3] 'Standards of Living and Labour. Report of Committee by Owen R. Lovejoy', *Proc. 39th N.C.C.C.* (Cleveland, Ohio, 1912), pp. 388–94, and *Proc. 41st N.C.C.C.* (Memphis, 1914), pp. 323, 324. See above, pp. 94–95.

community organisation and social action. Thus it may have seemed in 1934 that social action was to be recognized as a function of social work; but if that were the intention, the conference failed to act upon it. Six years later, it was pointed out, rather sadly, that little had been done within the Conference to provide a rational basis in theory or in method for this new area of social work. 'Excellent as have been the discussions of social problems', the speaker said, 'we have done little to define or outline the field, we have provided few guide posts for those who would practise in this area of social work, we have presented no comprehensive programme of action'.[1]

This self-reproach was to be often repeated. 'In recent years the profession has not made highly significant contributions in the field of social action', mourned one social worker in 1947,[2] while six years later, the retiring president of the American Association of Social Workers challenged his fellows on the ground that, in the field of social action, they were failing to meet their professional responsibilities. 'Is our function as social workers limited to the treatment of pathologies', he asked, 'or do we also have a positive or preventive function to perform? . . . the early development of social work gave emphasis to . . . social reform. (But) the pendulum has swung far over to the other side until today the greater emphasis is on the treatment of individual illness.'[3]

Of course, there were reasons for this. Historically, social work began in movements of reform, but during its career as a new and struggling profession, it had become preoccupied, perhaps inevitably, with the immediate task of developing its

---

[1] John A. Fitch, 'The Nature of Social Action', *Proc. 67th N.C.S.W.* (Grand Rapids, Michigan, 1940), p. 487. Defining social action as 'action within the framework of existing society', the writer described three types of activity which fell within the field of social action—group action for the purpose of achieving beneficial results on behalf of the group itself (e.g. consumers' co-operatives, associations of tenants, or labor unions), campaigns to influence group attitudes or patterns of behaviour which have an important effect upon general well-being (e.g. campaigns for freedom of speech or in support of democratic principles in government), and 'community action through the regularly constituted governmental or political channels' for goals considered socially desirable. (*Ibid.*, pp. 488, 489–90.)

[2] Eveline M. Burns, 'Social Action and the Professional Social Worker', *The Compass*, Vol. XXVIII, No. 4 (May 1947), p. 37.

[3] Benjamin E. Youngdahl, 'Social Work at the Crossroads', *Social Work Journal* (July, 1953), p. 111.

own skills. As Porter R. Lee had forecast in 1929, the change in social work's emphasis from 'cause' to 'function' meant that the social worker's role as an advocate of reform became subordinate to her task of rendering efficiently a technical service.[1] This meant that, although she acknowledged the importance of social problems, especially those such as slum housing and low incomes, which lay at the root of so many of the cases which she handled, the social worker saw herself primarily as a technician whose first responsibility was to her client, rather than as a crusader bent upon curing the maladies of society. This change of emphasis has had a dual effect. It has freed the social worker to develop the skills which her work demands, but it has also tended to reinforce certain characteristics implicit in the origin and development of her profession. Despite its heritage from early reform movements and its oft-acknowledged commitment to the improvement of social conditions, social work has always been firmly wedded to the existing order. Although, in its earlier days at least, it allied itself with the indigent and the disabled, whose interests would have been better served by a change of system, social work has always had a distinct distaste for any action which threatened to disturb the *status quo*. This could indicate that social work is not convinced that the ever-whirling wheel of change could or should radically alter the economic and social system. Or else it could be a tacit admission that, as a new profession still striving for recognition of its status, social work has such strong material and emotional vested interests in the existing order, that the voice of criticism must be tempered by the cautioning wind of expediency. The social worker is not unaware of the shortcomings of the present system. Nor is she unwilling to give moral support to reforms which would improve it. It does mean, however, that she considers her first duty is to provide a particular service to a client, rather than to concern herself with social reform, and if, willy nilly, she is drawn into the vortex

[1] 'Social Work as Cause and Function', *Proc. 56th N.C.S.W.* (San Francisco, 1929), pp. 3–20. This would not be accepted by all. E.g. See the *Social Work Year Book, 1960*, in which Elizabeth Wickenden claims that social action (which she defines as 'organised effort directed toward a change in social policy or the creation, modification, or elimination of a social institution'), is still an important activity of social welfare, although she admits that it has taken on a character different from that of its pioneer days. (*Ibid.*, pp. 529–34.)

of change, her part should be to contribute the specialized knowledge which her work has given her, rather than to present a blue print of a new society.[1]

In spite of these limitations, social work, especially when pranked in its newest garb of group work and community organisation, plays a role today which is in marked contrast to that which it has played in the past. Social casework, as we have seen, born as it was in a mid-Victorian world where poverty signified degradation and both constituted a danger to peace, was originally used as a social sedative and a 'regenerator'. As a social sedative, it was intended to damp down social discontent by stressing the duties which the rich owed to the poor, although denying that the poor had the social rights of a citizen. As a regenerator, it sought to discover, beneath the surface of dependence, apathy and hopelessness, some elements of character and will-power which could be used to restore the poor to self-dependence. In both cases, attention was focused on the individual rather than on economic and social institutions, and social work was conceived as a means of adjusting the individual to his environment, rather than of bringing environmental forces into play to assist the individual.

This concept of casework as a social sedative, though never wholly accepted, even by the C.O.S., cast an unhappy shadow over the later social work of England and the United States. Although many of the assumptions about human nature and society on which it was based have now been abandoned, wisps of the concept have remained to colour the social worker's conception of her role in society. During the depression in the United States, for instance, social work as 'the conscience of the community', certainly advocated reforms more radical than it envisaged before or since that time, but the mood of Lady Bountiful persisted to the extent that it was always

[1] E.g. Kenneth L. M. Pray has said: 'We do not know . . . all that must go into the organization and operation of an adequate and satisfying economic system. But we do know . . . the meaning to real people of inadequate income, of intermittent employment and unemployment; we know the meaning to the individual of real work, of creative, free, self-respecting participation in the economic process and in the determination of his own working conditions. This does not entitle us to prepare or to endorse a detailed blue print of a total reform of the economic system. It does obligate us to contribute of our special knowledge.' (*Social Work in a Revolutionary Age and Other Papers* (Philadelphia, 1949), pp. 43–44.)

assumed that there should be no radical change in the economic and social system. Because it accepted this assumption, social work conceived its role mainly in negative terms. It saw itself primarily as a 'shock absorber' whose task was to cushion the worst effects of the crisis, rather than as an advocate of a plan of action designed to make economic depression an anachronism. Within these self-imposed limits, however, social work gradually recast the social philosophy which it had inherited from the preceding century. It exchanged its once-cherished concept of charity for the newer concept of social welfare, which, concerned as it was with the citizen's social rights, prompted social workers to think not only in terms of adjusting the individual to his environment, but of mobilizing the community's resources to ensure the well-being of all citizens. Thinking positively in this way, social work is now undergoing a sea change. Especially in its newer garb of group work and community organisation, it is becoming a catalyst, bent on releasing human potentialities imprisoned by poverty, social fear, ignorance and sloth. No longer does it think exclusively in terms of the unprivileged poor, to be punished or rewarded according to their deserts; no longer does it see itself as a palliative of the present order; nor does it think only in terms of cure or even of prevention. The newer social work, while still accepting the existing framework of society, is becoming more concerned with mobilizing the community's resources to promote the well-being of all individuals. By identifying the needs which emerge in society with changing social conditions, and by seeking, through its professional organisations, to exert pressure on those with authority to implement those needs, social work is becoming more concerned with improving the social institutions through which the individual functions. In this role, it can have a more positive and constructive part to play than ever before. This has been recognized, both by social work itself and by other sections of the community. Consequently, there is a greater readiness today, both in England and the United States, to recognize the value of the social worker, to enlarge and to vary her function, and, in some cases, to invite her participation in the making of public policy. This has given social work a 'new look', which is in strange contrast to the 'old look' of the nineteenth century. It is to this that we must now turn, for it is only by comparing today's social work with that of the past, that we can appreciate how greatly it has enlarged its scope and activities and how much heavier are the responsibilities it has incurred in doing so.

IX

The 'New Look' in
Social Work

> Clara, Clara, Vere de Vere,
>   If time be heavy on your hands,
> Are there no beggars at your gate,
>   Nor any poor about your lands?
> Oh! teach the orphan-boy to read,
>   Or teach the orphan-girl to sew,
> Pray Heaven for a human heart,
>   And let the foolish yeoman go.[1]

Thus, in 1842, did Tennyson seek to expedite his unhappy yeoman's escape from the toils of the idle, enchanting, heartless daughter of the noble caste of Vere de Vere. In doing so, he presented a concept of social work—or rather, its predecessor, charity—which, to a large degree, reflected the attitude of his day. As a pastime for the wealthy and the leisured, attending to the poor at the gate or teaching the orphan boy to read was an activity sufficiently innocuous to be socially acceptable. Not only could it divert predatory women from the pursuit of men, but it could assuage a sense of personal guilt and create the illusion of purpose in an otherwise purposeless

[1] *Poems of Alfred, Lord Tennyson, 1829–1868* (London, 1929), p. 115.

life. Since no training was thought to be necessary, and, more-over, the well-intentioned could usually afford the luxury of spurning payment, philanthropy was a cheap, convenient, and often effective way of averting social discontent. To the Lady Claras of 1842, 'doing good' was an avenue of salvation, an insurance on the existing social order, an antidote to boredom, and a public expiation of the private sin of living comfortably in a comfortless world.

Today, more than a hundred years later, the motives prompt-ing men and women to take up social work are sometimes the same,[1] but there has been a dramatic change in the scope of the work they undertake, the type of service they render, the character and number of the persons they serve, and their own status as professional or near-professional people in the com-munity. This change is bound up with changes which have occurred, or are occurring, in other spheres. Today, more than ever before, social work in England and the United States reflects the society in which it lives, and this society, especially during the last twenty years, has changed quite drastically its ideas about the role which its social workers should play in the community. This is due not only to the discovery made during the war years that a trained social worker has a great deal to contribute to the arts of war and peace. It is also due to the fact that society itself has changed its notion about how much social welfare it can afford and what part the social worker can play in helping to create and man these new forms of social care.[2]

[1] Cf. *Four Decades of Students in Social Work*, issued in 1954 by the Research Board of the Faculty of Commerce and Social Science at the University of Birming-ham, in which Winifred E. Cavanagh analyses the answers to questionnaires sent to 595 social workers. The most frequent reason given for going into social work during the four decades from 1909 to 1949 was an interest in people and a wish to help them, which was 'sometimes coupled with feelings of guilt at being more fortunately circumstanced than many'. (*Op. cit.*, p. 15 and Table IV, p. 80.)

[2] There is a less optimistic school of thought which might deny, either outright or by implication, that this is so. E.g. Nathan E. Cohen, discussing (in 1958) American social work's choice between 'its broad purposes' (of social welfare) and a narrow professionalism, writes: 'Part of the answer to this dilemma may lie in recognizing the fact that greater acceptance in the community involves the status not only of the social worker but also of social welfare as an institution in a demo-cratic society. Unless the community is ready to see the value of social welfare services and pay for them through taxes and voluntary contributions, the role and status of the professional worker will not change significantly.' (*Social Work in the American Tradition* (New York, 1958), p. 346.)

In England, especially since 1945, the concept of the Welfare State has been built into the country's social and economic structure to the extent that the problem of acute want has largely disappeared. This is not to say that there is no poverty in the Welfare State. Unemployment may have been reduced, but far less progress has been made in removing other causes of poverty, inequality and chronic ill-health. Peter Townsend has reminded us of England's 'submerged fifth' of seven to eight million people, who, being old, disabled, widowed or handicapped, live perilously close to the margins of poverty,[1] while Brian Abel-Smith, posing the question, 'Whose Welfare State?', angrily concludes that it is the middle classes rather than the working classes who are the beneficiaries of England's system of social security. It is they, he claims, who get the 'lion's share' of the public social services, the 'elephant's share' of occupational welfare privileges, and who, in addition, enjoy 'hidden social services' provided by concessions in the income tax.[2]

In spite of these deficiencies and anomalies, however, the reforms of the immediate post-war period in England have gone a long way towards slaying the five giants of the Beveridge Report. In this slaughter of ignorance, idleness, disease, squalor and want, the English social worker, once regarded as a doer of good works in a voluntary organisation, has become an accepted part of the machinery of the State social services. For whereas her nineteenth-century predecessor almost without exception worked outside such statutory social services as existed in her day, the modern social worker is being summoned to staff those numerous and diverse social services which the British government has since created to ensure the well-being of its citizens. Thus the almoner has taken up her stance in the National Health Scheme; the caseworker has appeared on the National Assistance Board, and the psychiatric social worker and the child welfare officer play a vital part in manning the local authority health and welfare services. In this process whereby social work has become an integral part of the State's social services, many problems have been created or accentuated. Among those which have been most hotly debated in

[1] 'A Society for People', in Norman Mackenzie, ed. *Conviction* (1959), pp.103-4.
[2] 'Whose Welfare State?' in *ibid.*, pp. 63, 62.

post-war England, controversy seems to have centred on staffing, training, and the organisation of social work. Are there sufficient numbers of social workers to deal with the multifarious difficulties of old age, child care, sickness and insecurity? How can a better co-operation be achieved between specialist workers in the social services and between the voluntary and governmental authorities who employ them? What is involved in social work in the social services, and what kind of qualities and training are needed by those called upon to practise it? How can workers best be recruited? How best employed? These and other questions are vexing the mind of the English social worker at the moment, and in some cases are prompting her to examine her work in its entirety with a view to aiding the formulation of more realistic policies to recruit, train and employ social workers.[1] In addition, an ever-growing knowledge of man and society, combined with a greater desire to understand the lives of those for whom the services are intended, have led the makers and administrators of social policy to reject many inherited assumptions about how people ought to live and act. Need and behaviour are now conceived in terms of the family or the work group, rather than of the individual; the new social services cater for families and social groups in distress, rather than for classes of needy persons or for categories of disease and incapacity, and professions, such as social work, which are directly concerned with individual human welfare, have come to see that social intelligence is essential for professional competence. None of this is new; it is, in fact, a harking back to the

---

[1] See, for example, Barbara N. Rodgers and Julia Dixon, *Portrait of Social Work. A Study of Social Services in a Northern Town* (Oxford, 1950), who found that there were certain factors affecting the recruitment, training and employment of social workers 'which are only revealed, and whose importance can only be assessed, in such local field studies'; firstly, that there is a widespread confusion about the principles and practice of social work and of what can and can not be expected from social workers, which must be removed by making these principles and aims more explicit; secondly, that more of those engaged in social work need training in its principles and practice, which will be 'some guarantee of competence' and which will give them 'an assurance and status in the wider profession of social work which they at present lack'; and thirdly, that more thought needs to be given to the organisation of social work and to where and how social workers are employed in the social services, but that 'good co-operation depends more on the social workers having a "professional" attitude to their job than on any structural factor.' (*Ibid.*, pp. 222–52).

not so distant past when Mary Richmond deplored the undue emphasis placed upon social casework and a plea was made to 'put the social back into social work'.[1]

In this new, yet old, emphasis upon social factors, the social worker is learning to take a more comprehensive view of her responsibilities. She has found, for example, that human needs never come in neat specialist packets, and that a classification of people according to their age, handicap or social failure, although it may be logical for certain purposes, does not always provide the most appropriate grouping when it comes to social work. The personal needs of people suffering from varied handicaps remain the same, but if attention is concentrated on a single aspect of need, this reality of common human needs is often overlooked. The Younghusband Report has recently reminded us of this. 'There is always a risk in any type of specialization of concentrating on a particular aspect at the expense of the whole', it warns, '. . . . (and) this can lead to a focusing of effort on a particular need or handicap, rather than on the effect of these on the individual in his family or social setting'.[2] Accordingly, to do its job properly, a social service must understand the common social and personal factors in the needs of those using the services; it must take into account needs other than those it was set up to meet, and always the focus must be on the individual in his family and social setting. This has been recognized. Thus, more and more, the problems and needs of individual people are being studied and treated in terms of their family and social context. Juvenile delinquency and truancy, for instance, are seen as manifestations of tangled and unhappy relationships within the family. Child care has come to be regarded, not as an end in itself, but as a part, preferably a temporary part, of the help given to families unable to look after their children; and since, as a legacy of the Poor Law, many people still regard institutions as haunts of horror and fear, attempts are being made to give help to the

---

[1] Cf. Charlotte Towle's comment: '. . . the current scene (can) be described as one in which we are coming full circle in many aspects of our practice.' ('New Developments in Social Casework in the United States', in *Some Reflections on Social Work Education* (1956), p. 14.)

[2] *Report of the Working Party on Social Workers in the Local Authority Health and Welfare Services* (H.M.S.O., 1959), paras. 636, 640.

mentally ill, the old, and the handicapped within the familiar and comforting confines of the home.

Thus within fifteen years, administrative necessities, changing attitudes to people in need, and an increasing knowledge of human behaviour have created a demand for social work in England which even the most ardent charity organizer could not have foreseen. Demand has outrun supply,[1] and although recommendations have been made as to how the two may be brought closer together, recommendation, so far, has outrun achievement. The reason is not far to seek. Social work in England, far from being an honoured profession, is a depressed occupation. Despite the increasingly important role which its social workers are playing, England has been extremely loath to grant them payment and status commensurate with the work they do. Of course, it is not so long since the lofty social status of the social worker precluded the necessity for payment. 'The great evil in the East End', complained the Reverend J. F. Kitto, Rector of Stepney, 'was that there were very few persons who had leisure, and no persons of wealth, resident in the district to give their time and means to the work'.[2] This was the prevailing sentiment in 1887, but although the society which produced it has long since passed away, vestiges of the sentiment remain. Later salary standards have undoubtedly been influenced by this fact that social work began as a voluntary, missionary type of occupation in which the work done was considered to be its own reward, and many have been the complaints from those who have suffered because of it. 'The altruism of social work pioneers . . . has obviously had a negative effect on salary standards', mourned an American social worker in 1946,[3] while the following year, Professor T. S. Simey, investigating the salaries and conditions of English social workers, came to the conclusion that the reason why social workers earned incomes between £200 and £400 was that too strong an emphasis had been placed in the past on 'a

---

[1] According to the 1951 Census, there were 22,000 social workers in England and Wales—that is to say, as Barbara Wootton tartly pointed out, 'slightly more than one social worker to every two barmen or barmaids'. (*Social Science and Social Pathology* (1959), p. 263.)

[2] *Charity Organisation Reporter*, XIII, (June 7, 1887), p. 189.

[3] Harry L. Lurie, 'Criteria for Determining Salaries in Governmental and Voluntary Welfare Agencies', *The Compass*, XXVII (June, 1946), p. 27.

sense of vocation, a traditional approach, and the value to be placed on personality'.[1] 'In these days of full employment and high wages', *The Economist* tartly commented at the time, 'it is a particular shock to find that few, very few, social workers ever earn more than £400 per annum'.[2]

That these conditions are not merely a mischief that is past and gone is amply proved by the report which has recently emerged from the deliberations of a Working Party on Social Workers in the Local Authority Health and Welfare Services. Although the picture painted by the Younghusband Committee is not as gloomy as that presented by its two predecessors,[3] its findings are far from cheering. While investigating the problems of community care, the Committee discovered that there was an extreme shortage of trained social workers in the health and welfare services; that the great majority of workers have no systematic training, nor, under existing salary scales, is there any incentive for them to get it; that departments are undermanned, salary scales are low, opportunities for training and promotion are few; a shortage of senior appointments discourages officers from taking further training and deters new recruits from entering the services; and field workers, because of lack of facilities, spend an inordinate amount of their time in travelling, writing their own letters and reports and doing odd jobs that could be more economically done by someone less qualified.[4] The Working Party made it clear that no matter in which field of the health and welfare services it is practised—whether it be family casework, the home help service, or the provision of care for the sick, the aged, the mentally ill and the handicapped—social work faces the same problems of shortage of staff, low salaries, lack of opportunity

[1] *Salaries and Conditions of Work of Social Workers. Report of a Joint Committee of the British Federation of Social Workers and the National Council of Social Service,* under the chairmanship of T. S. Simey. (National Council of Social Science, 1947), pp. 26, 40.

[2] *The Economist,* 20 September 1947, quoted in British Federation of Social Workers, *Eleventh Annual Report, 1947,* p. 7.

[3] Eileen L. Younghusband, *Report on the Employment and Training of Social Workers* (Dumfermline, Fife, 1949) and *Social Work in Britain. A Supplementary Report on the Employment and Training of Social Workers* (Dumfermline, Fife, 1951).

[4] *Report of the Working Party on Social Workers in the Local Authority Health and Welfare Services,* paras. 732–5, 757, 365, 748, 397–406.

for training and promotion, and often unfavourable working conditions. Radical reforms, then, are necessary if community care is to become a reality.[1] Moreover, the Report delicately implies,[2] a systematic study of the training and employment of social workers in the whole field of the social services would produce for social work as a whole conclusions very similar to those which the Working Party reached in its own field.

This, however, is the darker side. Seen in happier light, the introspection, if not self-flagellation, which this Report reveals is the outward sign of inner strength. Both in its conception of social work's role in the community and its emphasis upon the need for training, the Report states the case for social work as a profession. This is a case which has long awaited an advocate, for despite a greater readiness to recognize its worth and to use its services, social work in Great Britain is less 'professionalized' than in the United States. This may be due partly to the circumstances in which it began, and partly to the fact that the British Civil Service gives discouragingly little recognition to the specialists it employs, particularly in positions where

---

[1] The main recommendation made in the Report is for a new type of training for social workers. The Working Party recommends that there should be three kinds of social workers to meet the three main gradations of need. Experienced social workers with a university qualification in social science and professional training in social work should provide a casework service for those needing the most skilled help with personal or family problems, to act as advisors or consultants to other social workers, and to undertake initial interviews when the information available suggests there might be a particularly difficult problem to handle. Next is needed a large supply of social workers with a general training in social work equivalent to two years' full-time training, to provide help with the more complex problems which form the greater part of the social work required in health and welfare departments. Finally, there should be a third group of 'welfare assistants' with a short but systematically planned in-service training, working under the supervision of trained social workers, and relieving them of a proportion of the simpler work and straightforward visiting. (*Ibid.*, paras. 24–28. For further detail of the training scheme, see paras. 567–74, 703–5, 575–601, and Chapter 9.)

[2] E.g. 'A number of witnesses commented on the difficulty of limiting their evidence to social workers in the health and welfare services, since this would mean considering only certain aspects of the total picture. . . . Through our inquiry we have been conscious that other local authority departments and branches of social work need the services of trained social workers. These are, however, outside our terms of reference. . . . Nonetheless we should like it to be clear that we fully recognize the importance of social work in other services. We are also aware that many of the principles on which our recommendations are based, though applied to the social workers within our terms of reference, are of general application.' (*Ibid.*, paras. 12, 13)

policy making is possible.[1] But mainly it is due to the circumstance that, operating as it does within a framework of statutory and voluntary organizations, social work in the Welfare State has usually been regarded as one aspect of the administration of a social service, rather than as a distinctive profession with its own body of theory, methods, ethical code and organisation. Thus the social worker herself, although possessing strong material and emotional vested interests in the outcome, has been extremely tardy in staking a claim for professional status. Inhabiting an age, as Professor Titmuss says, 'of more explicit discontents and of more articulate expectations',[2] she has managed to live at variance with both. Discontented though she may be with her lot, expectant though she may be of the future, she has seldom made her discontent articulate, let alone her expectations explicit.

Her cousins across the sea, however, have been more expectantly articulate, if not discontentedly explicit. Here, too, in recent years, social work has changed in scope, character and status, for the government of the United States, no less than that of England, has been busily enlisting its aid to deal with problems of dependency and poverty which exist in the midst of wealth. The last twenty-five years have seen a major acceptance of public responsibility for the unemployed, the handicapped, the disabled and the aged. Consequently there has been an increase in public expenditures in these areas of social welfare. It is now generally recognized that only the government can organize the kind of basic social insurance programme so necessary in an industrial economy, and so social insurance payments have increased dramatically from 384 million dollars in 1935 to nearly 16,000 million in 1958. Since it is recognized, too, that the government must provide at least a minimum income to persons in need, expenditure on public assistance during the same period soared from 624 million to 3,538 million dollars, while at the same time, the social services were expanded to play a variety of stabilizing, preventive and protective roles as they do in England. Public expenditure for child welfare services, vocational rehabilitation and veterans

[1] Cf. *Some Impressions of Social Services in Great Britain by an American Social Work Team* (U.S. Educational Commission in the United Kingdom, 1956), pp. 8–10.
[2] *Essays on 'The Welfare State'* (1958), p. 105.

welfare services has increased from 3 million dollars in 1935 to 719 million in 1958, while health and medical services, which in 1929 ate up 414 million dollars of government funds, by 1958 were devouring more than ten times that amount.[1] When it is considered, too, that despite this growth of public programmes, the private philanthropist has been busy raising funds to finance health and welfare services,[2] it is obvious that social welfare during the last twenty years has become a big business indeed. Moreover, it is a business which has come to stay. This acceptance of social welfare as a permanent feature of modern society is comparatively new in the United States. Before the depression of the 1930's, it was popularly believed that social welfare agencies were primarily emergency exits from a difficult situation which would cease to exist once regular social institutions, such as the family and the economic system, began to work again. But modern social developments have disproved this belief, and far from disappearing, social welfare has become an integral part of America's industrial, urban society.

This new demand for social welfare, combined with the increasing industrialization which has produced it,[3] has had a profound effect upon the scope, character and status of today's social work. It has meant that social work, bursting through its cocoon of traditional employment, is now practised in all corners of the country, under new auspices, in new settings, and often with a clientele whose middle class character contrasts strangely with that of a previous day. No longer an emergency service for the destitute, social work can now be found, if only in embryonic form, in programmes for public housing and child welfare, in mental hygiene clinics and recreation centres, and in the military forces and labour unions. For

[1] Ida C. Merriam, 'Financing Social Welfare Services', in *Social Work Year Book, 1960* (New York, 1960), pp. 268, 270–2, especially Tables I, II, III and V.

[2] E.g. In 1958, United Community Funds and Councils of America reported that 2,100 federated campaigns in America raised $427,262,622 for use, during 1959, by 27,700 participating agencies. (Russell W. Leedy, 'United Funds and Community Chests', *Social Work Year Book, 1960*, p. 586.) In 1957, too, 110 large foundations gave grants totalling $247,894,000, of which 47 per cent went to education, 14 per cent to health, 13 per cent to scientific research, and 9 per cent to social welfare. (F. Emerson Andrews, 'Foundations and Social Welfare', *ibid.*, p. 287.)

[3] For a closer analysis of the impact of industrialization on the supply and organization of social welfare services in the United States, see Harold L. Wilensky and Charles N. Lebeaux, *Industrial Society and Social Welfare* (New York, 1958).

it is the social worker who shares with other professional and non-professional groups responsibility for administering America's multi-billion dollar welfare programme. This is not to say that there is always a correlation between the amount spent on welfare and the number and quality of social workers employed. This varies too much for generalization.[1] But it does mean that there is a growing realization that the public interest can best be served by placing the administration of a programme, such as public assistance, which has now reached the stage where it affects the life of one American in every twenty-six,[2] into the hands of the professionally qualified welfare worker. She, one must suppose, can not only administer grants of money more efficiently than the unqualified, but her training fits her to understand more clearly the common human needs and feelings to which public assistance programmes should be geared. Thus public assistance today employs at least 41 per cent of all the country's social workers,[3] and although only a small proportion of these are professionally trained,[4] steps have been taken,

[1] E.g In public assistance programmes in 1950, approximately 94 per cent of the expenditure was for direct payment to persons in distress, and 6 per cent for administration and the services of those who performed social work. At the other extreme, there were voluntary welfare organisations, such as the member agencies of the Family Service Association of America, which, in 1949, reported that on an average they spent only 18 per cent of their funds on 'relief' and 82 per cent on other social work services. (Ernest V. Hollis and Alice L. Taylor, *Social Work Education in the United States. The Report of a Study made for the National Council on Social Work Education* (New York, 1951), p. 66.)

[2] The total number of persons receiving public assistance in December, 1958 (which is the last date available) was 6.9 million, or 3.9 per cent of the total civilian population. (Jay L. Roney, 'Public Assistance', *Social Work Year Book*, 1960, p. 460.) The two largest groups of recipients were the aged and young children—groups which are most likely to be dependent and which are increasing more rapidly than the total population.

[3] This is the figure given in the study made by the U.S. Bureau of Labor Statistics, *Social Workers in 1950. A Report on the Study of Salaries and Working Conditions in Social Work.* Prepared by the U.S. Department of Labor, Division of Wages and Industrial Wages (New York, 1952), Table I, p. 5. A similar study is being made by the Bureau of Labor Statistics in 1960, but the findings will not be available until late in the year. However, since the number of social workers and the public assistance programmes have expanded since 1950, this figure of 41 per cent is likely to be higher.

[4] In 1950, for example, 27 per cent of the social workers in public assistance agencies had a bachelor's degree, 31 per cent a bachelor's degree and some graduate work, and 7 per cent had no bachelor's degree but some graduate work. (*Social Workers in 1950*, Table D, 11, p. 44). Cf. the comment in the Hollis Taylor *Report*: 'Between three-fifths and three-fourths of the public assistance and related social workers of the nation have not had any professional education; moreover, with the

although hesitantly, to build up a supply of qualified personnel to man these and other services. In 1956, an amendment to the Social Security Act authorized more federal grants to help the states meet the cost of training personnel in public assistance programmes, while more recently, the Council on Social Work Education in New York has applied itself to the onerous task of formulating an educational programme,[1] in keeping with the changed conditions of today, which shall produce social workers numerous enough and competent enough to serve the present and the future hour.

Producing social workers to serve the present and the future hour is, indeed, a formidable task, for the future hour promises to make demands on social work even greater than those of the present. Straws in the demographic wind indicate that by 1975, programmes of social welfare will be faced with such an increase of dependants at life's two extremes, that it may necessitate expanding services for children by 71 per cent and those for the aged by 66 per cent.[2] Similarly, a study of the present American society suggests that industrialism and urbanization have wrought changes in social living which, even if they herald a more integrated society,[3] call for welfare services to protect and sustain the victims of change. Society itself must build the crèche for the child whose mother is at work and care for the aged emancipated from their children, and since there will always be those in travail, the community must help them to

general education of nearly half of this group being less than college graduation, a substantial proportion is not eligible to undertake graduate professional study.' (*loc. cit.*, p. 90.)

[1] *Curriculum Study of the Council on Social Work Education*, under the directorship of Werner W. Boehm (New York: Council on Social Work Education, 1959), 13 volumes.

[2] These are estimates drawn from Philip M. Hauser, 'Demography and Human Ecology in Relation to Social Work', *Proceedings of the Eighty-Third National Conference of Social Work* (St. Louis, Mo., 1956), pp. 195, 196. Professor Hauser estimates that by 1975 the increased birthrate will result in persons from 5 to 14 years of age increasing from 24.4 million to somewhere between 30.3 and 41.8 million, or by between 24 and 71 per cent. Persons between 15 and 19 years of age will increase from 10.7 million to between 17.3 and 20.3 million, or by 62 to 90 per cent. At the other end of the scale, persons of 65 and over will increase from 14.1 million to 20.7 million, or by 66 per cent. (*Ibid.*, pp. 195–6).

[3] See Harold L. Wilensky and Charles N. Lebeaux, *op. cit.*, Chapter V, for an analysis of 'Industrialism, urbanism and integration', and an optimistic conclusion that: 'A new welfare bureaucratic society emerges—more stable than its early forms suggest, richer and more varied than men had dreamed. . . .' (*Ibid.*, p. 133.)

cope with their lives. For just as the pauper and the unemployed have fallen by the economic wayside, so the delinquent and the neurotic reflect the fact that for some the pace of social change has been too great. Freed from old ties of family and neighbourhood, they have found no new allegiance to provide a centre of being and a new order of life; and so, feeling forsaken in an indifferent world, they seek fulfilment in behaviour condemned by their fellows. This our society is learning to accept —that just as it enjoys the rich fruit of social change, so it must bear the responsibility for those who come to grief as a result of it, that since in the complexity of modern life, the individual is unable fully to provide for himself and his needs, welfare services must be devised for his use which shall be accepted as a normal, integral part of modern industrial society.[1]

Demographic and social changes, then, combined with this 'institutional' conception of social welfare, favour a greatly extended role for social work, for not only do they foreshadow an increase in the kinds of services social workers can perform, but they promise, if not demand, an opportunity to help to shape social policy. This is a responsibility which in the immediate past has frequently been neglected.[2] So often has the individual, rather than society, been the centre of attention, that in the realm of social policy, social work has been more creature than creator. This reluctance to be involved in wider issues has led to a narrowing down of social work's conception of its role. Whereas the welfare worker of the nineteenth century, perceiving the effects of social factors on the individual, strove to improve the environment in which the individual lived, her modern counterpart, more concerned with individualized service, has been preoccupied with the shaping and refinement of technique.

This more modest conception of its task has dominated

---

[1] Wilensky and Lebeaux have christened as 'institutional' this conception of social welfare which accepts welfare services as 'normal, first line functions of modern industrial society', in contrast to the 'residual' conception which holds that social welfare institutions should come into play only when 'the normal structures of supply, the family and the market, break down'. (*Ibid.*, p. 138).

[2] Cf. the comment made in the Hollis Taylor *Report* on social work education: 'The social work profession in the last quarter century has . . . to an increasing degree, concentrated on the improvement of the quality of individualized service. . . The profession has accepted too little of a unified responsibility for appraising and improving social welfare institutions.' (*Op. cit.*, p. 142.)

American social work during the last four decades. From the 1920's to the early 1950's, except for the dramatic years of the depression, social work displayed little of its previous concern with reform and social policy. Perhaps in the initial period, this declining interest in social action reflected the conservatism of a post-war society anxiously searching for a return to 'normalcy'. Perhaps social work, pursuing the professional hare, wisely preferred to leave this broader public purpose to specialized agencies and professional groups better adapted than itself for reform. Or perhaps, reeling under the impact of the new psychiatry, it lacked time, energy and inclination fully to develop that branch of social work concerned with social change. Whatever the cause, community organisation, which might have become a laboratory for social action, turned its attention to safer study, and its practitioners, far from becoming a covey of reformers, confined themselves to helping community groups to evaluate their needs and find their own solutions.[1]

This tendency to abdicate responsibility in the field of social action has persisted until quite recent times. Certainly there have been voices raised in protest. The social worker of the 1940's was sternly reminded that social action was 'a motive force in democracy',[2] that she must see herself as a 'constructor' rather than a 'patcher-up of unconsidered trifles',[3] and that she had an individual and collective responsibility for social action as well as for the provision of a technical service. 'Each of us carries a dual responsibility', Kenneth Pray announced in 1945, 'to perform the particular services which are entrusted to us . . . and . . . to help the community . . . relate its institutions . . . to the fundamental needs of human beings'.[4] In the

---

[1] According to Elizabeth G. Meier, the community organizer 'no longer exhorted "reform" but attempted to help the community to evaluate its own needs and formulate its own objectives. This did not prevent the community worker from gathering data as effectively as possible, presenting it in ways and to the persons and groups upon which it would have the most effect, and judiciously stimulating these groups to take appropriate action in order to achieve socially desirable goals.' (*A History of the New York School of Social Work* (New York, 1954), p. 67.)

[2] Harry L. Lurie, 'Social Action: A Motive Force in Democracy', *Proceedings of the Sixty-Eighth National Conference of Social Work* (Atlantic City, 1941), pp. 631–41).

[3] Max Lerner, 'A Nation Worthy of Heroes', *Proceedings of the Seventy-First National Conference of Social Work* (Cleveland, 1944), p. 23.

[4] 'Social Work and Social Action', *Proceedings of the Seventy-Second National Conference of Social Work* (New York, 1945), p. 353.

following decade, too, some recognized that although the treatment of the individual was of vital concern, social work could
no longer cling to a pre-industrial individualism which had little
relevance to the conditions of the mass civilization of today. In
these conditions, it was argued, social work must not only
further its techniques to deal with mass situations, but it must
decide once again whether it could be content to treat the consequences rather than the causes of social discontent.[1] For just
as the welfare worker of the 1890's, influenced by the new
knowledge emerging from economics, sociology and political
science, was forced to turn her attention from the reform of the
individual to the reform of society, so her occupational descen-
dant had begun to realize that she must translate the new knowledge from today's social sciences into methods of dealing with
social institutions as well as individuals. And so, hesitantly at
first, and then with increasing firmness, the American social
worker was reminded that since she lived in what has been
called 'a society of masses',[2] she must temper her individualist
techniques to the requirements of the changing times. 'Social
work is not separable from social reform', Donald Howard
announced in 1954. 'If social work is to become a positive force
for change, new techniques and attitudes must be cultivated'.[3]
'Social welfare is our commitment', echoed Eveline Burns in
'58, 'We are all united in a common cause'.[4] 'What we need
. . . is . . . integrated social planning', added a third,[5] while
yet another warned his colleagues that there were 'needs to be
met, services to be created, vital functions to be filled', and that
if social work would not give adequate attention to social

---

[1] E.g. 'Social work today is at a crossroads much like that experienced by the
early humanitarians. Again it must decide whether it can be satisfied to deal with
the consequences rather than the causes of social breakdown.' (Nathan E. Cohen,
op. cit., p. 354.)

[2] C. Wright Mills, *The Power Elite* (New York, 1956), p. 302. Cf. also Wright
Mills' comment: 'The United States today is not altogether a mass society. . . .
We realize that we have moved a considerable distance along the road to the mass
society. . . . The top of American society is increasingly unified . . . at the
bottom, there is emerging a mass society.' (*Ibid.*, pp. 302, 304, 324.)

[3] 'Social Work and Social Reform', in Cora Kasius (ed.), *New Directions in
Social Work* (New York, 1954), pp. 159, 173.

[4] 'Presidential Address: Social Welfare is our Commitment', *Proceedings of
the Eighty-Fifth National Conference on Social Welfare* (Chicago, 1958), pp. 3, 19.

[5] Grace L. Coyle, 'The Bridge between Social Work and the Social Sciences',
(Eduard C. Lindeman Memorial Lecture), *ibid.*, p. 231.

policy, planning, community organisation, and social action, new professional groups would have to appear to fill the breach.[1]

The bolder spirits in social work responded to these pleas. In an effort to translate utterance into action, the National Association of Social Workers established a paid 'lobbyist' in Washington, appointed a committee to define a method to translate data from practice into social policy,[2] and repeatedly stressed its members' responsibility for social action in certain spheres. 'Social work is the profession which concerns itself with . . . strengthening . . . social relationships between individuals, groups and social institutions', it proclaimed in 1957. 'It has, therefore, a . . . responsibility . . . in . . . the identification, analysis and interpretation of unmet needs . . . (in) advancing the standard of recognized social obligation between society and its individual members . . . and (in) the application of specific knowledge, experience and inventiveness to those problems which can be solved through social welfare methods'.[3] Similarly, the American Public Welfare Association, since its inception in 1930, has become a leader in the field of social welfare, and the Council on Social Work Education, devising a programme to meet the demands of the future, has shaped its curriculum on the assumption that its graduates will be called upon to participate in the making of social policy.[4] 'Provided the profession makes the choice', the director, Dr. Boehm, has said, 'and consciously sets itself the task of developing the necessary knowledge and skill, it could become the profession *par excellence* which furnishes specialists in problems of social living'.[5]

[1] Alfred J. Kahn, 'The Function of Social Work in the Modern World', in Alfred J. Kahn (ed.), *Issues in American Social Work* (New York, 1959), p. 35.

[2] Raymond F. Gould, *Tentative Plans for Trend Study by D. C. Chapter* (New York, National Association of Social Workers, 1958, mimeographed), quoted by Bertram M. Beck, 'Shaping America's Social Welfare Policy', in Alfred J. Kahn (ed.), *op. cit.*, p. 214.

[3] *Goals of Public Policy* (N.A.S.W., 1957), Part I, p. 4. Also printed in *Social Work Year Book, 1960*, pp. 71–3.

[4] E.g. 'Social workers might participate increasingly in the formulation of social policy in such matters as general urban planning, income maintenance programs, the expansion of public and privately financed housing, industrial relations, the solution of such acute social problems as integration and many others where social work knowledge and skill may be called upon'. (Werner W. Boehm, *Objectives of the Social Work Curriculum of the Future*, vol. I of the *Curriculum Study*, pp. 17–18.) See also Appendix C in which Eveline M. Burns discusses 'Social policy and the Social Work Curriculum', *ibid.*, pp. 255–74.   [5] *Op. cit.*, p. 18.

Yet despite such exhortations, many social workers still tread the narrow way. Although they acknowledge the importance of social action, they still see themselves primarily as clinicians whose first responsibility is to their clients, rather than as reformers bent upon curing the ills of society. This may be due to several factors. It may be due to that innate conservatism which prefers adherence to the old and tried. It may be due to the difficulty of reaching agreement on policies of reform. It may be because caseworkers, who constitute 80 per cent of the country's social workers,[1] unconsciously assume that casework is the whole of social work and casework methods the extent of its professional skill. Or it may be because social work, striving for a place in the professional sun, has been preoccupied with method and technique. For despite the fact that it is acquiring its own body of theory, methods, ethical code and organization, social work in the United States is still not fully recognized as one of the professions.[2] Although it has travelled far since the days in 1915 when it was deemed 'the mediator' who summoned the expert,[3] social work in the United States has still not been able to gain complete professional acceptance. Studies made by sociologists show that its status is not high in the community, and that the 'average social worker' is 'a marginal person' who often feels herself underpaid and insecure.[4] A study

[1] E.g. It has been estimated that less than 20 per cent of the 1957 graduates majored in other fields. (Henry J. Meyer, 'Professionalization and Social Work', in Alfred J. Kahn (ed.), *op. cit.*, p. 337).

[2] There have, however, been claims to the contrary. To cite but three instances, Henry J. Meyer, *loc. cit.*, p. 319; Ernest Greenwood, 'Attributes of a Profession', *Social Work*, II, No. 3 (July, 1957), p. 54; Sir Raphael Cilento, 'The World Moves towards Professional Standards in Social Work', *Social Work Journal*, XXIX, No. 3 (July, 1948), p. 102.

[3] Abraham Flexner, 'Is Social Work a Profession?' *Proceedings of the Forty-Second National Conference of Charities and Correction* (Maryland, 1915), p. 588. Cf. also Felix Frankfurter's description of social work as a 'quasi profession' ('Social work and Professional Training', *ibid.*, p. 594), while even as late as 1951. the Hollis Taylor *Report* regarded it as being 'in its early adolescence'. (*Op. cit,*, p. 110.)

[4] Norman Polansky, *et al*, 'Social Workers in Society: Results of a Sampling Study', *Social Work Journal*, vol. XXXIV, No. 2 (April, 1953), p. 80. See also Polansky's later study, 'The Professional Identity in Social Work', in Alfred J. Kahn (ed.), *op. cit.*, pp. 293–318, in which he continues his 'social psychological analysis' of social work as a profession and a culture; Otto Pollak, 'Cultural Dynamics in Casework', *Social Case Work*, XXXIV, No. 7 (July, 1953), pp. 281–3; Clyde R. White, 'Prestige of Social Work and the Social Worker', *Social Work Journal*, XXXVI, No. 1 (January, 1955), pp. 21–23; William Oldys, 'Wages,

of the social worker's pocket book proves that there is just cause for complaint. For although the Bureau of Labor Statistics could point out in 1950 that average salaries in social work compared favourably with those paid to nurses, librarians, dieticians and teachers,[1] a later study made in '56 revealed that a trained social worker in the field of rehabilitation was paid less than a tool-maker, a factory worker, a railroad conductor and a brakeman.[2] This was the outward and visible sign of the value which the community was prepared to accord its social workers. Although they have now become trained specialists in a field increasingly well-defined, there are many people who still cling to the belief that any person with a warm heart and a cheery spirit can do the job. Thus even if conditions improve in the future—and there are signs already that, under the spur of competition, salaries may soar to a level which might almost be called moderate[3]—the social worker still faces the further difficulty of convincing the community that, since hers is a task which requires professional training as well as good intentions, the community will benefit from and should prefer the trained performance.

This struggle to gain professional acceptance in the community has accentuated some of the stresses within social work itself.[4] Some of these stresses spring from attempts to fix rightful boundaries to its domain; others from efforts to define

Budgets, Recruitments, Expectations', *ibid.*, p. 24; Herbert Bisno, 'How Social will Social Work Be?' *Social Work*, I, No. 2 (April, 1956), pp. 13–18; Alfred Kadushin, 'Prestige of Social Work—Facts and Factors', *Social Work*, III, No. 2 (April, 1958), pp. 37–43; and Alex Inkeles and Peter H. Rossi, 'National Comparisons of Occupational Prestige', *American Journal of Sociology*, LXI (July, 1955–May, 1956), pp. 329–39, in which social work is not even mentioned!

[1] *Social Workers in 1950*, p. 21. The study, though, carefully refrained from comparing social workers' salaries with those of physicians, lawyers and dentists.

[2] Sidney G. Tickton, *Rebuilding Human Lives: The Rehabilitation of the Handicapped* (New York, 1957), Part I, p. 21. The figures of salaries given were: social workers, $4,600; railroad conductors, $7,681; railroad brakemen, $6,239; tool and die makers, $5,574; and automobile manufacturing, $5,400.

[3] E.g. The National Association of Social Workers has adopted a programme urging that the beginning salary for a new graduate be $5,400 a year with a maximum of $10,000 after ten years of experience. (*Salaries: Official N.A.S.W. Policy* (N.A.S.W., 1959). This, however, is not a salary which would satisfy the whims of a sybarite.

[4] For an interesting analysis of these stresses, see Lydia Rapoport, 'In Defense of Social Work: An Examination of Stress in the Profession', *Social Service Review*, XXXIV, No. 1 (March, 1960), pp. 62–74.

its function in new areas and settings. Some spring from limitations of its knowledge and experience; others arise from the nature of its own activity. But perhaps the most serious source of stress has been the attempt to reconcile the caution of professionalism with social work's traditional commitment to reform. For social work is concerned with social ills. It protects a group which needs to be sustained. It serves society which fearfully seeks protection through its work. It embraces values which may be uncongenial to the dominant order; and it serves as a reminder that society has failed to fulfil its obligations. It is at once the expression of the conscience and the fears of the community, as well as an embodiment of its determination to change and yet remain the same. And yet despite the contradictions of its roles, there is a unity of purpose. Durkheim has said that professions, by their nature, are 'centres of moral life', for next to the family, they are the most important means by which values are evolved in the community.[1] In this sense, social work is already a profession, for in relation to the problems which have called it into being, the working out of ends and that analysis of means which we call 'a code of ethics' have developed a corps of values which has affected the surrounding society. In addition, social work has acquired many of the characteristics of a profession, while avoiding some of the pitfalls which professionalization brings. Thus although it has built an armoury of theory and techniques, this has not yet become so sanctified as to arrest the search for new knowledge and experience. Likewise although the adoption of a code of ethics and the creation of a national organisation have increased the consciousness of being a profession, this professional consciousness has not yet hardened into an unyielding exclusiveness. But although it may have escaped the crippling effects of a crabbed conservatism, social work has had to pay a price. In the process of clearing a space in the professional sun, the conception of social work was whittled down to a fragment of its former range. It was forced to concentrate on method and technique, and social action, perhaps because it is too precarious a basis for professional specialization, was relegated to a limbo large and broad.

[1] Emile Durkheim, *Professional Ethics and Civic Morals* (Glencoe, Ill., 1958) pp. 26–27.

Now, however, the tide is turning, and present preoccupation with technique is being tempered with concern for wider issues. For once again, social work is being summoned by its leaders to accept the challenge of a changing age. Once again, it is being inspired to re-assess its role in the community and to recast old ways of thought. For faced with an institutional conception of social welfare, many social workers have realized that the needs of American society can best be served if social work, too, adopts an institutional rather than a residual concept of the part it must play. Accordingly, it should regard itself as an essential element of modern society, serving the normal as well as the distressed, and helping to plan the better life as well as treating personal and social ills.[1] Thus social work, sensitively attuned to emerging needs, must be ready to play a variety of parts. Not only must it perform its traditional duties to the indigent and distressed, but it must assume new roles or extend old ones to meet the requirements of a changing age. It must recognize needs as they emerge and help to translate them into rights. It must encourage the group worker's concern for collective action in the common interest, and the community organizer's efforts to help to improve society's institutions. It must play a part in shaping social welfare, and stand on guard till it can applaud the deed. It must recruit, train and supervise more workers, and seek to improve their status and prestige. This recognition of a richer role has prompted a number of questions, for many people realize that American social work is about to make some vital decisions and that these decisions can now be made in the light of considered thought about their implications. How can social work best be organized? In which areas can it claim a special competence? How can it shape America's social welfare? What knowledge is needed for the tasks ahead? How can workers best be trained? What kind of profession will social work become? These and other questions are troubling more thoughtful minds at the moment, for they realize that upon their answers the fate of social work as a social institution must depend.[2]

Social work, then, both in England and the United States, is

---

[1] For the most mature statement of this concept, see Alfred J. Kahn, *loc. cit.*

[2] For a discussion of these and other issues, see the essays in Alfred J. Kahn, ed., *op. cit.*

being summoned to a richer role. This is a far cry from the days of Lady Clara Vere de Vere. In the hundred and twenty years which have elapsed since she was exhorted to teach the orphan-boy to read and the orphan-girl to sew, social work in both countries has changed quite dramatically. Although in neither does it yet enjoy the same status as the older, established professions, in both the scope of work which it undertakes has been extended, the number of people it serves has increased, the services it renders have been diversified, and the status of its workers improved. For the new societies may yet prove to be readier than the old to recognize the value of their social workers, to enlarge and vary their function, and even, as in the participation of some American social workers in the making of public policy, to give them a modicum of power. These developments have given social work a 'new look' which is in strange contrast to that which it wore in the nineteenth century. Not only does this 'new look' emphasize the differences between social work's past and present roles in the community, but it points, perhaps, the fashion of the future. For if the present trend continues and social work applies an institutional concept of its role, it can play a richer and more constructive role than ever before. No longer a sedative for social revolution, nor a shock-absorber for the unmerited blows of an unkind economic fate, social work can become a catalyst, bent on releasing human potentialities imprisoned by poverty, fear, ignorance and sloth. This is the challenge which faces social work both in England and the United States. If it can be met successfully, social work can fulfil an obligation, not only to itself, but to society as well. For in serving the needs of the future, it can not only advance its claim to be fully accepted as a profession, but it can make a unique contribution to the welfare of the community with whose interests its own are so intimately connected.

Bibliography

I. PRIMARY SOURCES:

1. PARLIAMENTARY PAPERS:

Hansard's Parliamentary Debates.
Returns of the Number of Deaths in the Metropolitan Districts (of London) in the Years 1868, 1869 and 1870. (1871).
Report of the Royal Commission on the Poor Laws and the Relief of Distress, Cmd. 4499, 1909.

2. MANUSCRIPT SOURCES:

The Solly Collection (in the possession of the London School of Economics and Political Science, University of London).
Diary of Charles Stewart Loch, 1876–92 (in the possession of Mrs. R. B. Mowat, Bristol, England).

3. ANNUAL REPORTS:

Proceedings of the (American) *National Conference of Social work:* formerly:
  Conference of Charities, 1874–79;
  Conference of Charities and Correction, 1880–83;
  National Conference of Charities and Correction, 1884–1916;
  National Conference of Social Work, 1917–50;
  The Social Welfare Forum, 1950–
Annals of the American Academy of Political and Social Science.
Proceedings of the Annual Conventions of the National Association of Manufacturers of the U.S.A., 1926–30.
Annual Reports of the Family Welfare Association (England):
  formerly *Society for Organising Charitable Relief and Repressing Mendicity,* 1870–76;
  Charity Organisation Society, 1877–1945;
  Family Welfare Association, 1946–
Annual Reports of the British Federation of Social Workers.

Annual Reports of the National Council of Social Service. (Eng.).
Reports of Association of Social Workers (of England).

4. BOOKS AND PAMPHLETS:

Addams, Jane. *The Second Twenty Years at Hull House.* (New York, 1930).
—, *The Spirit of Youth and the City Streets* (New York, 1909).
—, *et al. Philanthropy and Social Progress.* (New York, 1893).
Bailward, W. A. *The Charity Organisation Society: An Historical Sketch, 1869–1906* (1935 ed.).
Barnett, Henrietta O. *Canon Barnett: His Life, Work and Friends,* 2 vols. (1919).
—, *The Work of Lady Visitors* (1880).
—, *What has the C.O.S. to do with Social Reform?* (1884).
—, and Barnett, S. A. *Practicable Socialism: Essays on Social Reform* (1888).
Barnett, S. A. 'The Universities and the Poor', *Nineteenth Century,* Vol. XV, No. LXXXIV (February, 1884), pp. 255–61; reprinted in *Practicable Socialism,* pp. 96–108.
—, 'Distress in East London,' *Nineteenth Century,* XX, (November, 1886), pp. 678–92.
—, 'Sensationalism in Social Reform', *Nineteenth Century,* XIX (February, 1886), pp. 280–90.
—, 'Practicable Socialism', *Nineteenth Century,* No. LXXIV (April, 1883), pp. 554–60.
Beveridge, William. *Social Insurance and Allied Services* (1942), Cmd. 6404.
—, *Voluntary Action. A Report on Methods of Social Advance* (1948).
—, *Power and Influence* (1953).
Booth, Charles. *Life and Labour of the People of London.* Vol. I (1892) and Vol. VII (1903).
—, *Condition and Occupations of the People of the Tower Hamlets, 1886–1887* (1887).
Booth, William. *In Darkest England and the Way Out* (1890).
Bosanquet, Bernard (ed.). *Aspects of the Social Problem* (1895).
Bosanquet, Charles B. P. *A Handybook for Visitors of the Poor in London* (1874).
—, *The History and Mode of Operation of the C.O.S.* (1874).
Brace, Charles Loring. *The Dangerous Classes of New York and Twenty Years' Work among Them* (New York, 1872).
Breckinridge, Sophonisba P. *Public Welfare Administration in the United States. Select Documents* (Chicago, 2nd edn., 1938).

Channing, William Ellery. *Memoir of William Ellery Channing* (2 vols., 1850).

Charity Organisation Society. *Occasional Papers, Pamphlets, Leaflets, Reports of Committees, etc.*, 1870–1907 (For details, see footnotes).

Cobbett, William. *Selections from Cobbett's Political Works* (ed. J. M. and J. P. Cobbett, 6 vols., 1835).

Colcord, Joanna C. (ed.). *The Long View: Papers and Addresses of Mary E. Richmond* (New York, 1930).

Curriculum Study of the Council on Social Work Education, under the directorship of Werner W. Boehm (New York, 1959)

Devine, Edward T. *The Practice of Charity, Individual, Associated and Organized* (New York, 1901).

—, *When Social Work was Young* (New York, 1939).

—, *Misery and its Causes* (New York, 1909).

—, *Organized Charity and Industry* (New York, 1915).

Doré, Gustave, and Jerrold, Blanchard. *London: A Pilgrimage* (1872).

Eden, Sir Frederick Morton. *The State of the Poor* (Ed. A. G. L. Rogers, 1928).

Escott, T. H. S. *England, Its People, Polity and Pursuits* (1885).

—, *Social Transformations of the Victorian Age. A Survey of Court and Country* (1897).

Finley, John H. (ed.). *The Public Treatment of Pauperism, being a Report of the First Section of the International Congress of Charities, Correction and Philanthropy, June 1893* (Baltimore, 1893).

Giffen, Robert. *The Progress of the Working Classes in the Last Half Century* (1884). Reprinted in *Essays in Finance* (1886).

—, 'Further Notes on the Progress of the Working Classes,' *Essays in Finance* (1886).

Gurteen, Humphrey S. *A Handbook of Charity Organisation* (Buffalo, 1882).

—, 'Beginning of Charity Organisation in America,' *Lend a Hand*, XIII (1894), pp. 352–67.

Haber, William, and Cohen, Wilbur J. *Readings in Social Security* (New York, 1948).

Hawksley, Thomas. *Objections to 'The History' of the (Charity Organisation) Society* (1874).

—, *The Charities of London and Some Errors of their Administration* (1869).

Hicks, W. N. *A Contribution towards the History of the Origin of the C.O.S.* (1875).

Hill, Octavia. *Life of Octavia Hill as told in her Letters*. (Ed. C. E. Maurice, 1913).

—, *Our Common Land and other Short Essays* (1877).

—, *The C.O.S.* (C.O.S., *Occasional Papers*).

—, 'The Work of Volunteers in the Organisation of Charity,' *Macmillan's Magazine*, October 1872; reprinted in *C.O.S. Pamphlets, Leaflets*, 1884.

—, 'A Few Words to Fresh Workers,' *Nineteenth Century*, XXVI (September, 1889), pp. 452–61.

—. 'Common sense and the Dwellings of the Poor,' *Nineteenth Century*, LXXXII (December, 1883), pp. 925–33.

—. 'Our Dealings with the Poor,' *Nineteenth Century*, XXX (August, 1891), pp. 161–70.

—. 'Trained Workers for the Poor,' *Nineteenth Century*, XXXIII (Jan.–June, 1893), pp. 36–43.

Hollis, Ernest V. and Taylor, Alice T. *Social Work Education in the United States: The Report of a Study made for the National Council on Social Work Education* (New York, 1951).

Hood, Edwin P. *The Age and its Architects. Ten Chapters on the English People in Relation to the Times* (1850) (1852).

Hone, William. *The Every Day Book*. 2 vols. (1827).

Kahn, Alfred J. (ed.), *Issues in American Social Work* (New York, 1959).

Kellogg, Charles D. 'Charity Organisation in the United States,' *Proceedings of the National Conference of Charities and Correction*, 1893, pp. 52–93.

Kingsley, Charles. *Sanitary and Social Lectures and Essays* (1889).

Leighton, Baldwyn (ed.). *Letters and Other Writings of the Late Edward Denison, M.P. for Newark* (1872).

Loch, C. S. *Charity Organisation* (1892).

—. *How to Help Cases of Distress* (1883).

—. *Things Within* (Oxford, 1922).

—. *C. S. Loch: Pamphlets* (compiled by Family Welfare Association, London, undated).

—. *A Great Ideal and its Champion. Papers and Addresses by the Late Sir Charles Stewart Loch* (Ed. Arthur Clay, 1923).

—. 'Manufacturing a New Pauperism,' *Nineteenth Century*, XXXVII (April, 1895), pp. 697–708.

London Congregational Union. *The Bitter Cry of Outcast London. An Inquiry into the Condition of the Abject Poor* (Boston, 1883).

Low, Sampson, Jr. *The Charities of London in 1861* (1862).

Lowry, Fern (ed.). *Readings in Social Casework, 1920–38* (New York, 1939).

Masterton, N (ed.). *Chalmers on Charity. A Selection of Passages and Scenes to illustrate the Social Teaching and Practical Work of Thomas Chalmers, D.D.* (1900).

Morris, E. E. *Charity Organisation Societies in England and the United States* (Melbourne, Australia, 1890).

Menninger, William C. 'Psychiatric Experience in the War, 1941–46,' *American Journal of Psychiatry*, C III (March, 1947), pp. 577–86.

National Association of Manufacturers of the U.S.A. *The Platform of American Industry: A Presentation of Sound Business Principles, including the Resolutions and a Summary of the Reports adopted by the N.A.M.'s Congress of American Industry on 4, 5 Dec. 1935.*

National Association of Social Workers (American). *Standards for Social Work Personnel Practice* (New York, 1959).

—. *Salaries: Official N.A.S.W. Policy* (New York, 1959).

National Council of Social Service. *Partnership in Social Effort: Nineteenth Annual Report, 1938–39.*

Organisation of Charities—being a Report of the Sixth Section of the International Congress of Charities, Correction and Philanthropy (Chicago, 1893).

Pacey, Lorene M. (ed.). *Readings in the Development of Settlement Work* (New York, 1950).

Paine, Robert Treat. 'Pauperism in Great Cities: Its Four Chief Causes,' *Proceedings of the International Congress of Charities, Correction and Philanthropy*, 1893, I pp. 23–58.

Richmond, Mary E. *Friendly Visiting among the Poor: A Handbook for Charity Workers* (1914).

—. *Social Diagnosis* (New York, 1917).

—. *What is Social Case Work?* (New York, 1922).

—. *The Long View: Papers and Addresses of Mary E. Richmond.* Ed. Joanna C. Colcord (New York, 1930).

—. 'What is Charity Organisation?' *The Charities Review*, IX (1899–1900), pp. 490–500.

Riis, Jacob A. *The Children of the Poor* (New York, 1892).

—. *How the other Half Lives: Studies among the Poor* (1891).

—. *A Ten Years' War: An Account of the Battle with the Slum in New York* (Boston and New York, 1900).

Rosenman, Samuel I (compiler). *The Public Papers and Addresses of Franklin D. Roosevelt* (13 vols., New York, 1938–50).

Sartor Minor. *Philanthropic Tailoring and Historical Cobbling* (1875).

Slocum, William F. 'The Ideal of the Charity Worker', *Charities Review. A Journal of Practical Sociology,* II (November, 1892–June, 1893), pp. 10–15.

Social Workers in 1950: A Report on the Study of Salaries and Working Conditions in Social Work. Prepared by the U.S. Department of Labour, Division of Wages and Industrial Wages (New York, 1952).

Sterling, Katherine S. *Charity, Noxious and Beneficent* (1853).

Stewart, William Rhinelander (ed.). *The Philanthropic Work of Josephine Shaw Lowell* (New York, 1911).

United Nations Social Commission. *Training for Social Work: An Introductory Survey* (1950).

Warner, Amos G. *American Charities* (New York, 1894).

Warner, Amos C. *et al. American Characteristics and Social Work* (New York, 1894).

Waterston, R. C. *An Address on Pauperism: Its Extent, Causes and the Best Means of Prevention* (Boston, 1844).

Wilkinson, W. M. *A Contribution towards the History of the C.O.S.* (1875).

Younghusband, Eileen. *Report of the Working Party on Social Workers in the Local Authority Health and Welfare Services* (1959).

—. *Report on the Employment and Training of Social Workers* (Dunfermline, Fife, 1949).

—. *Social Work in Britain, A Supplementary Report on the Employment and Training of Social Workers* (Fife, 1951).

5. PERIODICALS, NEWSPAPERS, AND JOURNALS

NINETEENTH CENTURY:

Saturday Review of Politics, Literature, Science and Art.
Contemporary Review.
Charity Organisation Reporter.
Charity Organisation Review.
Nineteenth Century.
Annals of the Academy of Political and Social Science.

TWENTIETH CENTURY:

The Compass.
Survey: formerly *Charities* (1897–1905) and *Charities and the Commons* (1905–09).

Social Service Review.
Social Work.
Social Work Journal.
Case Conference.
Social Service Quarterly.
Sociological Review.
Social Work Today.
Journal of Social Casework (formerly *The Family*).
Social Work Yearbooks.

II. SELECTED SECONDARY WORKS:

Allport, Gordon W. *Limits of Social Service* (unpublished paper, 1954).

Bell, E. Moberley. *Octavia Hill: A Biography* (1943).

Bisno, Herbert. *The Philosophy of Social Work* (Washington, 1951).

Bourdillon, A. F. C. (ed.). *Voluntary Social Services* (1945).

Bosanquet, Helen. *The Strength of the People: A Study in Social Economics* (2nd. ed. 1903).

Bosanquet, Helen. *Social Work in London, 1869–1912: A History of the C.O.S.* (1914).

Bremner, Robert H. *From the Depths: The Discovery of Poverty in the United States* (New York, 1956).

—. *American Philanthropy* (Chicago, 1960).

—. 'Scientific Philanthropy 1873–93', *Social Service Review*, XXX (June, 1956), pp. 168–73.

Brown, Josephine. *Public Relief, 1929–39* (New York, 1940).

Bruno, Frank J. *Trends in Social Work, 1874–1956* (New York, 1957 ed.).

Buell, Bradley, and Associates. *Community Planning for Human Services* (New York, 1952).

Burns, Eveline. *The American Social Security System* (Boston, 1951 ed.).

Cohen, Nathan Edward. *Social Work in the American Tradition* (New York, 1958).

Cormack, Una M. 'Developments in Casework,' in A. F. C. Bourdillon, (ed.), *Voluntary Social Services* (1945).

—. *The Welfare State* (Loch Memorial Lecture, 1953).

Curti, Merle. 'The History of American Philanthropy as a Field of Research,' *American Historical Review*, LXII (January, 1957), pp. 352–67.

Dunham, Arthur. *Community Welfare Organisation: Principles and Practice* (New York, 1958).

Elliott, Lula Jean. *Social Work Ethics. Studies in the Practice of Social Work*, No. 3 (American Association of Social Workers, New York, 1931).

Fink, Arthur E. *The Field of Social Work* (New York, 1949 ed.).

Gray, B. Kirkman. *A History of English Philanthropy* (1905).

Heiman, Marcel (ed.). *Psychoanalysis and Social Work* (New York, 1953).

Jones, Maxwell, *et al. Social Psychiatry* (1952).

Keith-Lucas, Alan. *Decisions about People in Need. A Study of Administrative Responsiveness in Public Assistance* (Chapel Hill, 1957).

—. 'Political Theory Implications Implicit in Social Case Work Theory,' *American Political Science Quarterly Review*, XLVII (December, 1953), pp. 1076–91.

Klein, Alan F. *Society—Democracy—and the Group* (New York, 1953).

Kuenstler, Peter (ed.). *Social Group Work in Great Britain* (1955).

Lieberman, Joshua (ed.). *New Trends in Group Work* (New York, 1939).

Meier, Elizabeth G. *A History of the New York School of Social Work* (New York, 1954).

Miles, Arthur P. *American Social Work Theory* (New York, 1954).

Morris, Cherry (ed.). *Social Casework in Great Britain* (1950).

Mowat, Charles Loch, *The Charity Organisation Society, 1869–1913* (1961).

Perlman, Helen Harris. *Social Casework: A Problem-Solving Process* (Chicago, 1957).

Pimlott, J. A. R. *Toynbee Hall: Fifty Years of Social Progress, 1884–1934* (1935).

Pumphrey, Muriel W. 'Mary Richmond's Process of Conceptualization,' *Social Casework*, XXXVIII (October, 1957), pp. 399–406.

—. 'The First Step—Mary Richmond's Earliest Professional Reading, 1889–91,' *Social Service Review*, XXXI, (June, 1957), pp. 144–63.

Queen, Stuart Alfred. *Social Work in the Light of History* (Philadelphia and London, 1922).

Raynes, Harold E. *Social Security in Britain: A History* (1957).

Recent Social Trends in the U.S.: Report of the President's Research Committee on Social Trends (New York, 1933).

Russell Sage Foundation. *Report of the Princeton Conference on the History of Philanthropy in the United States* (New York, 1956).

Rich, Margaret E. *A Belief in People: A History of Family Social Work* (New York, 1956).

Robinson, Virginia P. *A Changing Psychology in Social Case Work* (Chapel Hill, 1939).

Rodgers, Barbara N. and Dixon, Julia, *Portrait of Social Work. A Study of Social Services in a Northern Town* (1960).

Rooff, Madeline. *Voluntary Societies and Social Policy* (1957).

Schweinitz, Karl de. *England's Road to Social Security* (Philadelphia, 1943).

—. 'Social Values and Social Action—The Intellectual Base as illustrated in the Study of History,' *Social Service Review*, XXX (June, 1956), pp. 119–31.

Simey, T. S. and M. B. *Charles Booth* (Oxford, 1960).

Smith, Cyril S. *People in Need and Other Essays. A Study of Contemporary Social Needs and of their Relation to the Welfare State* (1957).

Smith, Marjorie J. *Professional Education for Social Work in Britain* (1952).

Some Impressions of Social Services in Great Britain by an American Social Work Team (U.S. Educational Commission of the U.K., 1956).

Titmuss, Richard M. *Essays on 'The Welfare State'* (1958).

—. *Problems of Social Policy* (1950).

Trecker, Harleigh B. *Group Process in Administration* (New York, 2nd ed., 1950).

—. *Social Group Work. Principles and Practices* (New York, 1948).

Watson, Frank Dekker. *The Charity Organisation Movement in the United States. A Study in American Philanthropy* (New York, 1922).

Wilensky, Harold L., and Lebeaux, Charles N. *Industrial Society and Social Welfare* (New York, 1958).

Williams, Gertrude (ed.). *Voluntary Social Services since 1918* (1947).

Witmer, Helen Leland. *Social Work. An Analysis of a Social Institution* (New York, 4th. ed., 1950).

Wootton, Barbara. *Social Science and Social Pathology* (1959).

Young, A. F. and Ashton, E. T. *British Social Work in the 19th Century* (1956).

Young, Michael, and Wilmott, Peter. *Family and Kinship in East London* (1957).

Index

Abel-Smith, Brian, 209
Abbott, Edith, 86, 172, 173
Abbott, Grace, 70, 152
Addams, Jane, 62, 69n., 95, 135, 186–7, 186n., 201
Agricultural Adjustment Act, 169–70. *See also* New Deal
Allen, Nathan, 82n., 92
Almshouse, 84–5, 154–5. *See also* Poor Relief
American Association of Social Workers—then *see* National Association of Social Workers, 166, 166n., 202
American Public Welfare Association, 222
Arnold, Matthew, 5

Bagehot, Walter, 4
Bailly, Sylvain, 45
Barnett, Canon and Mrs. S. A., 59, 61–2, 157; and Toynbee Hall, 64–73, 184
Beers, Clifford, 125
Bernard, Sir Thomas, 9
Beveridge, Lord, 12, 20, 68, 144. *See also* Beveridge Report
Beveridge Report, 29, 144, 209
Boehm, Werner W., 218n., 222, 222n.
Booth, Charles, investigation of poverty in London, 9, 10–12, 14, 21, 34, 140; old age

pensions scheme, 58; and settlements, 64, 68
Booth, General, 6, 59, 59n.
Bosanquet, Charles P. B., 30
Bosanquet, Helen, 34, 58, 59–60
Brace, Charles Loring, 89, 122n
Brackett, Jeffrey R., 96, 160, 160n., 163
Brookings Institution, 153
Brown, Josephine, 156n., 162, 167n., 168n.
Bruno, Frank J., 86n., 171, 194n.
Buell, Bradley, 196–7
Burns, Eveline, 202, 221, 222n.
Burt, Cyril, 138
Butler, Amos, 158
Butler, Edmond J., 121
Buzelle, George B., 92–3, 120

Cabot, Richard C., 126, 128
Campbell, C. Macfie, 126, 128, 129
Canning, George, 12
Carlyle, Thomas, 12, 13
Carnegie, Andrew, 67, 81
Casework:—
    In England, C.O.S. and, 37, 39, 41–2, 43–4, 48–55, 57, 118–19, 203, 204; antecedents of, 44–7; C.O.S. training for, 53–4; and group work, 56–7; and community organisation, 56–7; Canon Barnett and, 70–3; influence of psychiatry on, in the

National Association of Manufacturers of the U.S.A, 134–
135
National Association of Social
Workers, 222, 224n.
National Conference of Charities
and Correction—from 1917,
National Conference of Social
Work, and from 1950, Social
Welfare Forum, 86, 107; views
on public relief, 87–8, 92, 94–5,
158–61; on pauperism and
poverty, 94–6; interest in psychology and psychiatry, 122,
124–9; in mental disease, 124–
126; in reform, 171–2; report
(1912) of Committee on Standards of Living and Labor, 95,
95n., 201; reports on social
insurance, 173–4, 173n.; interest in social group work,
187–9; in community organisation, 197–201, 201–2; in social
action, 203
National Council of Social Service, 181, 182, 183
National Industrial Recovery Act,
169, 170. See also New Deal
National Insurance Act of 1911,
143–4, 160–1
New Deal, relief programmes in,
163–8; Agricultural Adjustment Act, 169–70; National
Industrial Recovery Act, 170;
Social Security Act, 170–5;
social work during, 158–9,
162–3, 165–8, 171–2, 175–7

Old age pensions, 58, 143, 155–6,
160–1, 172–3, 172–3n.
Ozanam, Frederick, 45

Paine, Robert Treat, 83n., 94,
96

Paul, St. Vincent de, 44
Peek, Francis, 36
Philanthropy, in England, 18–23;
in U.S.A., 89–90, 207–8, 216
Pierce, President, 85, 156, 196
Poor Law Amendment Act of
1834, 17–18
Poor Relief, in Elizabethan England, 16–17; in eighteenth
century, 17; in 1834, 17–18;
Elberfeld system of, 45, 47;
attack on, 140–2; In U.S.A.,
in colonial times, 84–5; during
Great Depression, 153–62,
163–8; philosophy underlying,
82–4, 86–8, 154–62, 167–8;
arguments against, 87–8; attitude to public and private
relief, 158–61
Pound, Roscoe, 159
Poverty. See especially Chapters I
and IV:—
In England, and plenty in the
nineteenth century, 3–7; observations on, 6–8; lack of accurate knowledge of, 8–9; surveys of, by Sir Thomas Bernard, 9, 10, by Sir F. M. Eden,
9, 10, by Henry Mayhew, 9–10,
by Charles Booth, 9, 10–12, by
Lord Beveridge, 12; extent of,
8–9, 11–12; recognition of as a
social danger, 12–14, 48–50;
methods of dealing with, 14,
16–18, 19; English attitudes to
6–8, 58–9; English attitude
compared with American, 139–
140; in Welfare State, 209;
English attitude to in twentieth
century, 143–4
In U.S.A., and plenty in the
nineteenth century, 77–82;
American attitude to, 82–4, 88–
9, 92–5; attitude embodied in

243

School of Sociology (of the C.O.S.)—later Department of Social Science and Administration, L.S.E., 24, 54, 137

Schools, ragged, 57, 63–4; Sunday, 63–4; state aid to, 15

Schools of Social Work, 24, 54, 104, 137; 187, early proposals for, 53–4, 97; training schemes, 53–4, 137–8

Schweinitz, Karl de, 135, 165

Settlements, 50, 57, 69, 69n., 77, 189:

In England, motives for founding, 64–5; underlying philosophy of, 65–7; Toynbee Hall, 64, 66–74, 184; other Settlements, 64–5, 69, 72; appeal of, 68; and group work theory and practice, 70–74

Sewell, Margaret, 54, 72

Shaftesbury, Lord, 16, 43, 139

Shaw, Benjamin, 13

Simey, T. S., 212–13

Simkhovitch, Mary, 113

Slavson, S. R., 190, 190n.

Smallwood, William, 121, 121n.

Social Action, defined 202n., 203n.; in nineteenth century England, 57–61, 184, 184–5n.; *In U.S.A.*, in the nineteenth century, 93–4, 95–9; Mary E. Richmond on, 98–9, 103–4; tendency of social workers to abdicate, 219–20, 223, 225; call to, 220–2. 226–7; social worker's participation in, 201–204, 222

Social Casework. *See* Casework

Social Group Work. *See especially* Chapters III and VIII; definition of, 56–7, 57n., 191n. *In England*, and the C.O.S.,

57–61; and groups in Victorian England, 62–4, 180–1; and groups during the depression, 181–2; and community centres, 183–4; scepticism about function, 179–80; little attempt to develop theory, 184–6, 185n., 186n. *In U.S.A.*, during '40's and '50's, 179, 185; development of theory and practice of, 186–191; as part of the 'newer' social work, 204–6

Socialism, 11, 13, 14, 55, 59, 67, 68, 160n.

Social Insurance, 173–4, 215

Social Policy, 214–15, 219–22, 222n. *See also* Social Action

Social Science Association, 52

Social Security Act of 1935, 154, 169, 218; as landmark in history of social services, 170–171, 174–5; disappointing to many social workers, 171–2; shortcomings, 172–4; reversal of federal government's policy, 174–5; and community organisation, 195–6. *See also* New Deal

Social Service Exchange, 192, 199. *See also* Community Organisation

Social Services, 85–6, 194–7, 209–12, 215–18, 218–19. *See also* Welfare State

Social Survey of Merseyside, 182, 182n.

Social Welfare, new demand for, 208–9, 215–16; effect on social work, 171–2, 209–12, 215–219

Social Work, as a social sedative and 'regenerator', 50–2, 54–5, 135–6, 204–5; as 'shock-